Succession Development Planning: A Strategy Used To Help Future-Proof Your Workforce

SUCCESSION DEVELOPMENT PLANNING: A STRATEGY USED TO HELP FUTURE-PROOF YOUR WORKFORCE

Douglas E. Fenner, Ed.D., CPC, ELI-MP, EQP

ISBN-13: 9780692925003
ISBN-10: 0692925007
Library of Congress Control Number: 2017911506
Dr. Douglas Fenner, San Diego, CA

CONTENTS

PREFACE

Chapter one provides a historical perspective about the meaning of agnatic succession, the origin of which can be attributed to a biblical perspective. Although only in his thirties, Jesus was one leader who prepared for premature succession. For example, a quote from the Condition of Discipleship (Luke 9:23–24) states, "Then he said to all, 'If anyone wishes to come after me [succeed him], he must deny himself and take up his cross daily and follow me. For whoever wishes to save his life will lose it, but whoever loses his life for my sake will save it.'" Moreover, as life and history progressed from the second and into the third century AD, leadership succession did not reform itself. Military leaders of the Roman army, for example, filled the throne of the Roman Empire using their voting power. However, during these times, voting an emperor into power was a very risky process. If military leaders failed to secure broader support for their candidates, they would assassinate the current emperor and revert to the previous emperor. By the third century, specifically, between AD 268 and 285, frequent revolts instilled fear in the hearts of incumbent emperors and their successors. Around September 282, Marcus Aurelius Probus, the forty-seventh emperor of the Roman Empire, was murdered by his military leaders.

Marcus Aurelius Carus Augustus, the forty-eighth emperor of the Roman Empire, became the first emperor who attempted to end the assassinations. Resolving the question concerning his own succession, he promoted his two sons, Marcus Aurelius Numerius Numerianus Augustus and Carinus, to senior-level positions, which led to new laws being established around the turn of the fourth century. These various laws required sons to follow the professions of their fathers. By the sixth century, leadership succession continued to be a major issue throughout the European governments.

As a result, Europe's male ruling class organized leadership succession biologically: male heirs succeeded their fathers. If there were no sons, succession devolved to a male relative. One of the most tantalizing and controversial laws that existed was called the Salic Law, which specifically prohibited female succession. It did, however, permit a king's child, such as Clovis I of the Salian Franks, to gain the throne in 481 at the age of fifteen. Moreover, it was not until 1126 that the English king Henry I persuaded the barons to accept his daughter Matilda as his successor to the throne. Nonetheless, by 1317, civil law once again excluded females—and, by 1328, denied even males the right to claim inheritance through a female line. Research indicated this was a deliberate attempt to keep Edward III of England—a descendant of French kings through his mother, Isabel of France—off the throne, thereby sparking the Hundred Years' War.

Meanwhile, the influence of the Salic Law of 1316 (also called Salian Law) extended to modern times in Central Europe (e.g., France, Netherlands, Germany, Italy, Hungary, Balkans, Austria, Belgium, and Romania). Even Japan became a major enforcer of the agnatic (male-traced) succession formality in 1331, which led to a civil war against Hojo regents. By the early fourteenth century, the word "succession" was defined as meaning "fact or right of succeeding someone by inheritance," from the Old French *succession* (thirteenth century), which was from the Latin *successionem* (nominative *successio*) "a following after, a coming into another's place, result," from *successus*, past participle of *succedere*; the English term was "succeed."

Chapter two discusses the arrival and the path the first settlers traveled to reach the New World. During the last Ice Age, called the Pleistocene Epoch, some fifteen thousand to forty-five thousand years ago, Asian or Paleo-Indian immigrants began to populate the New World, later called North America. Genetic data from these immigrants were first discovered in the Paisley Cave site in Oregon. The genetic data revealed fourteen-thousand-year-old feces, human hair, and human

DNA. The path to the New World reflected Paleo-Indians migrating by foot across Beringia, which encompassed the area where the Bering Sea exists today. They successfully maneuvered across the Bering Sea because much of the Earth's water was frozen in glaciers. This, in turn, lowered the sea level that exposed the land bridge near the Arctic Circle. This landmass, the Bering Land Bridge, connected Asia and North America. This migration led to a variety of different languages and twelve hundred different dialects, cultures, religions, social organizations, physical characteristics, and different types of technologies that helped establish North America's cultural foundation. Moreover, North America continued to converge socially and demographically via a tenth-century influx of European immigrants by sea from Western Europe and Western Africa.

By 1492, Spanish colonization took root, followed by immigrants from the Old World (e.g., France, the Netherlands, the British Isles, and Portugal) and with them came, although against their will, a variety of black African slaves. By 1820, the United States' population had reached almost half of Great Britain's, 9.6 million and 20.9 million, respectively. In fact, by 1850, approximately 23.5 percent of the United States' total population of twenty-three million were foreign born. This labor had a huge impact on the economies across the thirteen British colonies in North America. This diverse group of foreign-born immigrants included the Irish, Chinese, Japanese, and Hispanic/Latino, all seeking to fill construction, mining, and various other types of job vacancies across the United States of America.

Chapter three provides a perspective concerning the first three industrial revolutions and the coming of the Fourth Industrial Revolution (FoIR). In the 1700s, Britain was the birthplace of the Industrial Revolution, during which manufacturing occurred using hand tools or basic machines from within people's homes. This was followed by a high demand for production of iron and growth in textile industries and steam engines, which all contributed improvements and growth in railroad transportation, banking, and electronic communication. Between 1712 and 1793, the first steam engine and cotton gin became part of this revolution. Great Britain was the technological innovator, and it led the transformation of hand-production methods to machines, iron, steam power, machine tools, and new chemical manufacturing. The Second Industrial Revolution (SIR) included textile manufacturing, the prime employment for this generation. Between 1837 and 1914, William Cooke and Charles Wheatstone, British residents, had transitioned the world into its own SIR. During this revolution technology, the extensive manufacture of machine tools and the SIR's impact on the economy played major roles, which laid the foundation for the first true globalization pertaining to the fundamentals of e-commerce. This revolution included stream-powered transportation (i.e., railroads, ships, electricity, oil, boats, etc.) and was synonymous with the term "Technological Revolution," which led to new innovations in steel manufacturing, telephone communication, and electricity and petroleum to support public transportation such as automobiles and airplanes as well as bring electricity to households. Between 1913 and 1920, with these new inventions, the United States was producing more than one-third of the world's industrial requirements, which led to approximately eleven million Americans transitioning from farm communities to various cities. In response, almost twenty-five million immigrants came from foreign countries to gain employment.

In the 1990s, the Third Industrial Revolution (TIR) was the digital, biological, and physical revolution in which we used information technology, information systems, and electronics to automate workload production. This revolution focused on the creation of a high-tech, twenty-first-century smart, green, and digital economy. It was the earmark for the 3D-printing phenomenon, computers, and the Internet. The TIR, powered by oil and other fossil fuels, began to spiral into dangerous territories. Food and gas prices climbed exponentially, unemployment reached an all-time high, the housing market crashed, and consumer and government debt soared. By August 6, 1991, when the World Wide Web made its debut, millions tried out the Internet for the first time. This led to the beginning of various electronic interactions from e-mails, YouTube, Wi-Fi, Google, e-commerce, and Facebook, to various digital satellite technologies. And by 1993, the dot-com bubble collapsed, along with many Internet-based organizations (e.g., pets.com, Webvan, etc.), while organizations such as Amazon, Cisco, and eBay saw stocks drop by large margins, but later recovered.

Nevertheless, by 2020, the Fourth Industrial Revolution (FoIR) will kindle a paradigm shift that will include numerous converging and extraordinary technologies such as advanced robotics, artificial intelligence, machine learning, renewable energy, autonomous transportation, 4D printing, human intelligence, virtual healthcare, genomics, biotechnologies, and other advanced materials. These developments will transform the way employees rejoice, live, and work.

Moreover, to support the FoIR, succession development planning will be in high demand because it will help provide solutions to the five unprecedented paradigm shifts that will greatly challenge many organizations' strategic business model. The five paradigm shifts will force C-suite executives and managers to

1. focus more on an adaptive functional organization model;
2. establish solutions in how to lead and manage a multigenerational workforce;
3. establish ideas and solutions for managing, leading, and engaging a more diversified and inclusive workforce;
4. draw upon a global perspective as to what futuristic and multidimensional competencies employees must have to remain future-proof; and
5. determine best business practices and solutions for dealing with the labor shortage in the US labor force.

Chapter four reflects the importance of establishing a succession development plan. In today's work environment, organizations have maybe two to three different generations working in them. In tomorrow's work environment, this workforce dynamic will change drastically. Organizations will encounter up to five different generations (e.g., traditionalists, baby boomers, millennials (gen Y), generation X, and generation Z). Although organizations can greatly benefit from a diverse and multi-generational workforce, they should have a well-designed succession development plan in place to help overcome unexpected challenges. Equally important, as the United States labor force continues to meet its retirement age, having a succession development plan in place will exceedingly enhance organizations' business success. Moreover, C-suite executives and senior managers must be aware that the continued effectiveness and success of their organization depends on having employees with the right multidimensional competencies in the right position at the right time to meet current and future job functions' demands. As private and public organizations continue to grow their workforces and international businesses continue to hire America's best and brightest, US companies will experience major reductions in qualified executives and midlevel managers needed to fill key leadership positions. And if the data continue to support the shortage of qualified candidates entering the workforce, there will be fewer staff-level employees available to advance to supervisory and middle-management positions; therefore, great care will be required to identify promising candidates and to actively cultivate their leadership development. At the same time, managers will deal with the challenges of leading and managing a multigenerational, diverse, and inclusive workforce. Chapter four discusses the problems impacting the future labor force in the United States and what solutions can be implemented to mitigate these problems. It also discusses future job predictions and the impact they will have on the United States' economy and job market for both public and private organizations.

Chapter five discusses traditional and nontraditional reasons for featuring diversity and inclusion in the succession development planning process. The traditional approach to diversity and inclusion was for employees to remain in their organization throughout their career, hoping to be the next in line for an executive or management position. At the same time, executives and managers did not care about workforce diversity and inclusion (D and I) and would hire and promote on the basis of human similarities and tenure. Today, in a nontraditional work environment, D and I have become major pillars in many organizations' business strategy plans. In 2015, for example, the Equal Employment Opportunity Commission (EEOC) processed 89,385 discrimination complaints. Over the eighteen-year period between 1997 and 2015, EEO complaints increased by nearly 10 percent. These high-profile complaints were about color (73 percent), retaliation—all statutes (54.2 percent), and religion (51.2 percent). Table 1 identifies the various complaints and percentage increases over the last eighteen years.

Moreover, while leading and managing in the Fourth Industrial Revolution (FoIR), C-suite executives and managers will not have the luxury of ignoring the importance of training, developing, hiring, and retaining a diversified and inclusive workforce. They are key pillars in the succession development planning process. The more D and I the workforce has, the more inspired, creative, and innovative it will become. D and I are also very important to the diverse communities and customers they serve. Jointly, they are catalysts for ensuring an organization remains reflective of the community it serves. Keep in mind people believe things because they are conditioned to believe them. If senior leaders, for example, think D and I are important to their business success, then they will include them in their succession development plan, human capital plan, and strategic business plan. If not, then they will exclude them. This chapter also defines the terms "diversity" and "inclusion" and the impact each has on an organization's current and future business strategies.

In contrast, there are disadvantages to workforce diversity and inclusion. Experts argue that seeking out diverse opinions from a homogenous group is one thing, but involving culturally diverse groups in problem solving and decision making can present significant challenges to a leader. Researchers who have completed studies on cultural diversity in the workplace, for example, indicated it took time to reach high levels of performance from culturally diverse groups, because homogenous groups were more likely to significantly outperform culturally diverse groups on measures of problem identification, quality of solutions, and overall performance in the initial weeks of a task. During the initial phase of the project, the study indicated homogenous groups were better at group processes than mixed groups. Nonetheless, after seventeen weeks into the study, the researchers acknowledged the differences in overall performance or group process disappeared, and as time elapsed, both types of groups improved. The diverse groups, however, improved more, and their performance converged. Keep in mind that the maturity of a diversity-and-inclusion program will take time. A D and I mission statement and goals should be established to include roles, responsibilities, and accountability for all C-suite executives, managers, and employees alike.

Chapter six focuses on the mind-sets of C-suite executives, managers, and employees as they pertain to the succession development planning process. Why is the mind-set challenge so important to succession development planning? Basically, many executives and managers do not understand the meaning of succession development planning or the positive impact it has on their organization. If the United States wants to remain the world's multipolar superpower, executives must alter their mind-set, which appears to be trapped in prehistoric times when it comes to succession development planning. The global success of the United States will depend greatly on its ability to develop and grow the country's next generation of top leaders and high performers. The time has come for these leaders to catch up with the way great executives operate and how they see their role in tomorrow's workplace. Traditionally, chief financial officers have argued that the primary purpose of business is to make money. After all, the more they make, the higher their yearly bonus becomes. This conveniently narrow image, deeply embedded in traditional corporate CFOs and other executives, constrains them to focus only on short-term profits. Their decisions are expressed in financial terms, not in employees' career development and growth. On the other hand, nontraditional CFOs and executives, those who think long term, are most likely to care about workforce training, development, retention, and building an enduring organization. Moreover, nontraditional executives believe in succession development planning and the importance of investing in the organization's future by building a twenty-first-century knowledge-based workforce. Additionally, they see succession planning as a choice, not a desperate obligation. This chapter provides constructive psychosomatic influencing (CPI) techniques to guide executives and managers through the Need-to-Got-to-Have-to-Want-to (*Nt-Gt-Ht-Wt*) Mind-set Transformation Process. It also provides a comprehensive step-by-step succession development planning framework.

Finally, **chapter seven** discusses the results of a workforce-competency-gap analysis case study that I implemented across my former information technology (IT) department, while serving as the chief information officer (CIO). As many organizations continue to deny the need for workforce succession development planning, they will also continue to be confronted with major increases in overhead costs associated with employees retiring and departing. These costs include training and developing new hires, salaries, benefits, recruitment, new workspace, technology equipment, geographic location expenses, and other related costs. Organizations may spend up to 150 percent of a manager's salary to prepare an employee for a management position. Costs may be even higher depending on the profession; for example, a person working in the information technology profession may earn $60,000 annually, but to backfill his or her position, the cost could be approximately $150,000. Moreover, US companies will face major challenges filling positions in the science, technology, engineering, arts, and mathematics (STEAM) career fields. Companies will also pay dearly in the areas of loss of productivity and knowledge, thereby leaving behind a heavy workload for those remaining, which will negatively impact workforce morale and generate an increase in work-related stress and absenteeism. To make matters worse, as US colleges and universities continue to benefit financially from international students filling their classrooms, the US student population wanting to enroll in STEAM curricula will continue to decline. Finally, this chapter discusses the importance of implementing succession development planning tools (e.g., competency-based alignment, competency modeling, competency mapping, workforce competency gap analysis assessment, competency comparative analysis, workforce economy of scale, and cost/benefit analysis) to help future-proof an organization's workforce.

Acknowledgments

T hose precious people who guided me through the many challenges in my personal and professional life hold a very special place in my heart. They earned the deepest gratitude that these words can only acknowledge. First, I am grateful to the many beloved family members and friends who sustained my emotional spirit throughout this work: my wife, Jacqueline Fenner; my adult children, Andrea and Brandon; my daughter-in-law, Tracie; and my two grandsons, Brandon II and Braxton. I want to give a shout-out to my mother, Ms. Gertrude Fenner, for her encouragement. I also want to give a special thank-you to my running, walking, and dining comrades, Pastor Robert Pope, Marcus Weathersby, Dr. Donald Chick, David Frost, Carl Caskey, Pete Copeland, and Willie Levett.

Moreover, I am profoundly grateful to the outstanding employees of the Naval Facilities Engineering Command Southwest Chief Information Office Department, who believed in the work we accomplished as it related to succession development planning and the quality of service we provided our warfighters and civilian customers. I am also thankful to the many federal agencies and their workforce-development professionals who assisted me in my research over the years: Department of the Navy Civilian Human Resources, US Office of Personnel Management Office (OPM), Aeronautical Radio, Incorporated, TRICARE Region Nine, Military Sealift Command, Marine Corps Systems Command, Naval Sea Systems Command, Naval Air Systems Command, San Diego Gas and Electric (SDG&E), Naval Supply Systems Command, and Space and Naval Warfare Systems Command.

About the Author

For the past twenty-five years, Douglas E. Fenner, EdD, has conducted research in the field of succession development planning. Other researchers and experts have used his doctoral dissertation research titled "Linking Succession Planning to Employee Training: A Study of Federal Employees." He is recognized as a leading expert in the field of succession development planning. Dr. Fenner is the founder/president of the Fenner Consulting Group, where he provided training in the areas of succession development planning; leadership development; workforce development; diversity and inclusion; and emotional, social, cultural, and personal intelligences. He provides professional executive coaching, corporate coaching, and focus group facilitation services. Dr. Fenner has authored mentoring and coaching handbooks and executive papers. He pioneered the first succession planning study for the Department of the Navy.

A graduate of the Federal Executive Institute's Leadership for a Democratic Society program, he holds a bachelor's degree in electrical engineering, a master's degree in computer resources and information management, and a doctoral degree in leadership and educational sciences from the University of San Diego. He is a retired federal civil servant and navy veteran with over thirty-three years of dedicated and honorable service to his country. He has held various positions such as chief information officer, deputy chief information officer, director of organizational development and training, regional contracting officer's representative, project manager, and more.

Dr. Fenner is a certified professional executive coach (CPC) with the International Coaching Federation (ICF) via the Institute for Professional Excellence in Coaching, a certified energy leadership index master practitioner (ELI-MP), a Lominger 360-degree leadership architect suite certified practitioner, and a certified Six Seconds emotional intelligence practitioner (EQP). He holds as a master black and lean six sigma certification. He is certified by the Defense Acquisition University information technology Level-III and information technology infrastructure library (ITIL) v3 foundation programs.

He is a member of the National Defense Industrial Association (NDIA), Armed Forces Communications and Electronics Association (AFCEA), National Society of Black Engineers (NSBE), and University of San Diego Black Student Alumni Association. He also supports the Asian American and Pacific Islander Association and National Society of Hispanic Engineers.

His hobbies include coaching youth league football, soccer, basketball, and baseball teams, as well as swimming, writing, and reading.

Chapter One

HISTORICAL PERSPECTIVE ON SUCCESSION DEVELOPMENT PLANNING

> Let our advance worrying become
> advance thinking and planning.
> —WINSTON CHURCHILL, FORMER PRIME
> MINISTER OF THE UNITED KINGDOM

Introduction

Policies are easy to develop, but what are the consequences of not having a succession development plan? If succession development planning is left to chance, it could have a detrimental impact on the business success of any organization. For twenty years, I have traveled across the United States, researching and interviewing senior leaders in government, academia, and business on the topic of succession development planning (SDP). I discovered two key common insights:

1. Most senior leaders (i.e., C-suite executives) knew little about succession development planning.
2. The majority felt succession development planning was the responsibility of their human resources officer (HRO).

Succession development planning can be either reactive or proactive. *Reactive succession development planning* is typically a crisis response, when a key employee or C-suite executive suddenly departs. When fifty-four-year-old United States Secretary of Commerce Ronald Harmon "Ron"

Brown was killed, for example, in a plane crash on April 3, 1996, the Department of Commerce did not have a successor groomed. Reactively, President Bill Clinton appointed Michael "Mickey" Kantor, the United States trade representative, as Brown's successor, thereby leaving a different void in the senior leadership.

Meanwhile, *proactive succession development planning* occurs when a senior executive anticipates a critical vacancy and develops a well-trained and developed talent pool of senior leaders to select from. In essence, succession development planning is vital at all times, crisis or no crisis. It also can serve as a tool to future-proof your workforce. Here is another key reason why your organization should implement a succession development plan. Can you relate?

> **Scenario:** In 2015, Bob announced he would be retiring in early 2016. The announcement of Bob's retirement did not come as a complete surprise to Jerry, Bob's supervisor. The organization also recently offered separation-incentive pay (SIP) to employees who qualify for early retirement. The SIP program allows the organization to buy out the employee's employment contract.
>
> Jerry has known for nine months that Bob would qualify, although Bob did not indicate until now that he would accept the SIP. Jerry also knows Bob is concerned about his wife's declining health and feels he should be at home to assist her during her time of need. Although Bob is not the only supervisor Jerry will be losing to retirement, Bob's departure causes Jerry the most concern; he has not prepared anyone to succeed Bob in his important, technically oriented, and challenging leadership position. To make matters worse, Jerry recently read two significant reports regarding the aging (maturing) US labor force and the increase in employment opportunities in the federal government.
>
> The first report by the Bureau of Labor Statistics (BLS) indicated approximately 267,000 of the Department of Defense's 2.1 million federal employees have met or will meet their retirement age of fifty-five by 2015. To add to Jerry's problem, the literature

indicated the labor force growth of young workers in the private-sector workforce decreased dramatically between 2013 and 2015. With the understanding that younger workers are unwilling to seek employment, Jerry is concerned that he may face stiffer competition in finding and keeping those who have traditionally started work in entry-level positions. Due to the United States' aging labor force, it is essential for Jerry and other senior leaders in his organization to meet and discuss the need for implementing a succession development plan for their organization.

Moreover, when planning for succession development, organizations must factor in the employee's performance and his or her leadership traits. Leadership traits should not only have value in high-performance candidates but also in candidates who are average achievers. Promoting ill-equipped top performers into leadership positions can be a disaster waiting to materialize. High performers can be horrific leaders. As a former member of the C-suite executive community, I have witnessed many C-suite executives who were excellent at managing projects and programs but failed miserably at leading people.

You can avoid this quagmire by making the correct decision about who should be groomed for key positions in your organization. To keep employees motivated and engaged in today's work environment, senior leaders must have experience in a diverse set of soft skills such as coaching, mentoring, emotional intelligence, social intelligence, cultural intelligence, diversity and inclusion intelligences, executive intelligence, and so on. Senior leaders must also develop a strong supply of candidates throughout their organizations in all directions—vertically, horizontally, and obliquely. Succession development planning should be conducted organization-wide, thereby giving you the opportunity to identify a continuous flow of diversified candidates. In addition, senior leaders should ensure employees are working at the right level. Leaders should clearly understand the organization's pipeline structure, meaning they have the ability to clearly communicate and assess the skills, time applications, and work values for each level throughout the organization. Moreover, other factors also come into play. According to Gene F. Brady and Donald L. Helmich, authors of *Executive Succession: Toward*

Excellence in Corporate Leadership, because many C-suite executives are quite charismatic, their departure may destabilize the power structure unless that charismatic authority is clearly and deliberately transferred to an incoming leader who shares many of the same qualities.[1]

Lyndon Baines Johnson's succession to the US presidency following the assassination of John F. Kennedy provides an excellent example of this succession process working well. While Johnson's personal style was very different from Kennedy's, he had not only his own kind of charisma but also a commitment to continue President Kennedy's vision, mission, and goals. As a result, the executive staff remained healthy and loyal. Johnson was also successful in working with both Democrats and Republicans.

Yet the smoothness of that sudden transition is something of an anomaly. I have witnessed far too many organizations invest millions of dollars in leadership and workforce succession development planning programs and management tools that just sit on the shelf collecting dust. I am hoping you will actually read and implement the strategies provided in this book. Please ask yourself several questions as you read:

- Why is executive leadership SDP important to your organization?
- Why is workforce SDP important to your organization?
- What do you need to do to establish a SDP culture?
- Who should be accountable for implementing the SDP?
- When should the plan be implemented?
- How should the SDP be implemented, and for which organizational roles (e.g., workers, managers, or senior leaders)?

There are two top executives who really understood their purpose as chief executive officers in their organizations. The first is the late Steven Paul "Steve" Jobs, who told *Fortune Magazine* on March 7, 2008, "We've got really capable people at Apple. My job is to make the whole executive team good enough to be successors, so that's what I try to do." The second is the late Liam McGee, former chairman and chief executive officer of Hartford Financial Services Group Incorporated, who told *Fortune* in 2014, "I focused on succession from day one. It's the CEO's most important job."[2] These two great leaders were true servant leaders.

They cared about the welfare of their organizations and the people who served under them, which led to their proactive behavior to plan for their own succession. This type of practical mind-set of leadership succession development planning embodies Robert K. Greenleaf's 1970 writings on servant leadership. In summary, he defines the servant leader as "a servant first, who consciously aspires to lead for the organization's benefit—unlike those who define themselves first as leaders and seek power or material possessions."[3]

The servant-leader concept is extremely different from the slave-leader concept. I call this leadership concept a "We, Us, and Team" philosophy. A servant-leader

- focuses on subordinate growth and well-being;
- shares power;
- puts the needs of others first; and
- helps people develop and perform as highly as possible.

Meanwhile, a slave-leader strives to accumulate and exercise individual power at the top of the pyramid. I call this type a "Me, Myself, and I" leadership philosophy. A slave-leader

- focuses on him or herself first;
- refuses to share power (controlling);
- puts his or her needs ahead of all others; and
- refuses to help develop others to become high performers.

Fortunately, most top executives I have interviewed who understood the importance of succession development planning possess the DNA of servant leadership. What is your perception of C-suite executives' and senior managers' mind-sets in your organization as it pertains to succession development planning? What is their primary purpose as C-suite executives and senior managers? If it is not to develop their successor, then you may want to seek new employment. Why is this important? If C-suite executives' and senior level managers' primary job is to improve their organization's financial bottom line and not to develop their successor, then they are only in the position to serve their stakeholders and themselves and not their employees. As senior leaders, your curiosity should pique new levels of concerns about your organization's future workforce and the competencies they should possess—if you want your organization to remain competitive and survive in the twenty-first century.

Origin of Succession

Before we move forward, I want to share with you how and where succession development planning originated. From a biblical perspective, although only in his thirties, Jesus was one leader who prepared for premature succession. For example, a quote from the Condition of Discipleship (Luke 9:23–24): "Then he said to all, 'If anyone wishes to come after me [succeed him], he must deny himself and take up his cross daily and follow me. For whoever wishes to save his life will lose it, but whoever loses his life for my sake will save it.'"

As life and history progressed into the third century AD, leadership succession did not reform itself. Take, for example, the throne of the Roman Empire, which was filled via a vote by military leaders of the Roman army. According to Roger Collins, author of *Palgrave History of Europe: Early Medieval Europe 300–1000*, voting an emperor into power was a very risky process. If these military leaders failed to secure broader support for their candidates, they would assassinate their current emperor and revert to their previous emperor. By the third century, between 268 and 285, revolts were frequent and instilled fear in the hearts of incumbent emperors and their successors. Around September 282, Marcus Aurelius Probus, the forty-seventh emperor of the Roman Empire was murdered by his military leaders.

The first emperor who attempted to end the assassinations was Marcus Aurelius Carus Augustus. Carus, the forty-eighth emperor of the Roman Empire, had dealt with the question of his own succession. He established the need for the emperor to be in more than one place at a time and nominated his younger son Marcus Aurelius Numerius Numerianus Augustus to the rank of Caesar, or junior emperor, and assigned him to rule the West. Later, when he undertook his Persian campaign in 283, he promoted his elder son, Carinus, to the superior rank of Augustus (full emperor), and he later became the forty-ninth emperor of the Roman Empire.[4]

In general, changes introduced around the turn of the fourth century by Diocletian and his successor Constantine I were aimed at the production of a more regimented and rigid society. Laws requiring sons to follow the professions of their fathers, laws that fixed prices, laws that established exact hierarchies in the civil and military administrations, and laws that forbade an increasing range of opinions and practices all reflected a common social ideology.

In the early sixth century, leadership succession continued to be an important issue across the European government. Europe's male ruling class organized leadership succession biologically: male heirs succeeded their fathers. If there were no sons, succession passed to a male relative. One of the most controversial laws that existed was called the Salic Law, a law that specifically prohibited female succession. It did, however, allow a king's child such as Clovis I of the Salian Franks to gain the throne in 481 at age of fifteen.[5] Moreover, according to Dictionary.com, the word "succession" originated in the early fourteenth century, meaning "fact or right of succeeding someone by inheritance," from the Old French *succession* (thirteenth century), which was from the Latin *successionem* (nominative *successio*) "a following after, a coming into another's place, result," from *successus*, past participle of *succedere;* the English term was "succeed."[6]

It was not until 1126 that Henry I, the king of England, persuaded the barons to accept his daughter Matilda [c. February 7, 1102–September 10, 1167] as his successor to the throne. Nonetheless, by 1317, civil law once again excluded females, and, by 1328, denied even males the right to claim inheritance through a female line. Research indicated this was a deliberate attempt to keep Edward III of England—a descendant of French kings through his mother, Isabel of France—off the throne, thereby sparking the Hundred Years' War.[7]

William Shakespeare claimed Charles VI of France rejected Henry V's claim to the French throne based on Salic laws, leading to the Battle of Agincourt. In fact, the conflict between Salic Law and English law was used to justify several struggles between French and English monarchs over the French throne. Meanwhile, the influence of the Salic Law of 1316 (also called Salian Law) extended to modern times in central Europe (e.g., France, Netherlands, Germany, Italy, Hungary, Balkans, Austria, Belgium, and Romania). Even Japan became a major enforcer of the agnatic (male-traced) succession formality in 1331, which led to a civil war against Hojo regents. Moreover, agnatic succession can be linked to the United States Constitution.

In 1787, during the writing of the US Constitution, our Founding Fathers understood the importance of agnatic succession. Amendment XX Section 3 of the US Constitution, for example, states, "If, at the time fixed for the beginning of the term of the President, the President-elect shall have died, the Vice President-elect shall become President." According to Article I Section 2 of the US Constitution, "When vacancies happen in the Representation from any State, the Executive Authority thereof shall issue Writs of Election to fill such vacancies."[8]

By the early sixteenth century, Holy Roman Emperor Charles V became the most powerful member of the House of Habsburg, ruling both the Spanish kingdom with its New World dominions (inherited from his maternal grandparents) and the Austrian and Burgundian dominions (inherited from his paternal grandparents). In 1520, a year after his election as emperor, he ceded his Austrian territories to his brother Ferdinand I of Germany. This appeased the prince-electors who feared he would be too powerful if he retained both. It also spawned the creation of two branches of the house of Habsburg: the Spanish branch and the Austrian branch. The Austrian branch later acquired the hereditary crowns of Bohemia, Croatia, and Hungary. Moreover, the throne of the Holy Roman Empire was virtually an Austrian hegemony; although nominally an elected post, the house of Habsburg held it from 1439 to 1806 with only a single five-year interruption. However, with the death of King Charles II of Spain, the Spanish branch became extinct in 1700. By September 1701, the Grand Alliance of the Hague, formed by England, the United Provinces, and Emperor Leopold I of Austria, declared war, which resulted in the War of the Spanish Succession and lasted for fourteen years, from 1700 to 1714.[9]

Because Charles V's popularity with his own people waned, his brother Charles VI dethroned him as emperor. Charles VI then developed his own will that deviated from the order of leadership succession specified in the Pactum of 1703. His will, which evolved into the Pragmatic Sanction of 1713, gave precedence to his own daughters ahead of his late brother's daughters. As the war progressed, Emperor Leopold I, head of the Austrian branch, established an explicit law of leadership succession within his surviving branch of the family. Leopold I and his two sons, Joseph and Charles, signed the *Pactum mutuae successionis* succession pact on September 12, 1703, which acknowledged females as successors only when all male lines became extinct. Leopold died in 1705 and was succeeded by his son Joseph I as emperor. Joseph I died in December 1711, leaving two then-unmarried daughters. Soon afterward, the Croatian Parliament, under the presidency of Imre Esterházy, voted its Pragmatic Sanction of 1712, in which the kingdom of Croatia accepted female inheritance of its crown after extinction of the male line and endorsed the position of the queen of Croatia.

While Charles VI spent incalculable hours preparing Europe for a female ruler, he lagged in preparing his own daughter, Maria Theresa. He refused to read official documents to her or take her to meetings, denied her the opportunity to be introduced to ministers, and failed to prepare her for the power she would later receive. More importantly, his refusal to prepare her implied an acceptance of his inability to produce a male heir. Nevertheless, a year later, Charles VI unilaterally issued the Pragmatic Sanction, and female rights of succession in Habsburg domains became acceptable. His elder daughter, Maria Theresa, at the young age of twenty-three, succeeded him after his death in 1740, leading immediately to the outbreak of the War of Austrian Succession. It was not until the Treaty of Aix-la-Chapelle of 1748 that Maria Theresa was finally recognized for her enduring leadership.[10]

Chapter Two

SLAVES AND IMMIGRANTS SUCCESSION IN NORTH
AMERICA

The Ice Age

During the last Ice Age, called the Pleistocene Epoch, some fifteen thousand to forty-five thousand years ago, Asian or Paleo-Indian immigrants began to populate the New World, later called North America. According Barry Lewis, Robert Jurmain, and Lynn Kilgore, authors of *Understanding Humans: Introduction to Physical Anthropology and Archaeology*, genetic data from these immigrants were discovered in the Paisley Cave site in Oregon. The genetic data revealed fourteen-thousand-year-old feces, human hair, and human DNA.[1] Paleo-Indians migrated by foot across Beringia, which encompassed the area where the Bering Sea exists today, as indicated in Image 1. They successfully maneuvered across the Bering Sea because much of the Earth's water was frozen in glaciers. In turn, this lowered the sea level that exposed the land bridge near the Arctic Circle. This landmass, called the Bering Land Bridge, connected Asia and North America. This migration led to a variety of different languages (and twelve hundred different dialects), cultures, religions, social organizations, physical characteristics, and different types of technologies that helped establish North America's cultural foundation.

Moreover, North America continued to converge socially and demographically via a tenth-century influx of European immigrants by sea from Western Europe and Western Africa. By 1492, Spanish colonization took root, followed by immigrants from the Old World (e.g., France, the

Netherlands, the British Isles, and Portugal). With them came, although against their will, a variety of black African slaves. By 1820, the United States' population had reached almost half of Great Britain's population, 9.6 million and 20.9 million, respectively.[2] In fact, by 1850, according to Bernard Grun author of *The Timetables of History: A Horizontal Linkage of People and Events,* approximately 23.5 percent (2.2 million whites and 3.2 million African slaves) of the United States' total population of twenty-three million were foreign born.[3]

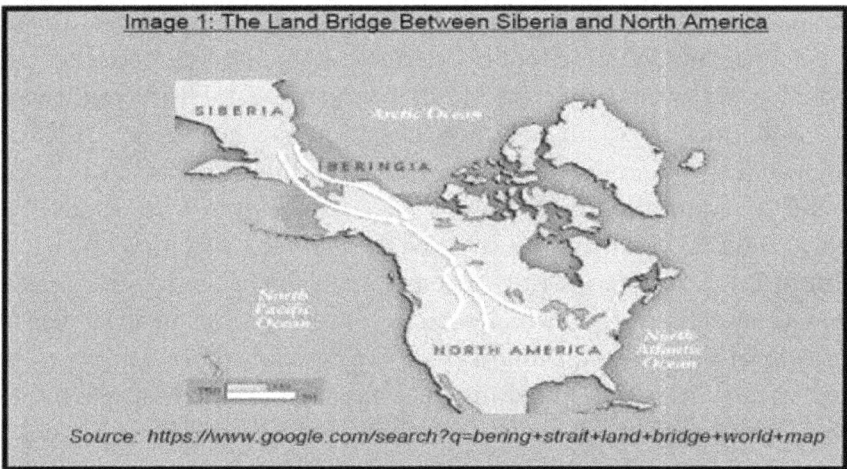

Image 1: The Land Bridge Between Siberia and North America

Source: https://www.google.com/search?q=bering+strait+land+bridge+world+map

African Slave Labor

For clarification, there are major differences between Africans being captured as slaves and transported by ship to America against their will and immigrants coming to America of their own free will. According to Toby Lester, author of *The Fourth Part of the World: An Astonishing Epic of Global Discovery, Imperial Ambition, and the Birth of America,* the enslavement of Africans began under Portuguese Prince Henry the Navigator (1394–1460), King Joao's third son. He spearheaded a raid in the mid-fifteenth century on the northern coastline of Africa. Henry tasked his Portuguese sailors to raid and defeat the Muslim Moors, who controlled immensely profitable items such as the trans-Saharan gold trade, the Canary Islands, spices, and the blubbery sea lions used for making sealskin and oils.

When this raid attempt failed, Henry directed his sailors to explore and seize control of the southern coastline of Africa. Controlling the southern coastline forced other Portuguese sailors to travel south along the West African coast, called the Royal Fifth, a place that had never been explored before by the Europeans. Sailors who wanted to sail south of Cape Bajado had to obtain Prince Henry's approval—and, upon their return, give him a fifth of their cargo.

Lester's explanations reflected that Prince Henry had several reasons for exploring Africa. First, he wanted to capture the most wealthy and powerful African kings who ruled the territory from east to west of the River of Gold, a river that desert traders used to transport gold and other riches north to the Mediterranean coast. His second reason was to identify Christian princes who had ingrained the love of Christ and would help him against those enemies of the Christian faith. Third, he did not want to enhance slavery succession, but to conduct an evangelical mission by saving the souls of the Africans and increasing their faith in the Lord Jesus Christ. Even though for centuries, traders and Genoan merchants had virtually monopolized the European side of the business of slave transportation from the African interior north to the Mediterranean, it was not until 1441 that the Portuguese slave trade became important to Henry's sailors, who felt it would be good luck to bring the first ten captive slaves to face Prince Henry.

By the early seventeenth century, workforce succession had become a critical element to the success of the thirteen British colonies in North America. Exporting black slaves from the coast of Africa created a new workforce that subsidized the labor needs of European white farmers known as Boers. Not only did the Portuguese procure slaves for the European colonists in Africa, in 1619, the Dutch raided a three-thousand-mile coastline of Africa and transported thousands of blacks by ship to the British colony of Jamestown, Virginia. These blacks were sold as slaves to plantation owners. Nevertheless, the earliest record of African and Native American contact predates English settlement by more than a century. It occurred in April 1502, when Spanish explorers brought an African slave with them to North America.[4]

By the eighteenth century, African slaves had replaced most other enslaved groups in England, although the slave population also included a significant number of Native Americans. In many cases, new tribes adopted captives to succeed fallen warriors. Some slave traders preferred captive Native Americans under eighteen years old, because they were more easily trained to handle new work. Nonetheless, as tea—England's greatest export—was being shuffled across the Atlantic, slave labor became an enormous commodity. This labor had a huge impact on the economies of these colonies.

Gerry Spence, author of *Give Me Liberty!*, argues that another primary reason for slavery was greed. Even one of our Founding Fathers, President James Madison (1751–1836), an intellectual contributor to the US Constitution, informed his visitors after the American Revolution that he could make $257 annually on every Negro, because the upkeep cost to him was only about $13 annually.[5] According to Walter Johnson, author of *River of Dark Dreams: Slavery and Empire in the Cotton Kingdom,* by the mid-eighteen hundreds, almost 70 percent of the small number of the wealthiest Americans whose wealth exceeded $100,000 resided below the Mason-Dixon Line in states such as Mississippi, North Carolina, and South Carolina. In fact, South Carolina was the richest state.[6] Europeans also made great profits from transporting slaves from Africa, which made many British entrepreneurs wealthy. These slaves were branded as the "building blocks"—the economic foundation—of North America.

By the early eighteenth century, the need for workforce succession became even more obvious; agricultural production had increased twofold both in Europe and across the thirteen colonies of the United States. The labor-intensive agriculture of the two countries equally demanded larger workforces. Crops such as sugar cane, tobacco, and cotton required a limitless and cheap supply of burly men to assure timely production for the European market. Several factors led to this change in the agricultural environment. First, Europe was cut off from Asia and the Middle East as Turkish power increased. Second, new economic theories came to fruition, directly affecting agricultural plantations. Third, many colonists died in the wars that took place in the colonies among England, France, and Germany. Finally, colonial agriculture not only fed the colonists, but it also produced cash crops for export, such as sugar, cotton, tobacco, tea, and animal products such as wool and hides, according to Rebecca Brooks Gruver, author of *An American History.*[7]

Nevertheless, while slavery became the new phenomenon in workforce succession in the United States in the nineteenth century, it had been a common practice in Africa since the seventh century, according to Bernard Grun. For five hundred years, between the seventh and twentieth centuries, Arab slave trade accounted for approximately eighteen million Africans being forcefully removed from their homelands in North Africa, the horn of Africa, and southeast Africa and transported by ship across the Indian Ocean to be sold as slaves. Although abolitionists saw it as a nefarious act, slaves were needed to succeed those who died, escaped, or converted to Islam. More importantly, they were needed to replenish England's labor force. Why was this succession of labor needed? Grun acknowledges that by 1349, one-third of England's population (25 million) had been killed by the plague called Black Death.[8] Outbreaks included the Great Plague of London (1665–66), in which one in five residents died. For the 250 years between 1530 and 1780, the number reached nearly 1.2 million (far less than the number of slaves who were transported to the Americas during this period). The deadly plague also migrated into Asia, thereby impacting its labor force.

By 1793, the Industrial Revolution—an industrialization pioneered by specialized machinery known as the cotton gin, designed for mass production of cotton—had taken root. The cotton gin, invented by a young Yankee schoolteacher named Eli Whitney, became critical to the South's economic success. This invention enabled slaves to clean (remove the green-seeded boll from) fifty pounds of cotton a day, compared with just a single pound per day, what was possible using the hand method. Within seven years, by 1800, daily cotton productivity skyrocketed to seventy-five thousand bales. According to Grun, between 1812 and 1830, the eleven most southern states' cotton productivity increased from 175,000 to 428,000 bales a day. By 1840, cotton accounted for half the value of all America's exports—the South was producing more than half of the world's cotton supply. As the tobacco crop began to diminish, cotton clothing had become a major commodity in Europe. The more money cotton produced, the more cotton the farmers wanted to produce on their farms—and the more slaves were needed to harvest the cotton. In fact, due to slave labor, Mississippi had more millionaires per capita than any other US state. The increased demand for slave labor resulted in additional raids on the African coastline.

During these raids, nearly four million blacks were captured, transported by ship to Jamestown, and sold as slaves to plantation owners to help harvest such lucrative crops as cotton, sugar, corn, wheat, and tobacco. The Americans called this system "cheap labor" because it supported the agricultural growth of the country's southern colonies. According to John Hope Franklin and Alfred A. Moss, Jr., authors of *From Slavery to Freedom: A History of African Americans*, these slaves were identified as being the healthiest, the largest, the youngest, the ablest, and the most culturally advanced. In fact, by 1860, slaves constituted approximately 45 percent of the population of Alabama, 25 percent of Arkansas, and 47 percent of Louisiana.[9]

By the mid-nineteenth century, an important machine-based manufacturing economic transition began to flourish in various areas within North America, creating a critical need for additional slave labor. The merger of the First and Second Industrial Revolutions emerged as technological and economic progress gained momentum with the development of steam-powered ships and railways, and later, the internal-combustion engine and electrical power generation. Work productivity again skyrocketed. The harsh work environments led to high demands for importation of indentured slaves from Europe to North America to construct railways. These indentured slaves, both black and white, also included prisoners from England who provided both skilled and unskilled labor, with the understanding that freedom would be granted after a certain number of years. Nevertheless, whites were granted their freedom while blacks were denied theirs.

Even though America's Northern states had abolished slavery, the United States Congress passed laws in favor of abolition in 1808, and British evangelicals or Quakers called for an immediate end to slavery, Southern states continued slavery. The slave population in the United States had nearly tripled by 1860, reaching approximately four million, with over half living in cotton-producing states of the South. According to the Funk and Wagnalls *New Encyclopedia*, to end slavery, the United Kingdom passed its Slavery Abolition Act of 1833, which abolished the owning, procuring, and selling of slaves; in turn, slaves across the British

Empire were allowed to participate in a four-year apprenticeship initiative. This initiative provided slaves the opportunity to learn a new trade; thereby, slave owners were provided the opportunity to retain their labor force. [10]

Robin D. G. Kelly and Earl Lewis, authors of *To Make Our World Anew: A History of African Americans*, acknowledge that Southern American states refused to surrender their beliefs. In fact, to plan for succession, slave owners began to rape their black slave women, forcing them to birth children who would later harvest their farm plantations. Moreover, when the Republican candidate Abraham Lincoln was elected president in 1860, seven of the eleven Southern states (South Carolina, Florida, Texas, Louisiana, Georgia, Mississippi, and Alabama) seceded to form the Confederate States of America from 1861 to 1865. Although Lincoln's antislavery views were well established, the war was not just about abolishing slavery; it was about preserving the United States as a nation.[11]

More importantly, at the start of the Civil War in 1861, the nation faced a shortage of military manpower, which was due to a growing antislavery sentiment in the North and the emancipation of many blacks who fled enslavement. Doris Kearns Goodwin, author of *Team of Rivals: The Political Genius of Abraham Lincoln*, contends it was not until well after the Union victory at Antietam in September 1862 that President Abraham Lincoln issued his preliminary Emancipation Proclamation on January 1, 1863, which stated, "slaves within states still in rebellion against the Union would be declared free, thenceforward, and forever."[12] By freeing over three million black slaves in the rebel states, the Emancipation Proclamation deprived the Confederacy of the bulk of its labor force, swaying international public opinion toward the Union. As a result, approximately 186,000 blacks joined the Union Army by the end of the Civil War in 1865. Nonetheless, slavery was not officially abolished until the adoption of the Thirteenth Amendment in 1865. In 1868, the Fourteenth Amendment provided blacks the rights of citizenship and the "equal protection" of the Constitution. In 1870, the Fifteenth Amendment instituted their right to vote, according to Julian E. Zelizer, author of *The American Congress: The Building of Democracy*.[13]

Irish Immigrant Labor

Succession in the United States for the Irish community took root as many ethnic groups began to immigrate to the United States of America, better known as the land of opportunity. What caused this migration? In 1695, the British began to impose immoral Anti-Catholic Penal Laws against the Irish for supporting the Catholic Stuart king, James II. They prohibited Irish Catholics from purchasing land, voting, practicing law, attending school, possessing weapons, practicing the Catholic religion, serving as officers in the British military, exporting trade, or holding government office. On June 18, 1798, the controversial law known as the Naturalization Act was passed. This law expressed the federalist distrust for not just Irish immigrants but for all immigrants attempting to enter the United States of America. These Irish immigrants favored the Republican Party, because the party better represented their democratic objectives and hostility toward the British Empire. Moreover, the Penal Laws existed for 140 years, until the Catholic Emancipation in 1829, which was spearheaded by Daniel O'Connell, a Catholic lawyer. Because of these restrictive laws and a large degree of poverty and new cheap labor requirements, by 1845, over one million Irish immigrants (mostly Presbyterians or so-called Scots-Irish) had immigrated to the United States, specifically in states such as South Carolina, North Carolina, Virginia, New York, Massachusetts, and Pennsylvania.

Seventy-five percent (or 650,000) of the Irish immigrants made New York their home during this famine era.[14] This migration was also associated with Ireland's great potato blight. Moreover, according to Adele Logan Alexander, author of *Homelands and Waterways: The American Journey of the Bond Family, 1846–1926,* nonenslaved blacks called Irish Negros also migrated to America from Ireland in hopes of joining the free-market labor force. Unaware of the federal statutes restricting naturalization in the promised land to only free white men, when these Irish Negros were not allowed to become American citizens, many were forced to work on plantations.[15] Nonetheless, in 1798, inspired by the American and French revolutions, the Irish staged a major rebellion against British rule, which led to the British Act of Union. As a result, in 1800, the British inducted Ireland into its United Kingdom, which abolished a five-hundred-year-old Irish Parliament in Dublin.[16]

Workforce succession began to unfold as Irishmen began to inhabit intricate labor jobs in transportation that served the railway, road, and canal industries. To build the 363-mile-long Erie Canal, for example, United States construction contractors needed workers. The rigorous task of building the canal led to the creation of the water route that ran from Albany, New York, along the Hudson River to Buffalo, New York, at Lake Erie, from New York City and the Atlantic Ocean to the Great Lakes. To establish this new labor force, American contractors solicited employment of Irishmen by placing recruitment advertisements in Ireland's newspapers overseas. The results of this workforce led to the stimulation of economic growth across the United States. These Irishmen also served as indigent servants and harvested farm plantations and have ancestral ties to twenty-two of the first forty-four US presidents, ranging from George Washington (first) to Barack Obama (forty-fourth).

According to John Mack Faragher, Mari Jo Buhle, Daniel Czitrom, and Susan H. Armitage, authors of *Out of Many: A History of the American People*, America's concern over Irish immigration and succession became secondary as slavery grew to be the primary issue during the start of the Civil War in 1861. Over 140,000 Northern Irish Americans joined the ranks of the Union Army, while many Southern Irishmen enlisted in the Confederacy. The all-Irish Sixty-Ninth New York Regiment, for example, earned its profound reputation for bravery and dependability during the battles at Gettysburg, Bull Run, and Antietam.[17]

Chinese Immigrant Labor

After the Slave Trade Act of 1807 was enacted, the United States was desperate to find its next succession of cheap labor, a labor force that would:

- build its transcontinental railroads;
- work its mining industry;
- harvest Southern plantations;
- establish agriculture and fisheries in the Southwest;
- serve in its military; and
- serve as construction workers, domestic servants, factory workers, and housekeepers.

Male Chinese immigrants were chosen for these roles. They traveled over twenty thousand nautical miles across the rough seas of the Pacific to be part of California's Gold Rush legacy. Many had other reasons for wanting to escape their homeland, such as fleeing from the turmoil following the British Opium Wars, the battle over fertile delta lands, and harsh economic conditions as a result of high taxes imposed by the Chinese government.[18] By the mid-nineteenth century, Chinese immigrants had become a major force in building the First Transcontinental Railroad. The Chinese population had grown from 2,716 in 1851 to over 63,000 by 1871, supplying the massive labor force needed to build the tracks for two privately owned railroad companies, the Union Pacific Railroad and Central Pacific Railroad. Railroad tracks, completed in 1869, were installed across the rugged Sierra Nevada Mountains and later throughout the state of Nevada.

Few white European construction workers wanted this difficult work, and hiring Chinese laborers was an enormous benefit to the two railroad companies, because they were not required to reimburse the living expenses of the Chinese. Chinese workers were recruited from gold and silver mines. It was the Chinese who made wagon trains obsolete as they saw railroad transportation as a faster way to transport goods. According to Lawrence M. Friedman, author of *A History of American Law*, even though the Chinese immigrants built a critical part of America's railroad system, they continued to face harsh treatment and racial discrimination. They were prohibited from owning land, seen as a degraded race, abused as cheap labor, and forbidden from marrying white women.[19] According to Faragher, Buhle, and Czitrom, in 1882, the United States Congress passed the Chinese Exclusion and Geary Acts, prohibiting immigration from China for a decade. The laws impaired the Chinese communities. First, they prevented thousands of Chinese men living in the United States who had left China without their children and wives from being reunited with their families. Second, the laws forbade new immigrants from entering the United States. The expulsion of Chinese farm workers in 1890 led them to cluster in Chinatowns of large cities.[20]

Moreover, because white European men felt the agricultural jobs were unappealing and refused to apply, Japanese, and later Filipinos, occupied the jobs. By this time, approximately 75 percent of all

California's agricultural workers—three hundred thousand, or a tenth of California's population—were Asian. According to the US Census, by 2010, the Chinese population had skyrocketed to 3.3 million, or 22 percent of the total Asian population in America. Many migrated to Arkansas, Louisiana, and other southern states to work on farm plantations. Just a few hundred immigrant Chinese women were transported over across the sea by boat, primarily as sex slaves.

By 1924, the laws denied all Asian immigrants except Filipinos entry into the United States; the Philippines came under US control following the Spanish-American War of 1898 (as did Puerto Rico, Hawaii, and Guam). Not until the early 1940s and World War II did the relationship between the United States and China improve. In 1943, the Magnuson Act facilitated Chinese immigration to the United States. Finally, in 1965, the Immigration and Nationality Act, formally known as the Hart–Celler Act, removed national-origin quotas and allowed not only Chinese immigrants but also Koreans, Indians, Vietnamese, and Japanese to immigrate to this beautiful country we call the United States of America. The Immigration and Nationality Act was established to attract skilled labor for the United States. [21]

Japanese Immigrant Labor

Because the federal legislation had excluded the Chinese immigrants from entering the United States, both American companies and farmers needed a new labor force. By the late eighteen hundreds, Japanese immigrants began to fill this labor pipeline. Thousands of Japanese immigrants began to immigrate to Hawaii and the Pacific Northwest from Japan to help build the railroads of the Northern Pacific (e.g., Portland and Oregon) and Columbia River Basin. By the early nineteen hundreds, approximately 40 percent of Oregon's railroad labor force was made up of Japanese immigrants, according to Laurie Mercier's online article, "Japanese Americans in the Columbia River Basin: Historical Overview." They worked as laborers in the sugar-beet industry, fish canneries, and in orchards and vegetable farms.

But this labor force of Japanese immigrants quickly came to a halt. In 1908, post–World War I activist organizations, including the American

Legion and the Hood River Anti-Alien Association, solicited their state and federal representatives to pass the National Origins Act of 1924, which forbade Japanese immigrants from entering the United States. This first generation of Japanese immigrants were called "Issei." Native-born United States Japanese citizens were called "Nisei." Forbidden from becoming US citizens, Japanese and Chinese Americans, even though faced with hostility and discrimination, fought for their civil rights, self-respect, and dignity. Rather than accepting the aforementioned acts, they filed thousands of lawsuits in local, state, and federal courts, challenging these unmerited laws. Basically, all they wanted to do was become part of the American DNA and contribute to its growth and prosperity. [22]

Hispanic/Latino Immigrant Labor

Since the sixteenth century, Spanish explorers (Hispanic or Latino) have been part of the American cultural society. In 1513, Juan Ponce de Leon was the first known explorer to reach the US coastline, which he called La Florida, in 1513. From 1513 to 1543, the Spanish were also the first Europeans to explore areas such as the Mississippi River, Great Plains, Grand Canyon, Maine, Appalachian Mountains, and along the Pacific Coast to Oregon. By 1565, they created the first permanent European settlement in locations such as Santa Fe, New Mexico, and Saint Augustine, Florida, which were founded before Jamestown, Virginia, in 1607. Nevertheless, it was not until the US-Mexican War of 1846–1848 that the Southwest (the area from Texas to California) became a Spanish-speaking territory. People occupying this territory were identified as Mexican-Americans, which resulted in a wave of immigrants from Puerto Rico, Cuba, the Dominican Republic, and Central and South America. These migrants were identified as Hispanics, or Latinos; approximately 117,000 immigrated to the United States by 1850 to backfill jobs in the areas of agriculture and mining, according to David G. Gutierrez's online article, "American Latino Theme Study: The Making of America."[23]

Between 1910 and 1920, during the Mexican Revolution, the United States was flooded with migrant laborers because they wanted to escape violent government attacks and seek employment and stability. US farmers exploited their physical and mental capacities. They were portrayed as temporary migrants and were seen as being mentally passive and reserved but physically robust and fit to perform the work at hand. These farmers trafficked the demand for Mexican immigrants. They understood that without Mexican migrants, they were unable to find the labor force needed to harvest their crops. By 1929, when the US stock market crashed, leading to the Great Depression, the number of available immigrant laborers decreased as Mexican migrants returned home to Mexico. The decade-long Great Depression resulted in the longest economic downturn in US history, wiping out millions of investments, leading to reductions in consumer spending and investing, and increasing levels of unemployment and layoffs. In addition, the US government implemented its unofficial deportation policies, causing many immigrants to return home. Nevertheless, by 1965, the US immigration law was modified to allow Hispanic and Latino immigrants to return to the United States and participate in its labor force. According to Renee Stepler and Anna Brown of the Pew Research Center, authors of *Statistical Portrait of Hispanics in the United States,* in 2016, they account for about 17 percent of the American population (approximately 55.4 million people) and account for 43 percent of the labor force. In addition, they occupy 69 percent of the jobs in areas such as forestry, farming, fishing, construction, cleaning, and maintenance.[24]

Whether we like it or not, immigrants have been and continue to be a major part of the United States labor force. In 2010, there were 23.1 million foreign-born persons in the civilian labor force, making up 16.4 percent of the total US workforce. As the foreign-born population continues to spiral upward, increasing America's total population, they have driven disproportionate growth as a share of the labor force. According to an online Brookings Institute report by Ron Haskins, in 1970, immigrants made up approximately 5 percent of the US population and 5 percent of the labor force. Four decades later, by 2010, 16 percent of the US labor force was immigrants, who accounted for 13 percent of the total US population. Moreover, during a fifteen-year period from 1995 to 2010, the US labor force was heavily populated with foreign-born workers. In fact, between 2000 and 2005, 67.7 percent of the US labor force was foreign born.[25]

According to Camille L. Ryan and Kurt Bauman of the US Census Bureau, by 2010, this number had reversed, with US-born occupying 58.5 percent and immigrants occupying 41.5 percent of the US labor force. Moreover, their educational status was equally competitive. The number of foreign-born immigrants who held a master's degree was nearly equal to native-born Americans, at 9.1 percent and 9.5 percent, respectively. They exceeded at the doctoral degree level (1.9 percent versus 1.2 percent, respectively). The drawback to foreign-born immigrants was that 28.9 percent did not have a high-school diploma, as compared to only 7.4 percent of the native-born workers who lacked their diploma. Within the next five to ten years, the impact to US organizations and the economy of 36.3 percent of the US workforce (both foreign-born immigrants and US-born) without a high-school education will begin to be felt. It may stifle innovation and creativity, which may lead to higher security threats to our nation.[26]

Chapter Three

THE COMING OF THE FOURTH INDUSTRIAL REVOLUTION

Industrial Revolutions

In the 1700s, Britain was the birthplace of the Industrial Revolution, during which manufacturing occurred using hand tools or basic machines from within people's homes. This was followed by a high demand for production of iron and growth in textile industries and steam engines, which all contributed improvements and growth in railroad transportation, banking, and electronic communication. The steam engine, for example, was an integral part of the Industrial Revolution. In 1712, Englishman Thomas Newcomen developed the first steam engine to help pump water out of mines. Because the majority of the world had become automated, work produced by the white-collar workforce, those who would herald the arrival of the Digital Age Revolution, began to show a decline. During the First Industrial Revolution in the eighteenth and nineteenth centuries, for example, United States and European companies attempted to replace humans with machines.

Prior to the invention of Eli Whitney's cotton gin in 1793, the laborious work of cotton picking by slaves was forever changed. A slave took an hour to pick 120 plants, but the new machine could harvest 144,000 plants in that same time. Along with the cotton gin was the invention of steam power, which propelled ships across the Atlantic Ocean in record time. With ships having the capability to transport cotton via steam power to Great Britain between 1760 and 1840, the First Industrial Revolution (FIR) was born. During these formative years, Great Britain was the technological innovator, which led to the evolution from hand-production methods to machine-produced products and services, including iron, steam power, machine tools, and new chemical manufacturing. This revolution included textile manufacturing, which was the prime employment for this generation. In addition, the rise in average household incomes and population growth was unparalleled.

The Second Industrial Revolution (SIR) was the successor to the First Industrial Revolution, in which technology, extensive manufacture of machine tools, and the economy played major roles between 1870 and 1914. It laid the foundation for the first true globalization pertaining to the fundamentals of e-commerce. This revolution included steam-power transportation (e.g., railroads, ships, boats, etc.) and was synonymous with the term "Technological Revolution," which led to new innovations in steel manufacturing, electricity, and petroleum to support public transportation such as automobiles and airplanes. As a result, businesses had to retool and retrain their workforce and, at the same time, search for the best and brightest people to fill critical construction job vacancies and telephone communication jobs, which resulted from Alexander Graham Bell's invention of the telephone in 1876.

Between 1837 and 1914, William Cooke and Charles Wheatstone, British residents, had transitioned the world into its Second Industrial Revolution (SIR). By 1866, the invention of the first commercial electrical telegraph led to a telegraph cable being installed across the country to enhance communications between telegraph systems and the banking industry.

Because of his limited hearing ability, Thomas Edison, a former railroad worker, learned the trade of telegraphy and became an apprentice engineer. During this time, he focused on the development of duplex telegraph technology, which allowed him to process dual messages at once. His brilliant mind did not stop with the electric telegraph or power lines, however. He continued to future-proof his mental state by creating the mimeograph and the electric pen, which led to the creation of the phonograph by other researchers and inventors. His embryonic development of a carbon-filament lamp was used for glass bulbs. The Second Industrial Revolution allowed new products from local communities to be transported via the innovations in transportation such as improved roads, the Erie Canal, steamboats, and railroads. With these new inventions, between 1913 and 1920, the United States was meeting more than one-third of the world's industrial requirements, which led to approximately eleven million Americans transitioning from farm communities to various cities, and almost twenty-five million immigrants arrived from foreign countries to gain employment.

By the early nineteen hundreds, the works of Frederick Taylor and Henri Fayol were being linked to the importance of succession planning. In 1911, Taylor wrote the book *Scientific Management*, in which he explained how synthesized various principles of work methods, measurements, and simplification ensured work efficiency. Born in 1856 in a middle-class suburb of Philadelphia, Pennsylvania, Taylor earned a mechanical engineering degree at Stevens Institute. His object of management was to secure the maximum prosperity for the employer, coupled with the maximum prosperity for each employee. *Maximum prosperity* sought not only to create large dividends for the company or owner; it was also committed to the development of every man to his state of maximum efficiency, where he became capable of producing his highest grade of work.

Taylor believed true scientific management required a mental revolution on the parts of both management and workers. He acknowledged that management could not be learned from just reading papers, books, or classroom theory; it had to be learned by doing. He supported the ideology of *functional authority*, in which all authority should be based on knowledge, not position. He was a true believer in the ideology of *functional foremanship*, in which staff members would be assigned to help shop foremen and supervisors in completing their task assignments. This action led to workforce cross-pollination. Providing incentive awards to his workers and foremen was contradictory to his philosophy of scientific management. Instead, he promoted intertwining professional education, technical training, and on-the-job-training. In turn, companies would receive a higher output of work by the workers and foremen.[1]

Meanwhile, Fayol's 1916 book, *Administration Industrielle et Générale*, scrutinized the nature of management and administration. His book has since been revised and printed in an English-language version titled *General and Industrial Management*. A French engineer and director of mines, Fayol used his classic fourteen principles of management to influence organizations as to the importance of management having the responsibility to ensure the stability of tenured personnel. His fourteen principles included the following:

1. Division of labor
2. Authority and responsibility
3. Discipline
4. Unity of command
5. Unity of direction
6. Subordination of the individual's interests to the common goal
7. Remuneration
8. Centralization
9. Scalar chain
10. Order
11. Equity
12. Stability of tenure of personnel
13. Initiative
14. *Esprit de corps* (team spirit)

If these were ignored, ill-prepared employees would fill key job vacancies.[2]

Moreover, his work supported the continuity of tenure among managers. His viewpoint of management contradicted Frederick Taylor's. Fayol's idea of management was top down, while Taylor supported a bottom-up approach. Fayol believed a manager's job was to carry out a business process, which consisted of five parts:

1. Planning for the organization
2. Organizing it
3. Coordinating its operating parts
4. Commanding it
5. Controlling it

In support of this business process, short-term and long-term plans of action were to be implemented; however, they had to be flexible and supported by management. Unlike Taylor, who did not support monetary incentives, Fayol supported them. Fayol believed these incentives would increase worker performance, and a reduction in supervision would be required, leading to larger numbers of workers being supervised by fewer foremen. Social order was also a concern for organizations. Social order presumed the successful execution of the two most difficult managerial activities: good organization and good selection of personnel. An organization should simultaneously identify its succession development needs and implement a career-development planning program that would proactively prepare employees to fill both unexpected and expected job vacancies. Meanwhile, a human-capital strategy plan could serve as an aid in identifying new positions, monitoring how changes in technology and industry would affect the performance of different jobs, assessing the special needs for training at all levels, and determining succession development needs that support the stability of tenure of all employees.

By 1973, Walter R. Mahler and William F. Wrightnour, authors of *Executive Continuity: How to Build and Retain an Effective Management Team,* pioneered the term "executive continuity," which became the authoritative reference on the subject of succession planning in America. Their argument was that in order for the executive-development process to be successful, a systematic approach requiring a ten-step solution had to occur to help senior managers avoid four major pitfalls:

1. Avoiding the mechanistic approach of developing a succession-planning program that was cluttered with a complex web of policies, pronouncements, procedures, and programs
2. Focusing on a holistic workforce-development approach, not just senior-executive development
3. Implementing an "early identification program" to include cross-pollination in order to provide high-potential employees with an opportunity to perform rotational job assignments between various divisions of the organization
4. Ensuring that top managerial support is granted, because without their support, the cross-pollination program would fail

There should, however, be a fifth pitfall included, which is to garner support from human-resources officers (HRO) during the initiation stage of designing and implementing a succession development plan. When senior leaders do not capture HRO support, the process may become subdued.[3] According to Cynthia McCauley, Russ Moxley, and Ellen Van Velsor, editors of *The Center for Creative Leadership: Handbook of Leadership Development*, one should be aware that the traditional approach to succession planning was to fit the most highly qualified candidates with the job, in the hopes that the candidate then carries out the responsibilities of the job more efficiently and effectively.[4] There are drawbacks to this approach, however: this approach focuses primarily on identification and assessment of job talent and pays little attention to the candidate's knowledge, skills, and abilities. As a result, senior management is provided with a list of candidates who may be qualified to fill particular positions, but it grants little consideration to what true experience the candidates might need to be prepared for the position or how the position might support the candidate's career-development needs. Meanwhile, when it comes to succession planning, organizations need increased depth and diversity of "bench strength" to have the right person available when the future reveals itself, according to Robert A. and Christina Gikakis, editors of *Shared Wisdom: Best Practices in Development and Succession Planning*. They also acknowledged that succession planning becomes more problematic when it comes to predicting future human-capital requirements, especially as it relates to easing executives out of their position in a timely manner.[5]

In the 1990s, according to Jeremy Rifkin, the Third Industrial Revolution (TIR) was the digital, biological, and physical revolution in which we used information technology, information systems, and electronics to automate workload production. This revolution focused on the creation of a high-tech, twenty-first-century "smart, green, and digital" economy. It was the beginning of the implementation phase of the 3-D printing phenomenon, computers, and Internet. The TIR, powered by oil and other fossil fuels, began to spiral into dangerous territories. Food and gas prices climbed exponentially, unemployment reached an all-time high, the housing market crashed, and consumer and government debt soared. By August 6, 1991, when the World Wide Web made its debut, millions tried out the Internet for the first time. This led to the beginning of various electronic interactions from e-mails, YouTube,

Wi-Fi, Google, e-commerce, Facebook, and various digital satellite technologies. And by 1993, the dot-com bubble collapsed, along with many Internet-based organizations (e.g., pets.com and Webvan), while organizations such as Amazon, Cisco, and eBay saw stocks drop by large margins but later recovered.[6]

Unlike the two previous industrial revolutions, where engineers used lathes, stamping presses, molding machines, and drills to accomplish their tasks, the Third Industrial Revolution relied heavily on technical-based workers who possessed one-dimensional skill sets and were major supporters of the Internet and e-commerce. These services radically reduced costs in how organizations generated and distributed information. Manufacturing companies, for example, provided opportunities using three-dimensional printing, which gave businesses the capability to produce and print 3-D products with computer-aided design software. Three-dimensional printing produced successive layers of various products using molten plastic, powder, or metals to create material scaffolding. This technology is identified as *additive manufacturing*, as compared to *medieval manufacturing*, which involved cutting down and pairing off materials and then assembling them together. Moreover, 3-D printing provided business with the ability to design and manufacture various other types of goods such as automotive parts, shoe prototypes, iPhone covers, and more, while at the same time reducing manufacturing time and costs. In addition, numerous computer-based, state-of-the-art software and hardware technologies began to emerge to support the operational functions of dexterous robots, the manufacturing of airplane parts, and a range of e-commerce-based services. With these new technologies, a technical-based workforce was at a high demand. Employees were forced to return to technical schools for retraining. Many executives began to turn their attention to the idea of replacement planning as short-term fix.

Replacement Planning versus Succession Planning

There are some commonalities between succession development planning, replacement planning and generic succession planning. To alleviate any confusion between replacement planning and succession planning, according to Rebecca Wolfe, author of *Systematic Succession Planning: Building Leadership from Within*, replacement planning focuses on risk management and ideas for coping with crisis, see table 1.[7] William Rothwell, author of *Effective Succession Planning*, differentiates between replacement planning and succession planning. Rothwell acknowledges that replacement planning is a form of risk management that is used to help reduce calamitous actions that take place as a result of unexpected loss of key human-capital resources. At times, the two activities may overlap, but they will always complement each other.[8] Meanwhile, succession development planning works toward continued leadership and proactive talent building, so an organization can continue with planned wisdom and foresight.

Table 1: Replacement Planning versus Succession Planning	
Replacement Planning	**Succession Planning**
Reactive	Proactive
Form of Risk Management	Planned Future Development
Substituting	Renewing
Narrow Approach	Organized Alignment
Restricted	Flexible

Workforce Development Planning versus Succession Development Planning

The power of succession development planning (SDP) will become transcendent as the one-dimensional workforce becomes historical. Organizations can no longer afford to have their employees focus on a single job function. Contrary to the various traditional definitions about succession planning, the nontraditional or twenty-first-century definition of succession development planning will focus on the importance of training and developing a multigenerational workforce that possesses multidimensional competencies to expeditiously fill both critical and noncritical job vacancies vertically, diagonally, and horizontally. Additionally, to ensure their organization is well prepared to confront this transformative knowledge-based workforce demand, C-suite executives must focus on more than merely implementing a succession development plan that would aid in developing executives', managers', and employees' technical and soft-skill competencies (e.g., knowledge, skills, abilities, education, experience, and certifications). To boost workforce morale, C-suite executives must indulge themselves in better understanding their organization's culture and workforce engagement. They must identify which employees have the right competencies to be promoted within the organization. In essence, succession development planning does not focus only on executive and management positions but encompasses all positions in the organization. It ensures proactive leadership continuity for all key positions by developing activities that will build personnel talent from within, while meeting an organization's immediate and future needs. Throughout this book, the term "C-suite executive" is defined as a senior leader who possesses the title of chief executive officer (CEO), chief operating officer (COO), chief information officer (CIO), chief financial officer (CFO), and so on.

Most managers, HR representatives, and training and workforce-development experts understand the difference between succession development planning (SDP) and workforce development planning (WDP). There are major differences between the two. Workforce development planning, for example, is the more traditional way organizations train and develop their employees. It is more aligned with the microevolution of training and development. WDP is an employee-centric approach to meeting organizational business needs. This approach, however, can no longer continue in a twenty-first-century multidimensional workforce. WDP focuses more on an individual development needs, while succession development planning focuses more on a macroevolution scale that transcends a holistic approach to group developmental needs.

Succession development planning is the nontraditional approach of the future. It is a holistic approach to meeting organization, employee, and customer needs. It supports an approach to workforce development to include diversity and inclusion awareness. It not only assesses employees' current and future competency strengths and deficiencies (e.g., knowledge, skills, abilities, education, certifications, etc.), but it is intertwined with how employees' task assignments are interconnected with the organization's overarching mission and goals. SDP not only measures gaps and deficiencies in the workforce competencies but also focuses on workforce diversity and inclusion, engagement, morale, age, ethnicity, productivity, flexibility, and adaptability. It measures employee soft skills such as emotional, cultural, personal, and social intelligence. In addition, it provides competency alignment, mapping, and modeling solutions. A living document, SDP delivers proactive solutions for how to future-proof your workforce. As such, it requires continuous review and updates.

In response to a changing workplace, SDP displays a forward-thinking mind-set that creates a competitive advantage in a twenty-first-century workplace. It provides a progressive approach to using a social-media framework that reinforces workforce engagement, collaboration, and connectivity via technology across a multigenerational and frequently dispersed workforce. It brings awareness of the generational balance or imbalance among the workforce and helps leadership bridge the gaps in managing and leading these diverse generations. SDP induces coaching and mentoring across all levels of the workforce to ensure both connectivity and a better understanding of organizational goals, objectives, vision, and mission. Implementing a SDP reinforces a workforce that is more agile, collaborative, and hyperconnected and supports future growth. SDP draws upon a knowledge-based workforce whose main capital is knowledge and who is inspired and grounded in globalization, and uses social media, social learning, and social networking as their action learning tools. It is also a tool that can be used for social recruiting, retaining, developing, and engaging employees at all levels of an organization. Table 2 shows other differences between the two plans.

Table 2: Workforce Development Planning versus Succession Development Planning	
Workforce Development Planning	**Succession Development Planning**
Traditional approach to workforce development	Nontraditional approach to workforce development
Reactive and current thinking (i.e., after employee retirement or departure)	Proactive and future thinking (i.e., before employee retirement or departure)
Focus only on current job vacancies	Focus on both current and future job vacancies
Training and developmental activities linked to individual department's goals and mission	Training and developmental activities linked to organizational overall goals and mission
Focus on individual approach to individual development	Focus of holistic approach to workforce development
Short-term or quick-fix approach	Long-term approach
Increase overhead cost	Reduce overhead cost
Status-quo-proofing the workforce	Future-proofing the workforce
Imbalanced workload demands	Balanced workload demands
Longer time frame to backfill job vacancies	Shorter timeframe to backfill job vacancies
Managers focus more time on administrative tasks	Managers focus less time on administrative tasks
Workforce competency gaps are reactively identified and measured	Workforce competency gaps are proactively identified and measured
Manual-based worker	Knowledge-based worker
Support quality improvement at individual level	Support quality improvement at all levels
Single-dimensional training and career development	Multidimensional training and career development
Suspension focus	Retention focus
Diversity and inclusion unawareness	Diversity and inclusion awareness

The Prominence of the Fourth Industrial Revolution

By 2020, the Fourth Industrial Revolution (FoIR) will kindle a paradigm shift that will include numerous converging and extraordinary technologies such as advanced robotics, artificial intelligence, machine learning, renewable energy, autonomous transportation, 4-D printing, human intelligence, virtual health care, genomics, biotechnologies, and other advanced materials. It is understood that various technology developments will provide the first major paradigm shift in the FoIR. These developments will transform the way employees rejoice, live, and work. It is also understandable that some jobs will disappear as others emerge, and that jobs that do not exist today will become commonplace in the new economy, according to Klaus Schwab's online article, "The Fourth Industrial Revolution: What It Means, How to Respond."[9] Nevertheless, my personal prediction is that the FoIR will be associated with five additional unprecedented paradigm shifts that will take place simultaneously and will greatly challenge the business models and human capital strategic plans (especially those focused on a more humanistic approach) of many organizations:

The first paradigm shift of this epoch will focus on organizational transformation that deals with a more adaptive, functional organization model incorporating team dynamics that leads to a more interdependent, interconnected, and flexible workforce, as compared to the antiquated traditional organizational model.

The second paradigm shift will address how organizations should lead and manage a multigenerational workforce that will consist of approximately five different generations.

The third paradigm shift deals with managing, leading, and engaging a more diversified and inclusive workforce.

The fourth paradigm shift draws upon a global perspective as to what futuristic and multidimensional competencies (e.g., hard skills, soft skills, postsecondary education, certifications, etc.) employees will need to ensure they remain future-proof in the twenty-first century. If employees want to remain marketable, they must learn to speak multiple languages. Even though they are important to have, I am not talking about languages such as English, Chinese, French, Spanish, and so on. I am referring to professional and vocational languages such as engineering, math, finance, construction, contracting, and science. Having the ability to communicate and collaborate in different languages will help employees to become more marketable when it comes to promotions and job opportunities.

The fifth paradigm shift deals with a shortage in the US labor force to fill both vocational and nonvocational or professional jobs (e.g., engineers, medical doctors, college professors, occupational therapists, mathematicians, machinists, ironworkers, coal miners, etc.), according to Jeffrey Sparshott's online article, "The US Occupations at Greatest Risk of a Labor Shortage."[10] To make matters worse, a 2010 Bureau of Labor Statistics jobs report indicated that the United States would need to fill twenty million new job vacancies during this period. In addition, historically, the job growth rate has been only about 6 percent; by 2020, it will increase twofold to a notable 14 percent, according to Hilda L. Solis, former secretary, US Department of Labor at the US Bureau of Labor Statistics.[11] This demand will lead to a massive labor shortage across America. Your competitors will seek to recruit your high performers in record numbers. Facing a very aggressive labor market, backfilling these highly skilled positions will be difficult and extremely expensive. This action will force C-suite executives to not only implement an organization-wide retention program but also a highly targeted retention program that is designed specifically for recruiting potential candidates with particular competencies. Having a well-established and active succession development plan will allow your organization to become the poacher, as opposed to the poachee. As a reminder, the business market will determine the movement of your employees, not your organization.

Paradigm Shift 1: Increasing Workforce Productivity via Technology
With the possibility of billions of people being connected by mobile devices having unlimited and unparalleled processing power, storage capacity, and access to knowledge, leaders will be facing competitive challenges of hiring, retaining, and sustaining a well-trained and developed workforce. FoIR will also consist of a knowledge-based workforce who possess a high degree of professional knowledge in the areas of artificial intelligence, human intelligence, autonomous transportation (self-driving vehicles), advanced robotics, genomics, machine

learning (such as IBM's Watson), biotechnology, cognitive technology, 4-D printing, web-based services, unmanned aerial vehicle (drone) delivery services, self-correcting communications networks, and so on. Moreover, these possibilities will be multiplied by emerging technology in fields such as nanotechnology, materials science, fossil fuels, solar, wind turbine, geothermal, hydroelectric, nuclear, cyber-based security (physical and remote surveillance), quantum computing (i.e., Big Data), reestablishment of cloud computing and storage, and so on. For example, the Big Data phenomenon will include IBM's Watson computer system, which will be used to collect and process huge amounts of data ranging from artificial intelligence to human intelligence to medical information, which will be used to collect and process more private and public raw data than any other machine in history. Data will be extracted from closed-circuit television (CCTV) and high-end cameras being posted on streets and buildings across the country. This data could be used to leverage data lakes to help drive value and assist federal, state, and local law-enforcement agencies in their antiterrorism force protection (ATFP) and national security efforts. According to experts at Tableau Corporation, a data lake is described as "a man-made reservoir in which you first build a cluster, then you fill it with water (data), and once the lake is established, you start using the water (data) for various purposes such as generating electricity, drinking and recreating predictive analytics."[12] For state and local law-enforcement agencies, the data can be used to help detect, prevent, and reduce neighborhood crime; enhance safety prevention; and address other community-related issues.

Consequently, if approved by the courts, federal, state, and local governments will have the capability to conduct facial recognition and track and monitor an individual's behaviors, locations, and more via the use of closed-circuit television (CCTV) and high-definition/resolution cameras posted on streets and buildings around the country. This technology will be used as preventive measures to help curb, detect, and prevent neighborhood crimes. More importantly, using CCTV as a prevention tool will help reduce incarcerations. Big-screen televisions will have the ability to be folded and stored away for later usage, which could help deter home invasions.

Manufacturing jobs will be a major contender for knowledge-based workers who have been retrained to work on high-end and complex robotic systems and computer systems. In their August 2011 online article, "Made in America, Again: Why Manufacturing Will Return to the US," Boston Consulting Group directors Harold L. Sirkin, Michael Zinser, and Douglas Hohner indicate that in areas such as transport, computers, fabricated metals, and machinery, 10 to 30 percent of these American-imported goods from China will be made at home by 2020. In turn, this would boost American output by $20 billion to $55 billion per year.[13]

Paradigm Shift 2: Traditional versus Functional Organizational Models
The traditional organizational model is associated with a workforce that is one-dimensional, meaning employees conduct one particular job function. Employees are required to work and remain in an organic culture that stiffens their ability to cross-pollinate or gain new work-related experiences. Employees are departmentalized and are required to follow an antiquated hierarchical structure in which power flows upward and vertically. In other words, employees are required to follow chain-of-command, like the military hierarchical structure. There are benefits associated with the traditional model. First, it provides employees with a transparent understanding about their work-related responsibilities and roles within the organization. Second, managers are provided many rules and regulations that allow them to better handle business- and workforce-related conflicts.

Meanwhile, a functional organizational model is associated with the competency-aligned organizational (CAO) structure. This is built on team-based performance, in which employees from other parts of an organization are assigned/loaned to other departments, to be inserted into integrated product teams (IPTs) to work on short- or long-term projects. Projects rarely exceed two years. Once the tasks are completed, the employee returns back to his or her official department. The key issue to ensuring CAO success is that an employee who is matrix into other departments must receive his or her performance review from his or her original or organic supervisor. The organic manager is also accountable for ensuring his or her employee receives proper training, career development, and annual performance reviews. The project manager, however, should provide his or her input on the employee's performance review. In addition, the CAO model should include the establishment of both an organic- and matrix-reporting structure and policies in which the employee would have dual reporting relationships to a functional manager and a product manager. This would protect both the employee and the organization from possible litigation issues.

More importantly, this new functional model incorporates team dynamics, which leads to a more interdependent, interconnected, balanced, and flexible workforce. The model also reinforces an employee's ability to strengthen his or her leadership and collaboration skills, career development, and overall workforce performance. In contrast, the traditional organizational model is independent based and does not necessarily encourage team dynamics, multidimensional learning, and high-performance ideology. Instead of integration, this stovepipe model can lead to workforce segregation in the areas of race, ethnicity, religion, language, sex, education, and salary.

However, there are disadvantages to implementing a CAO organizational structure:

1. If it is not properly communicated and employees are not adequately trained, internal complexity may result in havoc across the organization. Employees may become confused about their reporting chain and task prioritization, which could lead to conflict between supervisors and employees.
2. A second disadvantage is the increased overhead costs associated with having two different managers from different departments supervising the same employee.
3. The third disadvantage is having limited personnel with the right competencies to support current and future tasks or projects, which could have a negative impact on employee morale and productivity.
4. Finally, establishing a matrix organizational structure could enforce a more competitive work environment, which may lead to a hostile workplace. Employees with less experience may feel they are not being provided the opportunity to grow.

Paradigm Shift 3: Leading and Managing a Multigenerational Workforce
During the US Great Recession from December 2007 to June 2009, the country faced an eight-trillion-dollar housing bubble crisis. Personal bankruptcies and home foreclosures reached an all-time high for thousands of Americans. Overnight, millions of people became either unemployed or underemployed. Although the Great Recession had a huge, unconstructive impact on American families and the economy, it had a constructive impact on the ability of organizations to hire and retain high performers. C-suite executives and managers also began to witness three different generations fighting to remain employed. According to Allan Schweyer's July 21, 2015 online report, "Generations in the Workforce & Marketplace: Preferences in Rewards, Recognition & Incentives," traditionalists accounted for approximately five million, or 3.2 percent, of the 157 million people in the US workforce. Their primary reason for delaying their retirement was that they wanted to share their lifelong experiences with the other three generations. At the same time, the baby boomers workforce accounted for forty-four million. As a result of the 2009 economic downturn, in an effort to rebuild their retirement savings, they decided to prolong their retirement date too. Meanwhile, fifty-three million gen Xers and fifty-five million millennials comprised the remaining employees in the US labor force. Chart 1 shows the 2009 US workforce generational breakdown by percentage and overall population. Note: The inner circle represents the percentage, and the outer circle represents the five million millennials who made up the remaining employees in the US labor force.[14] Note: The inner circle represents the population percentage and the outer circle represents the population number in millions.

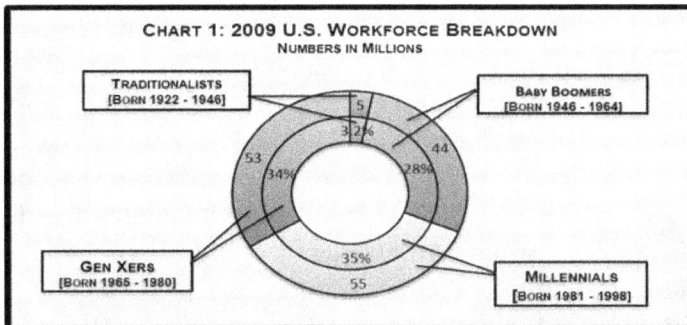

CHART 1: 2009 U.S. WORKFORCE BREAKDOWN
NUMBERS IN MILLIONS

TRADITIONALISTS
[BORN 1922 - 1946]

BABY BOOMERS
[BORN 1946 - 1964]

GEN XERS
[BORN 1965 - 1980]

MILLENNIALS
[BORN 1981 - 1998]

5
3.2%
44
53
34%
28%
35%
55

Generation Z, the fifth generation—those born between the early 1990s and mid-2000s—will be joining the US labor force at a prodigious rate: it is projected to be more than thirty million strong by 2020, according to Bruce Tulgan's 2013 online article, "The Great Generational Shift: The Emerging Post-Boomer Workforce." They will be entering the workforce with an optimistic perspective. Also known as iGeneration (iGen), they will become America's new poster-child generation. Generation Zers are considered to be the first true global generation. They are found to be smarter, speedier, and more tolerant of both work and workforce diversity and inclusion than their predecessors. They have a strong tendency to support the justice system and are disturbed about the environmental problems impacting the United States and the world.[15] According to Don Tapscott, author of *Grown Up Digital: How the Net Generation Is Changing Your World*, they are heavily engaged in performing their civic duty in their communities. Inspired by the first African American president, Barack Obama, many seek to engage in politics because they see government and democracy as critical tools for enhancing the world via progressive policies. Adapted to speed and freedom, this generation will transform the workplace culture.[16]

Meanwhile, traditionalists would have departed the workforce forever. And the baby boomers will gradually transition into the retirement phase of their life and will depart in massive numbers, taking with them tremendous knowledge, skills, and experience. Generation Xers will aggressively seek their independence. This may be associated with their childhood being impacted by high divorce rates, resulting in them becoming self-reliant, according to Susan G. Thomas's July 9, 2011 online article, "The Divorce Generation."[17] They do not believe in working long hours. They believe in working to live, not living to work. This generation will seek to ensure work/life balance becomes a reality. Although gen Xers are considered to be workaholics and technologically proficient, they will expect to have the freedom to conduct their work from anywhere they desire. If they are not provided this freedom, they will seek employment elsewhere that will grant them their freedom. If an organization does not have a well-executed and established succession development plan, it will be costly. For example, according to Christina Merhar's February 4, 2016, online article, "Employee Retention—The

Real Cost of Losing an Employee," the cost to backfill an employee who departs is the equivalent of approximately six to nine months of his or her yearly salary.[18] While employee replacement costs may be a one-time expense, it will take several years at a higher salary to equal the cost of replacing a seasoned employee one time.

Even though, in the past two decades, workforce succession development planning has become a leading topic, the mind-sets of C-suite executives and managers still reflect Industrial Age thinking, which is based on the antiquated command-and-control model. As stated earlier, an organization's business success can no longer depend on traditionalists and baby boomers, but must rely heavily on millennials, gen Xers, and gen Zers (iGen) to remain triumphant. These three generations will be the foundation of the global labor force, ranging from vocational to leadership and managerial jobs. The future workforce will not only depend on technical or vocational training but will also rely heavily on a high degree of soft-skills training (e.g., emotional intelligence, social intelligence, cultural intelligence, personal intelligence, executive intelligence, diversity and inclusion intelligence, and human intelligence). Training employees at all levels of the organization on these intelligences will proactively prepare the workforce for both current and future relationship challenges.

For the moment, both gen Yers and gen Zers are following their millennial counterparts in hot pursuit. They are entering the labor force with the highest intelligence quotient of any generation and will be expecting their executives and managers to possess the ability to communicate, collaborate, understand, connect with, and support them on various innovative ideas. Executives, managers, and career counselors should be prepared to interface with their potential new hire's helicopter parents. Because this is part of gen Zers' formative culture, organizations should include the helicopter phenomenon in their succession development planning strategy to help recruit, retain, and sustain a multidimensional, diversified, and inclusive workforce. In addition, gen Yers and gen Zers will be accountable for transforming every aspect of human life, from the workplace to politics to community to education. They are considered to be natural collaborators who are not afraid to adapt things to support their personal and professional needs. They believe in workforce engagement, and they look forward to sharing a seat or two at the decision-making table. In essence, those in leadership roles who embrace these innovative ways of collaborating and connecting will see better growth and higher productivity across their workforce.

On the other hand, millennials require the immediate attention of their bosses. They desire regular feedback from their managers and are always seeking a mentor. Because they see job-hopping as a very positive career strategy that will help catapult them to the top, 60 percent of millennials remain in their job for less than one year, according to Amy Adkins's May 12, 2016 online article, "Millennials: The Job-Hopping Generation."[19] These three generations also have different communication styles. Millennials prefer to communicate by text messaging. For example, over a four-year period, while lecturing at a prominent university in San Diego, California, I presented the following scenario to each class of undergraduate students.

> **Scenario:** "Imagine you are the project manager leading a top-notch team of coworkers overseeing a very important project. You have three months to identify business solutions for a technology problem impacting the company's customers. Once the solutions are identified, you must present them to the company's CEO prior to implementation. And if the project solutions are successful, you and your team would receive enormous bonuses. However, two weeks before the presentation is due, a key member of the team has fallen behind on his part of the project. The project manager's cubicle is located two cubicles down from the team member's cubicle. I asked the students the following questions:

> - What method of communication would you prefer to use to follow up with this important team member concerning the status of his part of the project?
> - Would you prefer discussing the issue via e-mail, text, face-to-face, fax, iPhone or desk phone, or have someone else follow up with him?

This scenario was presented to over twelve hundred undergraduate students, mostly juniors and seniors. Even though the project manager's cubicle was located two cubicles down the hallway from the team member's, 90 percent of the students stated that their preferred method of communication was to send the team member a text message.

C-suite executives, senior vice presidents and managers, if you want to hire, retain, and sustain a futuristic workforce that is multidimensional in its competencies, it is vitally important that you have an updated and active succession development plan (SDP). A SDP will help ensure your workforce remains future-proof by measuring and updating current and future competency gaps, while at the same time identifying ways to help close the competency-deficiency gaps. The SDP can be used to help identify employee strengths and weaknesses. It ensures employee competencies are updated to support current and future business strategies and job tasks. Moreover, as the world continues to become more competitive, the SDP will help ensure your organization is hiring and retaining a competitive labor force. More importantly, a SDP will help determine if your organization has the right people with the right competencies working in their passionate job at the right time to proactively meet the organization's short- and long-term business needs. In addition, the SDP will help mitigate human capital staffing deficiencies.

Paradigm Shift 4: Managing, Leading, and Engaging a Diversified and Inclusive Workforce
In workplace lingo, "diversity" is associated with accepting employee differences, and "inclusion" is associated with integrating and managing these differences to ensure organizational success. It does not matter whether you are a C-suite executive, manager, or employee; here are several questions you should ask yourself and your leadership team:

- Why should your organization concern itself with diversity and inclusion?
- Does your organization have a chief diversity officer (CDO)?
- If so, is he or she mentoring, training, and inspiring leaders and employees across the organization on the importance of having a diversified and inclusive workforce?

Organizations must understand the importance of knowing how to lead and manage a diverse and inclusive workforce. On January 13, 2016, Amy Adkins wrote a Gallup Poll article titled "Employee Engagement in US Stagnant in 2015." The article indicated that of the 80,844 US employees who participated in 2015, only 32 percent were "engaged" in their jobs, 50.8 percent were "not engaged," while another 17.2 percent were "actively disengaged." On a positive note, this was an improvement over the 2014 results.[20] What is causing this disengagement to occur? Karie Willyerd and Barbara Mistick, authors of *Stretch: How to Future-Proof Yourself for Tomorrow's Workplace,* believe low employee engagement can be associated with poor executive leadership, bad bosses, limited employee diversity, or lack of employee inspiration. They acknowledge that engagement is not a one-way street; it requires participation from top, middle, and bottom (T-M-B) of the organization—the employees, supervisors, managers, and C-suite executives. Karie and Barbara argue that employees have the power to change from disengagement to engagement and to realize their career dreams by future-proofing themselves. To support their ideology, they conducted twin studies that included executives and employees across twenty-seven countries to determine what the future workforce was thinking, wanting, and worrying over. The number-one concern employees expressed was that their ability and skills to perform rapidly changing jobs could render them obsolete. Meanwhile, only 50 percent of the employees from the survey believed the skills they currently use today will be the skills they would need three years later, according to Willyerd and Mistick. In addition, Karie and Barbara identified seven megatrends that will affect the future workforce:

1. Globalization
2. Demographics shifts
3. Explosion of data
4. Emerging technologies
5. Climate change
6. Redefined jobs
7. Complexity of government regulations.[21]

A critical solution for enhancing employee engagement and retention is to improve organizational leadership via training. If training does not work, you may have to redesign the organization's leadership hierarchy to support the effort. A second solution to enhancing employee engagement is for leaders to become more emotionally aware of the cultural thoughts, beliefs, and behaviors of their employees. According to Joshua Freedman, chief operating officer of SixSeconds and author of *At the Heart of Leadership: How to Get Results with Emotional Intelligence,* the words "trust," "loyalty," and "commitment" are critical ingredients of the word "emotion" and are major parts of an organization's culture. He argues that emotional intelligence is about "people smarts" and having the ability to relate to yourself and others. It helps leaders to better interact in a way that shapes a positive emotional context or climate. In turn, this drives employees and their interactions with customers. Moreover, according to Freedman, leadership is about "engaging people to go further and do better than they could on their own. It's about setting direction, and setting a context for people to do the impossible." Freedman associates emotional intelligence with having four distinct sets of branches.[22]

1. Perceiving Emotions: The ability to detect and decipher emotions in faces, pictures, voices, and artifacts; to include identifying one's own emotions.
2. Using Emotions: The ability to harness emotions to facilitate various cognitive activities, such as thinking and problem solving.
3. Understanding Emotions: The ability to comprehend emotion language and to appreciate complicated relations between emotions.
4. Managing Emotions: The ability to regulate emotions in both ourselves and in others.

Moreover, in a twenty-first-century workforce environment, low employee engagement can be linked to a lack of diversity in the workplace. Millennials, gen Xers, gen Yers, and even baby boomers understand the benefits of having a diverse and inclusive workforce; D and I have been part of their upbringing. According to Carol Harvey and M. June Allard, authors of *Understanding and Managing Diversity: Reading, Cases, and Exercises,* organizations that continue to succeed during economic downturns are the ones that encourage D and I training and development across the workplace. Executives in these organizations understand that diversity and inclusion are not only vital to their business success; they are legal necessities. D and I address the emerging needs that relate to workforce hiring, recruitment, retention, teambuilding, and decision making. When used holistically, D and I can help cultivate and create high-performing organizations. Diversity and inclusion are proactive, transformational, inspirational, appreciative, and generative. Implemented jointly, they will unleash the power of employee relationships and interactions. They can strengthen an organization's workforce recruitment practices and help internal retention strategies to sustain, develop, and leverage diversity of all employees. In essence, inspiring the need for D and I in the workforce and business processes will result in better decision making, higher employee retention, and a reduction in harassment and discrimination lawsuits.[23]

Furthermore, a more diverse and inclusive workforce will increase organizational effectiveness and alleviate complacency. Eric Klein and John B. Izzo, authors of *Awakening Corporate Soul: Four Paths to Unleash the Power of People at Work*, acknowledge that "when an organization's soul sleeps, the employees in that organization lose the sense of their purpose and place in the market. They become fundamentally impaired, going through the motions of their work without the breath of life."[24] The authors eloquently explain the four paths to corporate soul.[25]

1. Path of Self: Soul awakens when employees are aware of their own passion, in touch with their core values, and actively bring these alive in their daily work.
2. Path of Contribution: Soul and commitment become present when employees discover the deeper reason for their work. The value and meaning of their contribution comes alive as they recognize their daily efforts serve a worthy goal.
3. Path of Craft: When developing an intense enjoyment in the moment-to-moment action of work, craft begins to focus on the ongoing

process of learning and mastery. As a result, employees become engaged in activities that call forth their highest levels of skill.

4. Path of Community: When soul is found, connection among employees goes deeper than their job description, touches the heart, and transcends traditional teambuilding. Through this, employees join together to bring out the best in each other.

D and I can lift morale, bring greater access to new segments of the marketplace, and enhance productivity. In short, diversity and inclusion would be excellent for business. In his book *Building on the Promise of Diversity: How We Can Move to the Next Level in Our Workplaces, Our Communities, and Our Society*, R. Roosevelt Thomas Jr. acknowledges that organizations that make a conscious effort to establish a diversity-management program that promotes multiculturalism and diversity and inclusion awareness will become organizations of choice in the twenty-first century.[26] Furthermore, to reduce workplace diversity tension, organizations should establish diversity management and engagement practices, policies, and guidelines. Diversity professional coaching sessions should be established to help resolve emotional tension between managers and employees. A workforce engagement survey tool is included in appendix B.

Paradigm Shift 5: Determining Required Multidimensional Competencies
Organizations are transforming themselves, and with this transformation will come the need for the workforce competencies to transform from one-dimensional to multidimensional. In simple terms, competencies are a complex thought that focuses on what employees are capable of performing and not just what they understand. As workplace automation continues to grow, important manual-labor skilled jobs will continue to become obsolete. Even though manufacturing jobs may creep slowly back into the US labor market, they will require a high degree of technical knowledge and understanding to perform. Therefore, whether you are an executive, manager, or employee, the most important question you should be asking yourself is, "What innovative steps am I taking to ensure my professional competencies remain future-proof?" As a reminder, *the lack of motivation for innovation leads to stagnation.*

Organizations can no longer afford to have a competency-based workforce that is one-dimensional. Organizations of the future will require a competency-based workforce that is multidimensional. Employees working in future-based organizations will be required to have a comprehensive professional portfolio that is diverse in multiple competencies. In other words, employees must have the fortitude to speak and understand different competencies in the form of science, technology, engineering, art, math, finance, leadership, project management, construction, emotional intelligence, social intelligence, pipe-fitting, and so on.

Take the federal government IT workforce, for instance. Even though the government's Information Technology 2210 general scheduled job series covers multiple technical disciplines from information technology, information systems (programming), cyber security, information resource management, information assurance, portfolio management, to knowledge management, employees' competencies are one-dimensional. If you worked in the information-systems profession for the past ten years, for example, and you want to apply for an information-technology position, you would not qualify for the position because you do not have the required competencies to perform the job. In other words, your competencies are one-dimensional. They only perform work in the areas of programming, software applications, and administration and not testing, troubleshooting, and configuring IT networks and computers.

To make matters worse, if the government decides to outsource its IT work or the work is no longer required, where would the employees who perform IT-related work go? Would they be fired? Would they be retrained to do other job functions that may or may not be related to IT? This is why organizations must focus their attention on becoming futuristic by ensuring their employees' competencies are multidimensional. As previously stated in chapter one, the main goal of an executive is to develop his or her successor, which involves training and developing him or her across multiple professional disciplines. According to Anna Davies, Devin Fidler, and Marina Gorbis, authors of *Future Work Skills 2020*, this is a primary reason why organizations must reinforce the need for their employees to have multidimensional competencies that will help them adapt to changing work landscapes. In addition, their competencies must be transferable to support future job requirements.

Table 3 indicates the authors' eleven most important work competencies required for the year 2020.[27] I would argue for emotional intelligence to be added to this list of core work competencies.

Table 3: The Eleven Most Important Work Competencies in 2020	
Competency	Definition
Creativity	Ability to become more creative in order to benefit from upcoming changes in many new products, technologies, and new ways of working.
Sense Making	Ability to determine the deeper meaning or significance of what is being expressed
Social Intelligence	Ability to connect to others in a deep and direct way, to sense and stimulate reactions and desired interactions
Novel and Adaptive Thinking	Proficiency at thinking and coming up with solutions and responses beyond that which is rote or rule-based
Cross Cultural Competency	Ability to operate in different cultural settings
Computational Thinking	Ability to translate vast amounts of data into abstract concepts and to understand data-based reasoning
New Media Literacy	Ability to critically assess and develop content that uses new media forms and to leverage these media for persuasive communication
Transdisciplinary	Literacy in and ability to understand concepts across multiple disciplines
Design Mind-set	Ability to represent and develop tasks and work processes for desired outcomes
Cognitive Load Management	Ability to discriminate and filter information for importance and to understand how to maximize cognitive functions
Virtual Collaboration	Ability to work productively, drive engagement, and demonstrate presence as a member of a virtual team

So, when planning for succession development, C-suite executives and managers will be required to build a diverse and inclusive workforce, with each employee possessing multidimensional competencies such as the knowledge, skills, abilities, leadership, education, certification, and experience to perform multiple job functions. Moreover, having a multidimensional workforce that is well trained and developed to speak and understand multiple languages would greatly enhance employee morale, retention, and engagement. Even though this would be a highly desired skill set, the term "multiple languages" does not mean the ability to speak and understand a multitude of different languages such as French, Spanish, English, Chinese, Japanese, or Tagalog. In the new world of business, it means having a diversified portfolio of competencies and abilities to speak and understand various technical languages such as engineering, information technology, contracts, program/project management, finance, accounting, business operation, and marketing.

Furthermore, in both today's and tomorrow's business environments, if you are a chief information officer (CIO) leading an information-technology department, you would want your succession development plan to reflect an array of training and development opportunities to ensure all employees obtain diverse backgrounds and experiences in speaking and understanding a variety of different competencies: information systems (IS), information assurance (IA), customer relations (i.e., help desk), cyber security, telecommunications, contract management, smart energy technology, industrial-control systems, supply-chain management, business acumen, leadership, project management, or wireless communications. Having a workforce that is multidimensional in various competencies would greatly enhance workload productivity and improve morale. The succession development planning also becomes a salubrious equalizer when competing for top talent and should not be mistaken for replacement planning as used in the first three industrial revolutions. In essence, because employees are not as hungry for education as previous generations, C-suite executives have a responsibility to communicate to their employees that anything humans can do today, machine automation will do tomorrow. In short, C-suite executives must be seen as goodwill warriors who are always challenging their employees to future-proof themselves by growing and stretching their educational, technical, and soft-skill competencies.

Manufacturing Workforce

In an August 11, 2015 online report by Robert E. Scott, author of *Manufacturing Job Loss: Trade, Not Productivity, Is the Culprit*, between January 2000 and December 2014, the United States lost nearly five million manufacturing jobs (see chart 2).[28] Due to high labor costs and high taxes, of five million jobs, approximately 3.4 million were offshored to China. According to the North American Industry Classification System, manufacturing jobs consist of businesses promoting workload demands in the mechanical and physical areas that are mostly described as plants, factories, or mills that characteristically use power-driven machines and materials-handling equipment. Other businesses associated with the manufacturing profession are bakeries, candy stores, and custom tailors. Table 4 shows the states with the highest overall number of manufacturing jobs during this same time period. As referenced in

Tom Worstall's online article, "The US Lost 7 Million Manufacturing Jobs—and Added 33 Million Higher-Paying Service Jobs," even though the United States lost seven million manufacturing jobs to overseas competitors, it added thirty-three million higher-paying service jobs in the past two decades.[29]

CHART 2: US MANUFACTURING JOB LOSS, 2000– 2016, (4.838 MILLION)

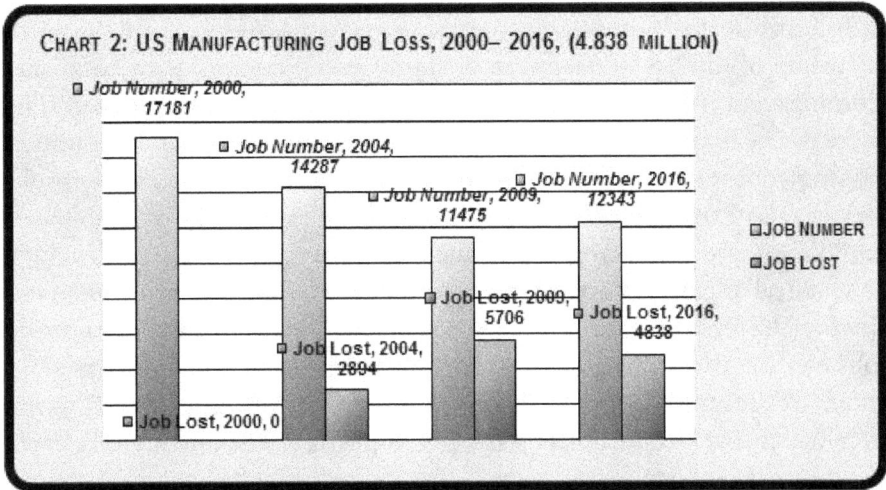

Table 4: States with Overall Highest Manufacturing Jobs (2012 versus 2016)		
State	2012	2016
California	1,231,300	1,275,400
Texas	847,000	845,700
Ohio	660,100	689,600
Illinois	598,700	568,500
Pennsylvania	571,500	564,400
Michigan	526,000	600,700
Indiana	488,900	514,000
Wisconsin	450,200	473,800
New York	448,200	448,900
North Carolina	439,700	460,300

According to Patrick Gillespie, author of *US Manufacturing Job Openings at 2007 Levels,* in October 2016, the United States had over 322,000 manufacturing job openings, as compared to 99,000 during the 2009 recession. However, only 271,000 of these jobs were filled, leaving 51,000 unfilled.[30] Moreover, in the FoIR, as manufacturing jobs begin to return to the United States, the skill sets required will drastically change.

Executives and managers will be seeking candidates with advanced competencies that will support the various types and quality of manufacturing jobs. In addition, to operate state-of-the-art and complex machinery, candidates will require advanced technical certifications and formal education. Since 2007, for example, more than half of all manufacturing workers completed some college courses, and the proportion will continue to increase, according to David Langdon and Rebecca Lehrman of the US Department of Commerce Economics and Statistics Administration and authors of *The Benefits of Manufacturing Jobs*.[31] The increase in manufacturing jobs will range from construction, utilities, mining, computer aid and design, computer networks, underwater welding, and vehicle assembly lines, to transportation. Several US-based companies are reshoring their manufacturing jobs. Companies such as General Electric, Ford Motor Company, Wal-Mart, Farouk Systems, Boeing, Caterpillar, and General Motors are bringing manufacturing jobs back to the United States from overseas. There are several reasons these US companies are reshoring manufacturing jobs, including an increase in overseas labor costs, high shipping costs, and speedy product delivery. Service providers are also importing jobs back to America. For example, in 2016, there were over five million Americans hired to support the sixty-six thousand call centers located across the United States, according to Michael Sauter and Samuel B. Stebbins, authors of *Manufacturers Bringing the Most Jobs Back to America*.[32]

Chapter Four

THE IMPORTANCE OF SUCCESSION DEVELOPMENT PLANNING

> The time to repair the roof is when the sun is shining.
> ~JOHN F. KENNEDY, THIRTY-FIFTH PRESIDENT
> OF THE UNITED STATES~

Why Succession Development Planning?

In today's work environment, organizations have maybe two to three different generations working for them. In tomorrow's work environment, this workforce dynamic will change drastically. Organizations will encounter up to five different generations. Due to the economic recession in the mid-2000s, traditionalists and baby boomers decided to hang around longer than expected, which limits promotion, training, and career-development opportunities for millennial, generation X, and generation Z employees. Although organizations can greatly benefit from a diverse multigenerational workforce, they should have a well-designed succession development plan in place to help overcome unexpected challenges. As the US labor force continues to meet its retirement age, having a succession development plan in place will exceedingly enhance an organization's business success. Moreover, C-suite executives and senior managers must be aware that the continued effectiveness and success of their organization depends on having employees with the right multidimensional competencies in the right position at the right time to meet current and future job-function demands. This will help ensure qualified employees are discovered inside the organization.

To add to this, C-suite executives and managers must identify current employees and recruit new hires who have the required multidimensional skill sets. Employees who are working in the electrical engineering profession, for example, may be required to possess contract management, financial management, leadership, and/or supply-chain management competencies in order to receive a promotion. In addition, they should have a strong foundation of soft skills such as emotional, social, cultural, and personal intelligences to help balance their interpersonal and intrapersonal skills. It is the responsibility of senior leaders to ensure their managers are developing future candidates to fill bottom staff positions. It is the C-suite executive's responsibility to develop middle-management and junior-level executives. This will help expedite the backfilling process of current and forecasted vacant positions throughout the organization. Equally important, succession development planning is the cornerstone to an organization's workforce development plan, talent management plan, succession plan, human capital strategy plan, staffing plan, and organizational development plan. It is designed to include critical elements from all of the aforementioned plans.

Meanwhile, as private and public organizations continue to grow their workforces and international businesses continue to hire America's best and brightest, US companies will experience major reductions in qualified executives and midlevel managers to fill key leadership positions. And if the data continue to support the shortage of qualified candidates entering the workforce, there will be fewer staff-level employees available to advance to supervisory and middle-management positions; therefore, great care will be required to identify promising candidates and to actively cultivate their leadership development. Moreover, coping with a multigenerational workforce is a key reason why it is important for organizations to implement a succession development plan. Executives and managers should also be aware of the importance of how to lead a multigenerational workforce and what impact a multigenerational workforce will have on their organization's business success. Succession development planning can help in this situation. It should serve as a living document intended to be reviewed by senior executive board members and updated by human-resources professionals and department managers.

As demands and circumstances evolve, it can be modified to benefit the need for new resources to achieve the organization's vision, mission, and goals. According to Richard Fry's April 25, 2016 online article, "Millennials Overtake Baby Boomers as America's Largest Generation," the total US population is approximately 324.4 million. In reference to the US labor force, there are five generations in the US labor market. Millennials/Generation Y represent almost 75.4 million (23.3 percent); baby boomers make up 74.96 million (23.1 percent); and generation X represents 62 million (19.1 percent). This means there is a shortage of gen X candidates to fill jobs being vacated by baby boomers in the next three to five years. Moreover, the 23.3 percent of the generation Y cohort (those ages eighteen to thirty-four) includes the youngest members of the population who have yet to or are about to enter the workforce. Recognizing the values each of these generations brings to the workplace will be critical as the baby boomer workforce declines and the gen X and millennial numbers continue to increase by the year 2020. In addition, the report reflected the 75.4 million millennials have surpassed the 74.9 million baby boomers as America's largest living generation. In 2016, approximately 4.1 million (or 6.1 percent) of generation Xers celebrated their fiftieth birthdays. By 2028, the generation X cohort is expected to exceed the baby boomer generation. Table 1 provides a generational breakdown by birth dates, ages, and workforce percentages.[1]

Table 1: Generational Breakdown			
Generation Name	Births Start	Ages	Workforce Percentage
Generation Z/iGen/Gen C/Centennials	1996 to the present	6–17	23.0 million
Millennials/Generation Y	1981–1997	18–34	75.4 million
Generation X	1965–1980	35–50	62.0 million
Baby Boomers	1946–1964	51–69	74.9 million
Traditionalists/Silent	1900–1945	70+	N/A

Generation Z (Gen Z), iGen, or Generation C (Gen C)

Born after 1996, generation Zers, iGens, or gen Cers are about to finish college or vocational school and will be entering the workplace in the next year. In America alone, they are twenty-three million strong and are the fastest-growing generation in the US marketplace and labor force. According to an online article by Roman Friedrich, Michael

Peterson, Alex Koster, and Sebastian Blum, "The Rise of Generation C: Implications for the World of 2020," the world population will be approximately 7.6 billion by year 2020. The letter *C* represents the words "connect," "communicate," and "change." For this book, the term "gen Z" will be used.[2] Although gen Zers have high expectations, many may decide to skip the traditional classroom educational system and complete their college education online. They will be the most highly educated of any current generation. Gen Zers will account for 40 percent of the population in the United States, Europe, and the BRIC countries, and 10 percent in the rest of the world. Their attention span will be limited because they will be always trying to keep track of global events and happenings. Because they refuse to be left out of the discussion, their iPhone, iPad, or whatever new digital device hits the market, will become their twenty-four-hour addiction.

Moreover, they will be attuned to processing information much faster than any of the four generations that preceded them. As a result, they will absorb a multitude of various tasks such as completing class assignments and conducting research on their iPhone while collaborating with friends located in another state or country. They will be doing all of this while sitting and watching television and listening to music and Face-Timing their friends via the television and not their iPhone. Moreover, because they want to become business owners someday, their mind-set is geared more toward capitalism. They will be actively working late at night and on the weekends to meet their goals, which means their iPhone will remain active at all times. They do, however, enjoy working independently and less in team environments but will not hesitate to conduct peer-to-peer social media and text messaging to communicate. Moreover, they believe in learning by trial and error. This generation will be the most hyperconnected of all generations. They will be considered the global generation, as more underdeveloped countries around the world become connected to the Internet, which means they will think, interact, and socialize more globally than any other generation. Because of technology, their face-to-face social and cultural intelligences will continue to be works in progress. They will, however, gain a great deal of social and cultural experiences via social media.

Nonetheless, they will require management oversight, because they will be expected to be available twenty-four hours a day, seven days a week. Therefore, they may become addicted to their electronic devices (iPhone, iPod, iPad, or any other multimedia device), which may cause them to enter into a mental state I call postdramatic technology stress disorder, or PDTSD. Currently there is no research data to support my claim, the acronym is being used to identify the reactions children and adults portray when their iPhone, PlayStation, Wii, Xbox, or other video games are being removed from their hands. What I have witnessed over the years is that most people would become agitated or upset when asked to shut down their electronic device during a family conversation, classroom, focus group, or at the dinner table. Their iPhone has become their pet at night and their alarm clock in the morning, as they sleep with it next to them in the bed. As a result, they may be the most sleep-deprived generation. They may suffer from a lack of memory sharpness, long-term memory loss, damaged brain cells, attention deficit, strategic thinking decrease, eating disorders, paranoia, and more. Entering into this state of mind may lead them to seek new employment, become disengaged, or depressed.

Millennials or Generation Y (Gen Yers)

Born between 1981 and 1997 this generation is technology savvy and is 75.4 million strong. Millennials are the most educated generation and are linked to a global environment. They witnessed and experienced terrorist attacks, school shootings, and the human immunodeficiency virus (HIV) and acquired immunodeficiency syndrome (AIDS) epidemics. Since their birth, technology and digital media (pagers, answering machines, desktop/laptop computers, video games, cellular phones, cable television, etc.) have been part of their everyday lives. Because they were wired at birth with these various technical gadgets, they will be expecting their employer to do the same. Technology is not a want; it's a *need* for this generation. They have a deep desire for speed. If not provided, they will seek other avenues to ensure they remain highly connected in this digital world. Their lives are based on collaboration, relationship building, and social learning. Because they are considered to be the most successful in the multitasking endeavor of the five generations, monotony must not become part of their daily work routine. According to Alexa Mantell and Barbara Brynko, authors of *Dealing with Hyperconnectivity*, millennials are identified as the hyperconnectivity generation in which everything is talking: person-to-person, person-to-machine, and machine-to-machine.[3] They will be confronted with innovating artificial intelligence in which they will be the first generation to develop computers that will speak, learn, read, play games, and think like humans.

Even though they experienced the upbringing in a single-parent household and were the most sheltered by their parents of the four generations, family values are still important. Their parents are known as "helicopter parents" who refuse to surrender them to real-world experiences. When people say this generation will be less successful than their parents, it is a fallacy. Gen Yers will benefit the most economically of the five generations. Moreover, millennials believe in having it all right now and are somewhat impatient. They believe in personal independence. They are patriotic, self-absorbed, and respectful of the competency of others. They think globally. They are innovative and creative, family oriented, and loyal to their peers. They believe in the work/life balance philosophy. They believe in diversity, inclusion, and multiculturalism in both the workplace and the community. They possess high morals and are highly competitive and ambitious. Leaders who have a divisive attitude concerning workforce diversity will not garner support from this generation. Millennials seek corporate integrity. They honor directness and openness, not radicalism. Likewise, they want work to be entertaining and goal oriented.

Millennials are very effective and productive workers but view the five-day work week as a pastime event between weekends. They are optimistic and self-confident but seek personal attention. Millennials are more prone to be electronically sociable (e-Social) by way of their iPhone or iPad. They remain individualist yet group oriented. They are the first generation to return home to hibernate with their parents after college and remain there much longer than any other generation. They are, however, very optimistic about what the future has to offer them. In addition, millennials are motivated by learning new things and ideas, which means they need to be trained and developed to reinforce their employment advantage. They personify the word "entitlement." It is a strong belief to them. This generation will enter the workforce with more theoretical and street experiences than any of the other three generations. Therefore, if you want to keep them employed, you must keep them challenged in the workplace, or they will seek the challenges elsewhere. It is okay to allow them to take a certain amount of risk, because they view this as learning and growth opportunities. Most importantly, because they believe in bargaining for the best product or service, they should be the organization's marketing and branding business strategists.

Generation X

Born between 1965 and 1980, generation Xers are sixty-two million strong. Douglas Coupland's 1991 novel *Generation X: Tales for an Accelerated Culture* universalized the term "generation X." Gen Xers are identified as being less successful than their parents. The letter *X* is associated with a group that was excluded from society and discovered that all the jobs were filled by their brothers and sisters when they attempted to apply. Because divorce was a common thing in their lives, they spent less time with their parents. They are individualists who crave independence and work/life balance over financial gains or successes. They are very confident in themselves, which may have contributed to their unwillingness to marry and high divorce rates.[4] Moreover, gen Xers felt the country was in major turmoil, because they were experiencing massive transformational changes such as the year 2000 transition, the end of the Cold War, Watergate, corporate rightsizing/downsizing, the advent of mainframe computers, the AIDS epidemic, Persian Gulf War, video-rental stores, Iran–Contra, and handheld calculators. They are self-reliant and do not care for authority. They are considered to be the generation of entitlement. When it comes to their professions, however, they expect feedback, rewards, and recognition from their leadership.

Gen Xers are willing to accept more responsibility than the other generations. In essence, they believe in working to live, not living to work. Struggling to survive on minimum wage and facing major economic conditions, they joined ranks and lived together to make ends meet. Gen Xers are global thinkers and are highly educated. They lack corporate loyalty and are identified as being skeptical and cynical about authority. They are results driven, highly productive, and technically competent. They couldn't care less about job titles. As a result of the various music events and television shows being displayed in their family rooms or bedrooms, gen Xers embrace diversity and inclusion and will not tolerate discrimination. Because they are more family oriented and drug-screening savvy, gen Xers are less likely to drink alcohol or do drugs.

Baby Boomers

The baby boomer generation was born between 1946 and 1964 and is approximately 74.9 million strong. In the 1960s and 1970s, this generation was confronted with social changes such as the Vietnam War, social justice, and school segregation. They are the civil rights fighters of the 1960s and 1970s and the yuppies of the 1980s. They are the Vietnam War heroes and sexual revolutionists of yesterday. They are linked to having the highest divorce rate among the five generations. They are team oriented and see win-win as a good thing. They are amenable to hard work and refuse to understand the importance of work/life balance. They are considered to be the most educated and are willing to relocate to secure that perfect job. Moreover, being valued is very important to baby boomers. If they see themselves as being unvalued, they will seek value elsewhere by seeking a new employer. They feel as though they have paid their dues to society. Therefore, they are considered to be the most threatening generation to any organization's business success, because they are the most able to retire and take all their knowledge, skills, and experiences with them when they depart.

They believe in merit promotions that are based on seniority and not necessarily on education, skills, and experience. They want to be front and center of the organization's success. This is where they find self-fulfillment. They do not, however, want to be micromanaged or denigrated. They believe in teamwork and are goal oriented. Be careful: they believe career development and training are important, but they do not want to be overloaded. If frustrated with too much training and career-development activity, they may rebel. Baby boomers believe in rewards and recognition and therefore want to be compensated for their hard work and contributions. What are the reasons behind their belief system? Because of the 2009 financial recession leading to financial losses, baby boomers remained in the workforce longer than expected to pay for eldercare, childcare, college tuition costs/debts, medical expenses, etc. This generation possesses the most social and cultural intelligence of the five generations. They believe in face-to-face conversations and enjoy communicating and collaborating with others.

Traditionalists/Silent Generation

Born between 1900 and 1945, the traditionalist (silent) generation professionals are identified as being hard workers and having strong work ethics. They are the wealthiest. They believe tenure leads to promotion. They are civic-minded. They are loyal to country and employer; many have committed to one company for an entire career. They have lived through good and bad times. Veterans of foreign wars, they experienced World War II and the Korean War. They survived the Great Depression. Traditionalists witnessed the Space Age, when President John F. Kennedy challenged NASA to be the first to put a man on the moon, which became a reality on July 20, 1969. They need to be wanted. Raised in a two-parent environment, they readily conform to authority and possess a high degree of respect for authority. They are seen as patriotic, conservative, and fiscally prudent. They believe in trustworthiness, honesty, and openness with teammates and family members. They enjoyed serving as role models when it pertained to ethical behavior. They would, however, not hesitate to challenge unethical behavior and disrespectfulness. From a cultural perspective, they are family focused and cherish eye-to-eye contact and face-to-face conversations. Traditionalists are slow to adapt to new technology to help them become more efficient and effective. They are technologically challenged but are very reliable in assuring task assignments are completed on time. Their technology world consisted of radios, black-and-white television, and handheld walkie-talkie devices. Nevertheless, when it comes to formal education, they believe in the traditional classroom-learning environment and not necessarily in online class participation.

US Future Labor Force

According to Marlene Lee and Mark Mather of the Bureau of Labor Statistics (BLS), in 1960 the median age of 40.5 years of the US population had reached its highest peak. Then came the baby boomer generation, and the median age decreased to 34.6 in 1980. In the next two decades, from 1992 to 2012, the median age of the US labor force rebounded to an average age of 36.2 years and 41.2 years, respectively. As indicated in table 2, by 2022, the average age of the US labor force will reach an all-time high of 42.2. By 2022, overall, the male labor force average age of 42.2 will be lower as compared to their female counterpart average age of 43.1. White labor-force members have always been older than other groups, and this will continue to be the case in 2022. The Hispanic labor force will continue to remain the youngest laborforce members in 2022, as white non-Hispanic members continue to lead the way with an average age of 44.8, making them the oldest age group. Meanwhile, the black/African American labor force will become the second-youngest age group, at 40.3, as the Asian labor force becomes the third-oldest population at an average age of 42.9.[5]

Table 2: Thirty-Year Median Age of the Labor Force, by Gender, Race, and Ethnicity				
Group	1992	2002	2012	2022
Men	37.2	39.8	41.8	42.2
Women	37.0	40.0	42.1	43.1
White	37.3	40.2	42.6	43.3
Black	35.5	38.1	39.7	40.3
Asian	36.2	38.8	40.9	42.9
Hispanic origin	32.5	34.0	36.9	38.9
White non-Hispanic	37.8	41.1	44.2	44.8
Average Age	36.2	38.9	41.2	42.2

Nonetheless, as the average age continues to increase, the biggest challenge for tomorrow's C-suite executives will be finding well-qualified executives, managers, and employees who have multidimensional competencies to help their organization sustain business growth in the twenty-first century. To make matters worse, as indicated in table 3, the

US annual growth rate is decreasing as compared to previous years. This will lead to a lack of potential candidates to fill job vacancies. For this reason alone, it is important for C-suite executives to use succession development planning as a strategy to help future-proof their organization. You should be asking yourself the following questions:

1. What are you doing to ensure your workforce does not become obsolete in this twenty-first-century competitive business environment?
2. What workforce competencies will be necessary to identify new markets and opportunities to help grow the company's business?
3. What pros and cons should be evaluated or considered before determining whether or not your organization should seek a new business opportunity?
4. Which junior-level managers can executives forecast to run the organization's business?
5. What can your organization do to promote the baby boomer reemployment?

Table 3: US Twenty-Year Annual Growth Rate Percentage							
Group	Level				US Annual Growth Rate Percentage		
	1992	2002	2012	2022	1992–2002	2002–2012	2012–2022
Total, 16 years and Older	128,105	144,863	154,975	163,450	1.2	0.7	0.5
Age and Years							
16 to 24	21,617	22,366	21,285	18,462	.3	−.5	−1.4
25 to 54	91,429	101,720	101,253	103,195	1.1	.0	.2
55 and older	15,060	20,777	32,437	41,793	3.3	4.6	2.6
Gender							
Men	69,964	77,500	82,327	86,913	1.0	.6	.5
Women	58,141	67,364	72,648	76,537	1.5	.8	.5
Race							
White	108,837	120,150	123,684	126,923	1.0	.3	.3
Black	14,162	16,565	18,400	20,247	1.6	1.1	1.0
Asian	5,106	6,604	8,188	10,135	2.6	2.2	2.2
All Other Groups	-	1,544	4,703	6,145	...	11.8[2]	2.7
Ethnicity							
Hispanic origin	11,338	17,943	24,391	31,179	4.7	3.1	2.5
Other than Hispanic origin	116,767	126,920	130,584	132,271	.8	.3	.1
White non-Hispanic	98,724	103,349	101,892	99,431	.5	−.1	−.2

Equally important, executives must decide whether or not they want to build upon their organization's history or its destiny. To think futuristically, it would be imperative for C-suite executives and senior managers to recognize and accommodate the differences and values each generation brings to the table when it comes to hiring, promoting, and retaining the preeminent and brightest across these four generations. Moreover, another major concern for organizations is the evolution of the gig economy workforce. This workforce is well educated and is determined to become entrepreneurs. They want to be unshackled from day-to-day office reporting. They want to have the freedom to work from anywhere in the world without being restricted to an office cubicle.

Take, for example, a 2016 report by Intuit titled "Twenty Trends that Will Shape the Next Decade," which indicated that by 2020, 40 percent of American workers will be part of the gig economy, in which they will serve as independent contractors and should be included as a pillar in the succession development planning process. They will be associated with the term "knowledge workers."[6] They will be the most educated of all generational groups and will seek to make work/life balance a reality. Sarah A. Donovan, David H. Bradley, and Jon O. Shimabukuro, authors of *What Does the Gig Economy Mean for Workers?*, identify the gig economy as being "the collection of markets that match providers to consumers on a gig (or job) basis in support of on-demand commerce via an Internet-based technological platform or Smartphone application."[7] According to Camille L. Ryan and Kurt Bauman, authors of *Educational Attainment in the United States: 2015 Current Population Reports*, the population between the ages twenty-five and forty-four have the highest educational attainment of the four generations. They are highly adaptive to change and technology. They are self-reliant, resourceful, flexible, motivated, and have an entrepreneurial mind-set.[8] Table 4 shows the educational breakdown by age, gender, and race. In essence, people associated with the gig economy will become the workforce of the future.

The diffusion of knowledge is the only
guardian of true liberty.
—JAMES MADISON, FOURTH PRESIDENT OF THE UNITED STATES

Table 4: 2015 Educational Attainment in the United States						
Characteristic	Total (#s in thousands)	High-School Graduate	Some College	Associate's Degree	Bachelor's Degree	Advanced Degree
Population						
Age 25 and Older	212,132	88.4%	58.9%	42.3%	32.5%	12%
Age						
25 to 34	43,006	90.5%	65.0%	46.5%	36.1%	10.9%
35 to 44	39,919	88.7%	62.8%	46.7%	36.3%	13.8%
45 to 64	83,213	89.4%	59.0%	42.6%	32.0%	12.1%
65+	45,994	84.3%	49.7%	34.1%	26.7%	11.3%
Sex						
Male	101,888	88.0%	57.6%	41.2%	32.3%	12.0%
Female	110,245	88.8%	60.1%	43.4%	32.7%	12.0%
Race						
White	168,420	88.8%	59.2%	42.8%	32.8%	12.1%
Non-Hispanic White	140,638	93.3%	63.8%	46.9%	36.2%	13.5%
Black	25,420	87.0%	52.9%	32.4%	22.5%	8.2%
Asian	12,331	89.1%	70.0%	60.4%	53.9%	21.4%
Hispanic	31,020	66.7%	36.8%	22.7%	15.5%	4.7%
Nativity Status						
Native Born	175,519	91.8%	61.3%	43.3%	32.7%	11.9%
Foreign Born	36,613	72.0%	47.6%	37.6%	31.4%	12.5%
Disability Status						
With a Disability	28,052	78.6%	41.6%	24.9%	16.7%	5.7%
Without a Disability	183,351	89.9%	61.5%	45.0%	34.9%	12.9%

The information-technology (IT) gig economy, for example, has grown drastically over the past decade. The gig economy will become the primary workforce of the future. According to Lawrence F. Katz and Alan B. Krueger, authors of *The Rise and Nature of Alternative Work Arrangement in the United States, 1995–2015*, between 2005 and 2015, the IT gig consultant workforce (those who work with "alternative employment arrangements") grew by 5.7 percent, from 10.1 percent to 15.8 percent, an increase of 9.4 million. During this decade, the US total employment only increased by 9 million, from 140.4 million to 149.4 million. Why is this important? There are several reasons for my conclusion.

- First, in the past, people joined companies because of their health-care benefits and salaries. But if the Affordable Care Act (ACA) remains the law of the land, gig economy consultants will be provided the opportunity to purchase their own health-care coverage. As a result, health-care benefits may no longer be a true marketing strategy for many companies.

- Second, working as a gig consultant would allow him or her the opportunity to become financially independent; the individual can serve as a participant and contribute directly to his or her own 401(k), IRA, and so on. Even though baby boomers may be retiring, they are still young at heart and want to contribute to the economy; therefore, they are seeking a second career.
- Finally, a gig consultant can be recruited to work on special projects that are to be completed in a specific time frame, with no additional overhead costs to the organization.[9]

According to John Egan's online report, "The Top 14 Self-Employment Hubs in America," this new generational workforce is already in motion. For instance, as illustrated in table 5, below, 16.24 percent of the Provo-Orem, Utah, working population is self-employed. The cities of McAllen, Texas (16.18 percent), San Francisco, California (15.68 percent), and Los Angeles, California (15.62 percent), are in close pursuit of this new generational workforce. The table also provides a breakdown of the top fourteen cities with households reflecting self-employment. Having a robust, updated, and active succession development plan will help in keeping the generations engaged. In turn, it will allow them to have a sense of purpose and meaning in their work.

Table 5: Self-Employment Households		
Location	Number of Households	Self-Employment
San Jose, California	651,352	12.30%
Honolulu, Hawai'i	307,703	12.35%
Denver, Colorado	1,075,919	12.91%
Nashville, Tennessee	686,640	13.08%
Austin, Texas	723,914	13.46%
San Diego, California	1,113,610	13.56%
Portland, Oregon	901,402	13.67%
Bridgeport/Stamford/Norwalk, Connecticut	333,528	13.76%
Boise, Idaho	245,109	14.47%
Oxnard/Thousand Oaks-Ventura, California	269,566	15.59%
Los Angeles, California	4,315,637	15.62%
San Francisco, California	1,689,907	15.68%
McAllen, Texas	225,692	16.18%
Provo-Orem, Utah	158,270	16.24%

Moreover, a gig economy is defined as "an environment in which temporary positions are common, and organizations contract with independent workers for short-term engagements."[10] Gig workers are freelancers (e.g., TaskRabbit, Uber, etc.) and will not be associated with traditional desk or office settings, but can work on jobs as temporary employees around the world. This is a culture change in this new work environment. These workers can select what jobs they are willing to support. Employers hiring gig workers will greatly benefit from a reduction in office-space requirements, training, development, health-care benefits, retirement matching, improved work/life balance, job vacancy reduction, and more.

Finally, implementing a succession development plan can help C-suite executives identify their most indispensable employees. In an era of ferocious competition, processes must be reengineered to decrease costs, for example, to reduce cycle time and increase work quality and productivity. These processes must be continually reexamined and not be taken for granted merely to maintain the status quo. In such an environment, organizations should not need employees to simply fill a vacancy. They need employees who can figure out what the job takes, while recognizing that the role will keep changing. Moreover, succession development planning can improve employee morale by encouraging promotions from within. Indeed, promotions from within will allow organizations to use employee skills and abilities more effectively, which can serve as an incentive. Promotions within will also improve workforce morale and productivity.

Furthermore, when managers and executives make their hiring decisions, they must consider the individual's potential for long-term advancement as well as his or her suitability for filling an immediate job vacancy. At the same time, hiring an internal or external successor should not be based on ceremonial relationships. According to Rosabeth Moss Kanter, author of *Men and Women of the Corporation*, when succession planning is informal and unplanned, job incumbents tend to identify and groom successors who have similar habits, appearances, backgrounds, and values that are based on a bureaucratic kinship system. This is a system in which managers look for protégés with social, cultural, or ethnic similarities. Kanter acknowledges that these similarities can promote a *masculine ethic*. For male managers, masculine ethic is associated with having a tough-minded approach to problems, analytic abilities to abstract and plan, a capacity to set aside personal or emotional considerations in the interests of task accomplishment, and a cognitive superiority in problem solving and decision making. On the other hand, female managers may portray a *feminine ethic.* Because they had a better understanding of people, female managers were hired to fill primarily personnel-related staff functions.[11] Nonetheless, this structure sets in motion forces leading to the replication of managers as the same kind of social individuals. Therefore, men and women who manage have a tendency to reproduce themselves in kind. Males, for example, tend to pick other males as successors. This practice perpetrates such problems as employment discrimination. According to Rothwell, these problems can be avoided by promoting diversity and multiculturalism in the work-place. He recommends using systematic efforts to identify and groom the best successors for key positions, not just those who resemble the present key job incumbent.[12] In essence, to ensure the coherence and coordination needed for implementing a successful succession plan, top executives should link individual and organizational demands both con-ceptually and procedurally in the succession development process.

Future Job Predictions

Since the early 1980s, blue-collar manufacturing jobs in the Northeast and Midwest have perished, while white-collar service-producing jobs continue to grow exponentially. Since 1973, for example, nonfarm jobs in manufacturing have declined by 14 percent, from 24 percent to 10 percent, in 2007. Meanwhile, jobs in the service sector increased by 13 percent, from 70 percent to 83 percent, during this time. As the blue-collar jobs continue to decrease, the white-collar service-providing sectors will account for most of the projected job growth. The largest job-growth areas will be in the service-producing sectors—health care, social assistance, and professional and business services. In the goods-producing sectors, employment will be driven by growth in construc-tion. Nevertheless, manufacturing jobs are beginning to return. Table 6 reflects the seven states with the highest manufacturing job growth. In addition, an online Bureau of Labor Statistics report, "Monthly Labor Review Industry Employment and Output Projections to 2024," projects that fall between 2014 and 2024, the total employment will reach 160.3

million, which is an increase of nearly 9.8 million additional jobs in the United States. The report also indicated that nearly 95 percent of these jobs will be nonagricultural. Where will the human capital derive from to fill these future white-collar and/or vocational-related jobs? Twenty-first-century organizations must prepare themselves for this challenge. To remain competitive, they must refocus their attention on future-proofing their workforce in order to take on these new jobs and opportunities. Table 7 reflects the twenty-year employment industry sector projection.[13]

Table 6: States with Highest Manufacturing Job Growth (2012 versus 2016)

State	Number 2012	Number 2016	Loss %	Job Difference
California	1,231,300	1,275,400	3.46%	44,100
Ohio	660,100	689,600	4.28%	29,500
Michigan	526,000	600,700	12.43%	74,700
Indiana	488,900	514,000	4.88%	25,100
Wisconsin	450,200	473,800	4.98%	23,600
New York	448,200	448,900	0.156%	700
North Carolina	439,700	460,300	4.47%	20,600

Table 7: US Twenty-Year Employment Industry Sector Projection

Industry Sector	Number of jobs (in thousands)			Change (in thousands)	
	2004	2014	2024	2004–14	2014–24
Goods-producing sectors, excluding agriculture	21,815.3	19,170.5	19,227.0	-2,644.8	56.5
Mining	523.2	843.8	924.0	320.6	80.2
Construction	6,976.2	6,138.4	6,928.8	-837.8	790.4
Manufacturing	14,315.9	12,188.3	11,374.2	-2,127.6	-814.1
Service-providing sectors	110,646.9	120,641.0	129,904.6	9,994.1	9,263.6
Utilities	563.8	553.0	505.1	-10.8	-47.9
Wholesale trade	5,663.0	5,826.0	6,151.4	163.0	325.4
Retail trade	15,058.2	15,364.5	16,129.1	306.3	764.6
Transportation and warehousing	4,248.6	4,640.3	4,776.9	391.7	136.6
Information Technology	3,118.3	2,739.7	2,712.6	-378.6	-27.1
Financial activities	8,105.1	7,979.5	8,486.7	-125.6	507.2
Professional and business services	16,394.9	19,096.2	20,985.5	2,701.3	1,889.3
Private educational services	2,762.5	3,417.4	3,756.1	654.9	338.7
Health care and social assistance	14,429.8	18,057.4	21,852.2	3,627.6	3,794.8
Leisure and hospitality	12,493.1	14,710.0	15,651.2	2,216.9	941.2
Other services	6,188.3	6,394.0	6,662.0	205.7	268.0
Federal government	2,730.0	2,729.0	2,345.6	-1.0	-383.4
State and local government	18,891.3	19,134.0	19,890.1	242.7	756.1
Agriculture, forestry, fishing, and hunting	2,111.3	2,138.3	2,027.7	26.9	-110.5
Agricultural wage and salary	1,149.0	1,384.0	1,307.3	235.0	-76.7
Agricultural self-employed workers	962.3	754.3	720.4	-208.1	-33.8
Nonagricultural self-employed	9,473.6	8,590.2	9,169.5	-883.4	579.3
Total	144,047.0	150,539.9	160,328.8	6,492.9	9,788.9

The future workforce climate of economic rehabilitation will take on the concept that a lifelong employee is a lifelong learner. Organizations can no longer afford to promote a workforce that is ill-prepared for the future. Because technology—not immigration—is the moocher of today's jobs, both the new and the old workforces will be required to gain the needed competencies (e.g., formal education, vocational, retraining, training, certifications, etc.) on their own time. Organizations may, therefore, want to offer incentives to promote self-development after working hours. AT&T, for example, uses a social content in its workplace by offering financial incentives to help employees invest in their training, retraining, education, and career development outside the work environment. Managing workforce strengths is easy; however, managing workforce weaknesses is very difficult. Managing workforce weaknesses is tied to underdeveloped, ill-prepared, untrained, and uneducated employees. Organizations must develop a workforce that simultaneously builds pluralism and individualism. *Pluralism* is the culture of energetic engagement of self-restructuring and commitment. Pluralism is an achievement in which you hold yourself accountable for becoming a multidimensional employee by diversifying your knowledge, skills, aptitude, education, certification, and training. Meanwhile, the *individualism* aspect requires employees to focus on their own development outside the work environment and not depend on their employer to guide their career destiny.

After serving in the information-technology profession for the past thirty-six years as a network technician up to the chief information officer–level positions, I found that the three commonalities employees had were:

1. They wanted to feel emotionally, socially, and technologically connected (*"eC"*).
2. They wanted to be emotionally and legally protected (*"eP"*).
3. They wanted to be emotionally and humanly respected (*"eR"*).

Because the pace of change is faster than ever, C-suite executives must ensure the workplace culture is attuned to an *"eCPR"* inclusive work environment. Executives must ensure the workplace is well connected, to help maximize productivity and minimize risks. An emotionally, socially, culturally, and technologically well-connected workforce is the workforce of the future. By 2020, for example, 50 percent of the workforce will consist of millennials and gen Xers who are emotionally, socially, culturally, and technologically connected and will accept nothing less. They want to feel valued by being involved in day-to-day decisions concerning their peers and work/life balance. Moreover, a digitally connected workplace allows all employees to succeed, not just the ones at the top. Working in a digital-intelligence work environment, employees will have the ability to enhance their experiences and enable mobility flexibility.

A connected workforce will consist of wearable technology such as Fitbit, which can be used to alter and improve employees' emotional and physical health by alerting them to take a work break. Another example of technology to be used to ensure a connected workforce is the Google Glass. Google Glass is a wearable optical head-mounted display shaped like a pair of eyeglasses, which can be used in the supply-chain management environment to order supply parts via a smartphone. Employees can also use smart-watch technology to help locate stock items more efficiently, which in turn would expedite service delivery to the customer. It can also be used to organize delivery or pickup points, which are similar to Uber's ride-service business.

C-suite executives can no longer afford to have their employees be handcuffed to a desk or locked in a secluded office environment. They must acknowledge the revolutionary benefits of new technologies to encourage innovation, creativity, learning, development, and productivity. In addition, according to a March 2015 online article by Antonia Cusumano of Price-Waterhouse-Cooper, "The Connected Workforce Is Talking SMAC. Are You Ready?", combined four technologies—social, mobile, analytics, and cloud, or SMAC—to inspire its connected workforce in becoming more productive, innovative, and engaged.[14]

Protecting the dignity of the workforce is a critical lifeline for all workers. Employees want to feel protected from neglected workspaces, sexual harassment, discrimination, job loss, job outsourcing, job offshoring, wage inequality, or regulations that may impact their employment. They want to ensure the Fair Labor Standards Act of 1938 (FLSA) is being enforced. Finally, the workforce wants to be respected. Whether we work in construction, health care, hospitality, or other economic sectors, we all want to be respected. Every demographic group must learn to respect each other's culture, social, religion, gender, and race differences. Sondra Thiederman, author of *The Diversity and Inclusion Handbook*, acknowledges that the single most important characteristic of an inclusive workforce is the overriding presence of respect. She defines respect as an "attitude—and the behaviors that accompany that attitude—that everyone has the right to be acknowledged as a valuable individual capable of making positive contributions to the team."[15] Moreover, organizations that enforce a respectful work environment will become more energized and productive. In addition, organizations that support a respectful workplace will gain trust, reduce absenteeism, reduce workplace bullying, minimize work-related conflicts, feel energized, and feel healthier and safer. A respected workforce creates a work environment that encourages employees to have different values, backgrounds, perspectives, and contributions. Moreover, implementing a CPR strategy is also a proactive approach to avoiding competency degeneration. If a CPR strategy is not supported, finding the right people with the right set of competencies to fill critical job vacancies will become much harder for many organizations.

Federal Government and Succession Development Planning

Let's take a glance at the federal government's workforce. In 2014, Robert Goldenkoff of the US Government Accountability Office (GAO) provided an online report entitled "Federal Workforce: Recent Trends in Federal Civilian Employment and Compensation," which indicated that of the federal workforce of 2.1 million, about 31 percent will be retirement eligible by 2017.[16] As a result, federal agencies would lose institutional knowledge and skills that are difficult to restore. Replenishing this workforce pipeline will be difficult. Keep in mind the private sector is not impervious to this problem. A September 1, 1999, online article *Leadership Void*, written by Susannah Zak Figura in *Government Executive* magazine indicated the birth rates in the late 1960s and 1970s were relatively low compared with the baby boomer rates in the 1950s. During the 1960s and 1970s, there were only 14.8 births per 1,000 people, compared to 25.3 per 1,000 people in the 1950s, indicating there is a smaller pool of younger talent available to succeed both private- and public-sector retirees. The loss of this expertise and the realization that it cannot be easily replaced with new hires has created a sense of urgency among C-suite executives across the country.[17] Along with limited resources to fill key vacancies and teenagers dropping out of school, where will organizations find these new hires? For example, William J. Hussar of the National Center for Education Statistics and author of *Projection of Education Statistics to 2020*, indicates that of the fifty-five million students in the K–12 school system in the United States today, approximately 3.4 percent (or 1.87 million) drop out of high school annually. The good news is that this number has declined since 1995, when the dropout rate was at 5.7 percent.[18] Senior leaders and managers must not only focus on recruiting and career development but also focus on the establishment of succession development and workforce engagement plans.

Department of Veterans Affairs

The Department of Veterans Affairs (VA) is a federal agency that oversees three major administrations: Veterans Health Administration (VHA), Veterans Benefits Administration (VBA), and National Cemetery Administration (NCA). Of the eighteen largest federal agencies, VA is the second largest, with an annual budget of $182.3 billion, approximately 340,000 employees, 1,221 inpatient and outpatient facilities, national cemeteries, and benefit offices across the nation. Under the direction of the VA, the VHA is accountable for delivering high-quality medical and administrative services to nearly nine million military veterans. VHA operates one of the largest health-care delivery systems in the nation, which is organized around twenty-three Veterans Integrated Service Networks (VISNs). In May 2014, VHA was confronted with a sense of urgency when America's veterans began to return home from war in massive numbers. By failing to deliver timely health-care services to thousands of US veterans, the VHA found itself in reactive mode. During this same time, minority veterans' enrollment into the VHA health-care system increased by nearly 29 percent. As a result, veterans became victims—not beneficiaries—of this failure, which contributed to the death of approximately forty veterans.[19] To make matters worse, when the attraction and retention of qualified and engaged employees were critical factors in VHA's business success, many senior leaders and managers found themselves out of touch with a workforce that was undergoing an emotional transformation. As employee workload began to increase, so did their stress levels. In turn, their engagement and attitudes began to dissipate. Together, these factors contributed to devastating losses in both employee energy levels and organizational agility.

According to the Office of Personnel Management's (OPM) Climate Assessment Survey 2016 Partnership for Public Service's report titled "2013 Best Places to Work in the Federal Government," of the eighteen largest federal agencies' best places to work, the VA ranked seventeenth in 2016, as compared to ranking twelfth in 2013.[20] Although the VA's overall climate assessment results reflected an uptick of 1.6 index points in 2016, the report indicated that in the last decade, the VA dropped approximately 10 index points, from 66.2 index points in 2005 to 56.7 index points in 2016, respectively. Additionally, according to Robert A. Pretzel, author of *Interim Workforce and Succession Strategic Plan 2014* (the VHA's equal employment opportunity and succession planning reports), between 2013 and 2019, 40.6 percent of VHA's workforce will reach retirement eligibility. The VHA's employee-retention rate also added fuel to this fire. It loses between 26 and 32 percent of its new hires within the first five years of employment and 10 to 15 percent of its new hires within the first year of employment.[21] The reports indicated the top two reasons employees gave for leaving were limited career advancement and professional development opportunities. Equally important, of the senior executive's service (SES) members, the organization's most senior leaders who are responsible for leading the organization out of this destructive path, 84 percent will meet retirement eligibility by 2018, with approximately 56 percent retiring. Additionally, 58 percent of those who fall just below the SES rank, the general schedule (GS-14/15) grade levels, will also meet retirement eligibility.

In an effort to improve timely access to medical service for our military veterans, Donald J. Trump, president of the United States increased the VA's fiscal year 2017 budget by nearly 10 percent. At the same time, the VHA implemented various programs including workforce engagement and retention, Telehealth/Telemental/Teleretinal, employee training and development, coaching, senior executive development, diversity and inclusion, educational programs, and succession planning. In addition, under the VA's Department of Veterans Affairs Plan to Consolidate Program to Improve Access to Care initiative, the DVA implemented an enterprise-wide intervention transformation program called MyVA, which is designed to help modernize the organization's culture, processes, and capabilities to put the needs, expectations, and interests of veterans and their families first.[22] Nevertheless, with the implementation of all these various initiatives and programs, military veterans continue to complain about timely access to medical care, and employees continue to depart the organization in unprecedented numbers. So why are these problems continuing?

First, it appears the VA and VHA's strategic goals are out of alignment. For example, the VA's top three strategic goals are to

1. improve veteran access to VA benefits and services;
2. eliminate the disability claims backlog; and
3. eliminate veteran homelessness.

Meanwhile, VHA's top three strategic goals are to

1. provide veterans with personalized, proactive, patient-driven health care;
2. achieve measurable improvements in health outcomes; and
3. align resources to deliver sustained value to veterans.

The VHA's strategic goals do not support the reduction in timely access to care for America's veterans. Their goals need to be realigned and communicated to support the improvement of quality and timely service to our veterans.

Second, senior leaders across the DVA organization understand they cannot enhance timely medical services to veterans when their employees are not fully engaged, their work performance shows little to no passion, or they are constantly seeking ways to leave the organization. Employees are devoted to their work but are stressed by a lack of resources and opportunities, and this is why the foundation of any business strategy should focus first on the employees and then on the customers. I agree to a certain degree with experts who think improving workforce climate starts at the top. In reality, the actions start at the bottom with the employees. Everyone should have a role and responsibility for improving workforce climate. Empowering, inspiring, and respecting policies can be accomplished by integrating them into the solution process. If not, they will become disengaged. Once this happens, their mind-set will transition into a defiant state. Negative thoughts, behaviors, and emotions will begin. Once this happens, it is too late. They are mentally out the door, followed next by their physical departure. A team approach is the best solution.

The team dynamics must include both active participation and support among top leadership (T), middle managers (M), and employees (B), or T-M-B. It also tells the detractors that senior leadership cares and values employee feedback. In other words, employees are given the opportunity to integrate their "corporate soul" with the organization's soul. According to Eric Klein and John Izzo, authors of *Awakening Corporate Soul: Four Paths to Unleash the Power of People at Work*, corporate soul is about employees wanting their work to have meaning, and even more, to engage more of them at the deepest levels of their capacity and desire.[23] I must give a high degree of credit to the DVA and its senior leaders for having the fortitude to develop a succession plan, because many federal agencies have been unwilling to accomplish one. *Kudos to the Department of Veterans Affairs and its workforce!*

Department of the Navy

In 2004, I researched and studied the impact to organizations not implementing a succession development plan. To complete my doctoral dissertation research, I conducted a comprehensive research study on the Department of the Navy (DoN) titled *Linking Succession Planning to Employee Training: A Study of Federal Employees.*[24] The study consisted of ten different DoN federal organizations or commands. The quantitative study examined whether differences emerged in senior and middle federal male and female managers' and supervisors' perceptions concerning four distinct areas:

1. Organizational career-development culture
2. Succession development planning components
3. Reasons for succession development planning
4. Barriers impacting succession development planning

The comprehensive survey included 85 statements and was administered to 300 middle and senior managers (150 male and 150 female) within the federal agency. Of the 300 surveys, 152 (approximately 51 percent) were returned. Participant grade levels ranged from general schedule GS-12 to GS-15. The GS-15 grade level, for example, is a very senior-level manager in the agency. The GS-13 and GS-14 grade levels are more middle-level managers. The GS-12 grade level is defined as a more junior-level manager. Employees serving in the SES were not included in this study. According to the Office of Personnel Management's (OPM) online site, the term "manager" is defined as a "person who oversees one or more supervisors." The term "supervisor" is defined as a "first-line supervisor who does not supervise other supervisors. Typically, those who are responsible for employee performance appraisals and approval of their leave." The term "nonsupervisor" is defined as "anyone who does not have supervisory responsibilities." The term "federal agency" was used to ensure anonymity.[25]

In the late 1990s, the federal government made a major paradigm shift in how it would conduct business in the twenty-first century. Its primary mission was to rebuild its military forces. In an effort to support this mission, federal training budgets were abridged. While civilian managers and supervisors gravitated toward ensuring the military war-fighting mission was being met, they failed to provide a gravitational balance as it pertained to training, educating, and developing their most important resource, their civilian employees. If senior leaders are to effectively and efficiently manage the tasks and programs assigned to their organization via legislation, they must have a well-trained, educated, and developed civilian workforce.

Ensuring such a workforce would be in place in the future requires senior leaders across the federal agency to know what civilian human-capital requirements would be needed, as well as what competencies (e.g., technical and soft skills) employees should possess to support their organization's future business and succession development needs. To make matters worse, a 2000 online report by *Federal Government* magazine indicated 54 percent of the federal workforce (baby boomers) who joined the federal workforce in the 1960s and 1970s would meet retirement eligibility by 2005. These baby boomers would depart with a wealth of knowledge and experience, leaving federal agencies inadequately prepared to meet their business needs. However, because of the 2008 stock-market crash, many civil servants lost a good percentage of their retirement savings, thereby causing them to postpone their retirement dates.

Meanwhile, the study identified numerous individual and significant differences. Based on the findings of the research, the federal government is in dire need of a unified strategy to establish a career development culture and succession development plans to support its current and future human-capital development and retention requirements. As represented by high mean scores, findings suggest the mentality among most federal senior and middle managers and supervisors is that federal agencies continued to ignore the need to establish succession development plans. This requirement appears to be ignored because Senior Executive Service members, the government's most senior-level managers, continue to rely on the merit promotion system (MPS) and employee individual development plans (IDP) to fill job vacancies and reactively identify training needs as they arose.

Research Findings

The research study reflected fourteen key findings impacting succession development planning in the federal agency. The study also revealed that 71 percent of female participants at the GS-13 and GS-14 grade levels responded with negative perceptions concerning these findings.

Finding 1: Action Learning

The topic generating the most significant differences in support by both management level and gender was to implement action-learning events such as job-shadowing assignments and rotational assignments. Even though action learning can be used to deliver a learning experience that is tailored to both the organization's and the employee's own career development goals, 55 percent of all female respondents disagreed with their organization using action learning, career-development workshops, simulations, and experiential learning as career-development tools. In contrast, male respondents as a whole provided a high level of support for their organization using these ideas as career-development tools. Female respondents rated these two themes as their top priorities for linking employee-training activities to their organization's business and succession needs. In contrast, male respondents provided a high degree of support for the use of mentoring and coaching, nonmonetary incentive awards, and job promotions as key components. Meanwhile, female respondents were less supportive of the ideas of using succession development planning to communicate upward and lateral job moves. Male respondents were more favorable to the idea of using an automatic database to link action learning activities, training, education, and career-development activities, as compared to an unfavorable rating by female respondents.

Finding 2: Reasons for Succession Development
The five topics identified as participants' primary reasons for succession development planning were

1. increased job opportunities;
2. changing workload demands;
3. database automation;
4. identifying organizational short- and long-term human-capital goals; and
5. monitoring individual development plans.

Finding 3: Barriers Impacting Succession Development
Research indicated there were several systemic barriers consistently impacting the succession development planning process. Major barriers ranged from insufficient support from senior leaders to workload overburden. Several independent variables appeared to create significantly different levels of support as to the reasons for implementing a

succession development plan. Significant differences were noted among the eight management levels on the themes of increased job opportunity, changing workload demands, key elements for implementing strategic business plans, developing an automatic database, following up on employee career development, identifying short-term and long-term goals and objectives, aiding in the job-selection process, and monitoring IDPs. The following list of items was identified as barriers impacting the succession development planning process.

a. Lack of Executive and Management Support: The first major obstruction to implementing a succession development plan may be a lack of support from C-suite executives, managers, or employees. According to William Rothwell, if executives and managers do not see or understand the urgency, a succession development plan will not succeed.[26] *So how do you transform impossible thinking into reality thinking?* If this is the case, your best strategy is to practice using influence techniques on yourself first to see how well you respond. Once you are comfortable using the techniques, use them on one or more credible executives and managers to garner their support for the plan. We will discuss several influencing techniques in chapter six.

b. Company Politics: A second obstruction may stem from organizational politics. Instead of promoting employees based on merit and qualifications, C-suite executives and managers may promote their favorite friend or family member, regardless of talent or experience. To alleviate this problem, executives, managers, and HR must collaborate and establish formal policies and procedures for promoting high performers.

c. A Short-Term Mentality: A third obstruction may be associated with C-suite executives and managers having a short-term mentality. This mind-set is well known across the federal government. Most military and civil-service leaders do not understand the importance of succession development planning. The culture within is that they can fill a critical position with an inexperienced person (e.g., retired military or active civil servant) and will train and develop him or her over time by way of on-the-job training. This is associated with a "short-term" mentality. Most of the time, candidates do not possess the necessary competencies (e.g., knowledge, skills, abilities, experience, certification, training, and/or education) to perform the necessary job functions. A short-term-mentality approach sacrifices effectiveness for expediency, which may prompt higher-than-normal turnover among both employees and leaders. This mind-set can also lead to workforce morale problems.

d. Limited/Low Visibility: The fourth barrier may be associated with what William Rothwell calls "low visibility."[27] Because most C-suite executives are constantly attending board and/or stakeholder meetings, they are removed from the daily business activities and may not realize the benefits of implementing a succession development plan. To make matters worse, they may feel they do not have a stake in the development of the plan. Therefore, your succession development plan must be made a high-visibility issue. The plan must employ active support and direct participation from all parties (e.g., C-suite executives, managers, supervisors, and employees alike).

e. Lack of a Competency Aligned Organization (CAO): During organizational realignment, vacancies could be predicted, candidates could be trained for targeted jobs, and a traditional homogenous workforce could lead to an easy transition and assured continuity. The CAO process should include the establishment of matrix organizational policies in which project managers or integrated product team (IPT) members would temporarily relocate to a different department to work with team members in that department to complete various short-lived projects or programs. Once the projects/programs are completed, the employee would be organically relocated back to his or her official department. This would also ensure that the employee meets his or her required yearly training and career-development activities. In this digital age, the rapid pace of organizational change may raise serious questions concerning the value of the traditional "fill-in-the-box-on-the-organizational-chart" approach to replacement-oriented succession development planning versus a more functional organizational approach. To solve this problem, human-resources managers and C-suite executives must see beyond a simple technological solution. Developing competency requirement models (CRM) for each department would greatly support the CAO process. The use of succession development planning software that is designed to accelerate the organization's ability to keep pace with staffing needs, retention, and changes will be inadequate on its own to assure sound succession development.

f. Limited Time: C-suite executives may feel there are not enough hours in the day to do their own job, let alone those of their managers. They may feel a succession development planning program may take too long or become a waste of time because no one will maintain or execute the plan. Some may take the approach that SDP will only generate the need to cut down more trees, due to additional paperwork, during a time in which the organization is attempting to become paperless. They may obstruct the process by focusing on the need for automation, thereby causing a delay in the process, until a database system is developed. This way, management can focus their attention on locating high-potential talent to fill critical positions needed for implementing the organization's business strategies. Having limited time may cause managers to have limited time for follow-up to ensure planned actions such as employee development plans are completed and accurate.

g. Heavy Reliance on HRO: When succession development planning becomes the responsibility of human-resources personnel, middle management will ignore the process. This is a common reason for the limited effectiveness of succession development planning efforts. In addition, because succession development planning in most organizations focuses on replacing positions as they exist today, they are divorced from any long-term plans or business strategies, which are linked to the primary reasons succession development planning fails.

h. Lack of Accountability: Walter Mahler and Stephen Drotter, authors of *The Succession Planning Handbook for the Chief Executive,* argue that management accountability can be increased by making specific outcomes of the succession plan visible through the use of semiannual reports to summarize the progress and outcomes of the plan.[28] The report should also be discussed at the progress-review meetings. Indicators might include the number of successors who actually filled jobs for which they were slated or the number of positions staffed using the performance-management database. Progress measures, such as number of positions filled internally, time taken to fill these positions, and the effectiveness of individuals who fill these positions, also demonstrate the "bottom-line value" of succession planning and help convey the importance of succession planning to top management, according to William Rothwell.[29] Moreover, to ensure accountability and follow-up on developmental plans, experts suggest quarterly individual development plan (IDP) meetings, wherein managers from each department of the organization report on their employees' IDP progress. Alternatively, a succession development planning coordinator should periodically meet with individual managers to review progress on the IDPs in their area of responsibility. Finally, according to Robert Fulmer and Marshall Goldsmith, authors of *The Leadership Investment: How the World's Best Organizations Gain Strategic Advantage Through Leadership Development*, accountability for development can be established by tying development to a bonus or appraisal system. At General Electric, for example, executives are held accountable for the development of managerial talent, and employee performance is a factor when bonuses are determined.[30]

Finding 4: Coaching and Mentoring
Coaching and mentoring were major contributing factors relating to dissimilarity in male and female respondents' perceptions. Findings indicated females and males have different perceptions of how they should receive coaching and mentoring. The perception of general scheduled (GS) male managers and supervisors at grade levels twelve and fifteen gravitated toward using interpersonal networking activities, whereas 66 percent of the female participants at the same grade levels associated coaching and mentoring with being linked to skill-development activities such as rotational job assignments, shadowing assignments, employee exchange programs, and collateral duties to aid them in their career development and advancement. The remaining 34 percent of the female participants (GS-13s and GS-14s) and all management levels of male participants were in consensus as to these training activities being provided. Moreover, because my assumptions were incorrect about females

wanting to receive coaching and mentoring from their senior leaders, I conducted face-to-face and one-on-one telephonic interviews with ten female participants to capture their true perceptions. Their reasons for not wanting to receive coaching or mentoring from their male senior leaders included fears that their peers may perceive them as having a sexual affair or that they may be perceived to be "kissing up" to or "brownnosing" their senior leaders. Nonetheless, both male and female participants were reluctant to ask a senior leader or manager to become their coach or mentor.

Finding 5: Limited Career-Development Tools

Findings indicated female participants at the GS-13 and GS-14 grade levels were not receiving support from their senior leaders as to what career-development tools and materials can be used to support them in their career advancement. The findings also indicated that the gender variable contributed to thirteen of the twenty-one survey statements (62 percent) meeting the rejection criteria in support of their organization promoting a career-development culture. Tests of significance were also conducted on the level of support by gender. Seventy-one percent of the females at the GS-13, GS-14, and GS-15 grade levels denied having a career-development culture, as compared to 19 percent of female participants at the GS-12 grade level who supported having an established career-development culture.

Finding 6: Organizational Hierarchal Culture

Findings suggested there were implications for culture change, which meant the government's hierarchal structure is not just typical top-down male dominant but also male-lateral dominant, thereby explaining why female managers and supervisors may prefer *not* to receive coaching and/or mentoring and are willing to rely on their knowledge, skills, and abilities (KSAs) and education for promotions. Meanwhile, male job-promotion culture appeared to be linked to a friendship-based culture, whereas female promotion culture is linked to a KSA-dependent culture. Thirty-four percent of male participants at the GS-13 grade level were more supportive of career-development culture as compared to the remaining 66 percent of their male counterparts. On average, 54 percent of female middle managers and supervisors agreed that their organization supports promoting a career-development culture, as compared to 56 percent of male participants.

Finding 7: Using IDPs

This finding suggested 58 percent of female participants at the GS-12 and GS-13 grade levels did not have written individual development plans (IDPs), which indicated IDPs were not being used as an assessment tool for linking employee-training activities to their organization's business and succession development needs. Overall, findings suggested managers and supervisors are ensuring their employee IDPs are being updated to support the business needs of the organization.

Finding 8: Using Performance Appraisals

Using performance appraisals as a development activity generated a high degree of interaction by management level and by gender. Female participant perceptions at the GS-12 grade level generated a 58 percent approval rating concerning performance appraisals not being used as a development activity, as compared to 53 percent level of support among female participants at the GS-13, GS-14, and GS-15 management levels. Meanwhile, the perceptions among the four male management levels favored female participants' perceptions at the GS-12 grade level. This finding may suggest an antidevelopmental mind-set may have contributed to the unwillingness of only 39 percent of GS-13 and GS-14 female managers and supervisors to participate in the study. At the same time, antidevelopmental consequences can be linked to those managers and supervisors who realize they are on the fast track becoming concerned about their promotion opportunity and therefore are taking fewer risks and consequently to avoid activities that lead to career development.

Finding 9: Morale and Engagement

Indeed, internal promotions permit an organization to use the skills and abilities of individuals more effectively, and the opportunity to gain a promotion can serve as an incentive for high morale and workforce engagement. This finding revealed 27 percent of female respondents at the GS-14 grade level agreed that major morale and engagement problems exist in their organization, and 58 percent of female participants at the GS-13 and GS-15 grade levels indicated the morale in their organization was on the borderline of becoming a major problem that contributed to low workforce engagement. The perceptions among female participants at the GS-12 grade level were favorable of the morale status in their organization. Meanwhile, the individual mean scores of male participants at all grade levels indicated that morale was not an issue in their organization. The findings also supported the study on how male and female respondents differed in the way they thought and acted. The statistical data supported the theory of gender differences in perceptions concerning workforce morale and engagement, career development, leadership influence, social interaction, and communication between male and female respondents.

Finding 10: Limited Leadership Support
This finding indicated 23 percent of the GS-12 respondents favored senior leaders supporting the implementation of a succession development plan. In contrast, respondents at the higher-grade levels (GS-13, GS-14, and GS-15) indicated that senior leaders are less supportive; as such, they are barriers to implementing an organizational succession development plan. Females, in particular, indicated that a lack of support by senior leaders was a barrier. This finding also indicated there were significant differences in the participants' perceptions in the areas of communication and morale. The lack of support for career development activities and communication from top management emerged as major contributors.

Finding 11: Merit Promotion
This finding revealed the utilization of merit promotion–generated disparity in the level of support between male and female respondents. Even though the system was designed to provide greater uniformity in the succession development process by promoting federal employees based upon their knowledge, skills, and abilities, 64 percent of the respondents rated the merit-promotion system as the fourth-most-perceived barrier to organizations implementing a succession development plan. Female respondents' perceptions of the merit-promotion system in particular supported the literature reviewed, which identified the system

as adding little or no value with regard to achieving organizational succession development needs and career advancement.

Finding 12: Limited Promotion Opportunity

As a reflection of the low mean scores, this finding suggested there was a "glass ceiling" or "bottleneck effect" for female managers and supervisors at the GS-13 and GS-14 grade levels when trying to get promoted and there was limited support for them to grow and develop in their organization. This perception became a reality, for example, when I witnessed a female manager who was acting in a senior management position. She possessed all the qualifications for the position but was not promoted into the position. A male candidate with less experience and education who had come from a different department was given the position. In essence, this is a reflection of low scores from female participants, indicating a low level of support for career-development culture and succession development planning in their organization. In addition, during a December 2005 Federal Government Executive Leadership Conference in Washington, DC, the Department of the Navy had over 15,219 federal employees at the GS-13 grade level, but female employees accounted for only 27 percent of this workforce structure. As the grade levels increased, the female demographic population decreased; for example, of the 5,230 GS-14 employees, females made up approximately 23 percent. Within the 2,656 GS-15 grade level positions, females represented only 18 percent. Demographic data on male and female employees at the GS-12 grade level were not provided.

Finding 13: Grade-Level Differences

This finding indicated male and female participants at the GS-12 grade level provided the highest level of support for the list of barriers impacting succession development planning, at 38.1 percent. The other three grade levels (GS-13, GS-14, and GS-15) provided similar percentages of 30.65, 31.95, and 33.1, respectively. Overall, the statistical analyses presented a high-neutral percentage among the four grade levels in response to the survey statements concerning barriers impacting succession development planning in their organization.

Finding 14: Career Growth

This finding indicated 52 percent of male and female respondents acknowledged their organization has not established proactive solutions to support employee growth without a move to managerial positions and that new work procedures, activities, and responsibilities are critical elements in the career-development process.

Even though my research study concerning succession development planning in the federal government was conducted in 2004, the problem appears to have a direct correlation to and impact on today's private organizations. A 2015 online report by Deloitte University Press (DUP) titled "Global Human Capital Trends" described a comprehensive study pertaining to talent, leadership, HR challenges, and readiness across 3,300 businesses and human-resources leaders from 106 countries around the world. The survey asked businesses and HR professionals to assess the importance of specific talent challenges facing their organization and to judge how prepared they were to meet those challenges. The report highlighted substantial capability gaps in ten major talent challenges. Of the ten, the top three talent challenges were the following:

1. Culture and engagement
2. Leadership
3. Learning and development

The report also indicated that leaders have identified these three challenges as being "urgent priorities" in their organizations. More importantly, but not surprisingly, challenge number three (learning and development) climbed five spots, from eighth in 2014 to third in 2015. In addition, what is more disturbing is that the report indicated only 40 percent of respondents rated their organizations as "ready" or "very ready" in learning and development in 2015, as compared to 75 percent the previous year.[31]

Chapter Five

Diversity and Inclusion in the Fourth Industrial Revolution

> If we cannot now end our differences,
> at least we can help make the world safe for diversity.
> —John Fitzgerald Kennedy, thirty-fifth
> president of the United States

Diversity and Inclusion

The traditional approach to diversity and inclusion (D and I) was for employees to remain in their organization throughout their career, hoping to be the next in line for an executive or management position. At the same time, executives and managers did not care about workforce diversity and inclusion and would hire and promote based on human similarities and tenure. Today, D and I have become major pillars in many organizations' business strategy plans. In 2015, for example, the Equal Employment Opportunity Commission (EEOC) processed more than 89,385 discrimination complaints. Over the eighteen-year period from 1997 to 2015, EEO complaints increased by nearly 10 percent. The breakdown and percentage of the discrimination complaints include the following: color (73 percent), retaliation—all statutes (54.2 percent), religion (51.2 percent), and disability (32.5 percent), and national origin (28.9 percent), age (21.6 percent), respectively.[1]

Meanwhile, organizations such as San Diego Gas and Electric (SDG&E), its parent company, Sempra Energy, and the City of San Diego have established accountability for commitment to their diversity and inclusion initiatives into tier-management evaluation systems. SDG&E

has long been one of the top one hundred private companies to make headlines in *DiversityInc* magazine. Its understanding of the importance of developing and maintaining a diverse and inclusive workforce has led to its ability to expand into international marketplaces, including Mexico, Asia, and Europe. D and I initiatives are built into organizational business models at all levels, and this reinforces the hiring of diverse groups to support the geographical areas they serve. In the organization's customer call centers, for example, sixteen different languages are spoken.

Why is workforce D and I so important? While leading and managing the Fourth Industrial Revolution (FoIR), C-suite executives and managers will not have the luxury of ignoring the importance of training, developing, hiring, and retaining a diversified and inclusive workforce. Diversity and inclusion are key pillars in the succession development planning process. The more diversified and inclusive the workforce is, the more inspired, creative, and innovative it will become. D and I are also very important to the diverse communities and customers they serve. Jointly, they are catalysts for ensuring an organization remains reflective of the community it serves.

Keep in mind that people believe certain things because they have been conditioned to believe them. If senior leaders, for example, think D and I are important to their business success, then they will include them in their succession development, human capital, and strategic business plans. If not, then they will exclude them.

What does the term "diversity" mean? According to the Equal Employment Opportunity Commission, this term is associated with race, color, religion, sex (pregnancy, gender identity, and sexual orientation), national origin, age (forty or older), disability, or genetic information. The term has become a key discussion within many organizations, because it brings about cultural competency and awareness surrounding gender, ethnicity, religion, professional experience, education, disability, race, and so on. To ensure their organization remains competitive, C-suite executives can no longer just talk about the need for diversity and inclusion; they must take critical steps toward ensuring their workforce reflects their organization's customers and communities. According to Taylor Cox Jr., author of *Creating the Multicultural Organization: A Strategy for Capturing the Power of Diversity,* the term "diversity" is defined as "the variation of social and cultural identities among people existing together in a defined employment or marketing setting." In Cox's definition, the phrase "social and cultural identity" refers to the personal affiliation with groups that research has shown to have significant influence on people's life experiences.[2]

In today's global economy, organizations must seek candidates who speak not only the English language but also those who are proficient in other languages (Spanish, Chinese, Japanese, etc.). Having a diversified and inclusive workforce will lead to higher work productivity, improved problem resolution, innovation, and recruitment and retention. Meanwhile, the term "inclusion" is about meeting the needs of all employees and taking premeditated actions to create work environments where all employees feel included, protected, and respected, thereby ensuring equal access to opportunities in order for them to achieve their full potential. These affiliations include gender, race, national origin, religion, age, and work specialization. Although the emphasis of succession development planning has traditionally focused on senior executive positions, smarter organizations are now employing succession planning for a broader range of jobs, both vertically and horizontally across the organizations, to include middle managers and downward. World-class organizations not only pay attention to the aforementioned affiliations but also focus on retaining and recruiting people who are diversity competent. This effort must start at the very top of the organization. C-suite executives and managers must ensure their business and marketing strategies are D and I focused.

The phenomenon of including diversity in the workplace is due to a very tight labor market and the limited amount of people with the required technical and soft skills to do the work. Fourth Industrial Revolution (FoIR) organizational leaders must become aware of their unconscious D and I biases. As Sandy Sparks from the University of Warwick explains, "Unconscious bias refers to a bias that we are unaware of and which happens outside of our control. It is a bias that happens automatically and is triggered by our brain making quick judgments and assessments of people and situations, influenced by our background, cultural environment and personal experiences." Sandy also acknowledges that unconscious biases are prejudices we have but are unaware of. They are mental shortcuts based on social norms and stereotypes. Sparks's unconscious bias examples are identified in table 1. The Society for Human Resource Management and other experts acknowledge that there are major differences in definitions of equal employment opportunity, affirmative action, and diversity. Table 2 provides a baseline breakdown of the three terms.[3]

Table 1: Unconscious Bias Awareness	
Workforce Recruitment	
	Generational bias
	Name recognition of underrepresented groups
	Criteria for person with specific and essential criteria
	Résumé bias
	Candidate reminds you of someone you know
	Anonymous short listing
	Interview panel reflect single gender on panel
Workforce Promotion	
	Gender differences in promotion opportunities
	Difference by gender of time spent at each career field
	Clear work objectives
	Merit pay
Workforce Appraisals	
	Monitor the appraisal process among staff
	Gender difference in the outcome of appraisals
	Appraisal recognizes the variety of work
Workload Allocation	
	Gender difference in time allocated to various work areas
	Volunteering or carrying out work that is more positive to career progression o work that is not highly valued
	Ensure administrative work is not disproportionately allocated to one particula group
Other	
	Diversity in guest speakers and/or instructors
	Marketing and website
	Awareness of team dynamics are gender, race, and age
	Candidate speaks the language

Table 2: Equal Employment Opportunity, Affirmative Action, and Diversity Comparison		
Equal Employment Opportunity (EEO)	**Affirmative Action**	**Diversity**
Freedom from discrimination based on protected classes such as race, color, sex, national origin, religion, age, disability, or genetic information	Employer's standard for proactively recruiting, hiring, and promoting women, minorities, disabled individuals, and veterans; aims to eliminate barriers in hiring, advancement, and education; is deemed a moral and social obligation	Goals devised to measure acceptance of minorities and women by embracing cultural differences within the workplace; leverages the differences and values the diverse perspectives within the workforce to achieve better results
Focuses on employment practices	Numerical measures with the intent of increasing the representation of minorities	Concept of diversity extends to the work environment, as well as individual attitudes and behaviors
Mandated by federal law and government initiated	Federally mandated, legally driven, and directed by public law and consent decree	Is achieved through awareness, education, and positive recognition of cultural differences within the workplace; is voluntary; not directed or leadership driven
Assumes assimilation and mitigates discriminatory practices	Brings previously excluded groups into an organization and changes the way an organization "looks"	Changes the way an organization "works"
Provides equal access to benefits and privileges of employment	Covers specific groups and/or unprotected categories	Provides inclusion of total workforce, not specific groups; ensures an inclusive and fair climate
Is problem- and internally focused	Is problem focused	Is strategic and has an operational focus as well as productivity, efficiency, and quality-performance focus
Is reactive	Is reactive	Is proactive
Is measured quantitatively with goals and quotas	Is measured quantitatively with goals and quotas	Is measured qualitatively

US Demographics

The US population will drastically change in the FoIR. For example, in 1950, the total US population was 152.3 million. By 2016, the US population had more than doubled to 324 million. By the year 2030, nearly 37 million people (or 23 percent of the population) will be reaching their retirement age of fifty-five or older. According to Marlene A. Lee and Mark Mather, authors of *US Labor Force Trends*, in 2005, non-Hispanic whites represented 70 percent of the US labor force. This number, however, is expected to change dramatically by 2050, as Asians and Hispanics are the fastest-growing populations in the US workforce. The Asian and Hispanic labor forces will reach nearly 24 percent and 8 percent, respectively. Meanwhile, the African American labor force is expected to have a small increase of 3 percent (from 11 to 14 percent), while the white non-Hispanic labor force will decrease nearly 18 percent by 2050.[4]

As listed in table 3, according to Conner Forrest, author of *Diversity Stats: Ten Tech Companies That Have Come Clean*, between 2014 and 2015, ten major high-tech companies tracked diversity and inclusion in their organization. These organizations understood the importance of their business strategy revolving around continuous D and I knowledge awareness, leadership development, and retention. They also understood the importance of continuously preparing and developing a diverse and inclusive workforce as it pertains to the future growth of their organization. To enhance workforce culture, having a defined and focused diversity and inclusive strategy would help their organization attract and hire top talent, retain high-potential employees, and enhance their bottom line.[5] Using D and I tools such as metrics and human-resources systems to track workforce demographics also ensured their organization met their D and I goals. In addition, management accountability was key. Managerial incentives were linked with their D and I success, employee engagement, creativity, and innovation. Implementing a diversity and inclusion strategy also helped mitigate litigation in their organizations.

Table 3: Top Ten High-Tech Companies Tracking Diversity and Inclusion										
Company / Report Date	Twitter	Apple	eBay	HP	Pinterest	Pandora	LinkedIn	Yahoo	Facebook	Google
# of Employees	2.91k	92.6k	21.4k	317.5k	0.6k	5k	4.24k	7.4k	5.5k	32.53k
Female %	10%	30%	42%	32.5%	40%	49.2%	39%	24%	31%	30%
Male %	90%	70%	58%	67.5%	60%	50.8%	61%	62%	69%	70%
Monitors Diversity	Yes	Yes	Yes	Yes	Yes	Yes	Yes	Yes	Yes	Yes
% of Female Managers	22%	28%	29%	25.6%	N/R	15%	30%	24%	23%	22%
% of Male Managers	78%	72%	71%	N/R	N/R	85%	70%	76%	77%	78%
AA/Black	2%	7%	7%	6.9%	1%	3%	1%	2%	1%	2%
White	59%	55%	61%	71.5%	50%	70.9%	53%	50%		61%
Asian	29%	15%	24%	14.22 %	42%	12.3%	38%	39%	41%	30%
Hispanic	3%	11%	5%	6.06%	2%	7.2%	1%	4%	3%	3%
Two or more races	3%	2%	2%	0.74%		5.7%	1%	2%	N/R	4%
Native American	1%	N/R	N/R	0.48%	N/R	N/R	N/R	N/R	N/R	N/R
Native Hawaiian/ Pacific Islander	1%	N/R	N/R	0.10%	N/R	1%	N/R	N/R	N/R	N/R
Other race	2%	9%			5%		1%			1%

N/A = Not Reported.

Gender Diversity and Start-Up Companies

How diversified are US start-up companies? In 2015, of the 186 newly established global companies, 100 with revenue worth one billion dollars or more were located in the United States. Fifty percent of the founders and/or cofounders of these one hundred companies were born outside of the United States. Their formative years were spent in countries such as Ireland, Canada, India, Israel, and Iran. Gender diversity remains a problem for these companies. Although the gender diversity numbers were small, two of the companies had female CEOs, and 10 percent of the cofounders were females. Approximately seventy of the hundred companies did not reflect gender diversity at the board level, and 30 percent failed to hire females in leadership roles, according to Aileen Lee, author of *Welcome to the Unicorn Club, 2015: Learning from Billion-Dollar Companies.*[6] In essence, succession development planning in small start-up companies must also include gender, social, cultural, and multigenerational trends. C-suite executives, managers, and employees alike must become aware of these trends and how each impacts their organization's overall business success. In an increasingly global society, organizations will continue to encounter people of different backgrounds, religions, races, and ethnic groups. People of all races and ethnic groups must therefore learn the importance of tolerance when interacting with diverse coworkers. Consider, for example, the case of gender diversity in today's college enrollment.

According to Taylor Cox Jr., in the 1950s, three of every four college degrees in the United States went to men; in recent years, the majority (around 54 percent) of college graduates have been women. By 1971, US women earned less than 4 percent of all graduate-level business-management degrees; by the early 1990s, that figure had multiplied more than sevenfold to around 30 percent. In hot technical fields like engineering, according to Cox, the rates of increase in the participation of women have been even higher.[7] In essence, in both today and tomorrow's business environments, C-suite executives and managers must learn to value coherence and celebrate diversity and inclusion. To ensure D and I are taken seriously, C-suite executives must hold themselves and their managers accountable. This can be accomplished by proactively incorporating D and I results into yearly incentives. They can also monitor the profile of succession development candidate pools for key dimensions such as gender, race, national origin, work specialization, and so on. The work specialization element is very important because it will help alleviate the notion of limited access to C-suite executive positions only to people with certain professional specialties.

Moreover, gender diversity is very important because it helps increase female promotional opportunities to C-suite executive positions. According to an online news article by the Economic Cycle Research Institute (ECRI) tilted "Women's Labor Force Participation Down, Capping Jobs and Economic Growth," by 2025, the United States has pledged to add 25 million new jobs. Without a surge in women and immigrants entering the job market, this may be an impossible task.[8] According to an April 2017 US Department of Labor online report "Women in the Labor Force: A Databook," for the past seven decades the female labor force has shown a steady increase from 31 percent in 1948 to 58 percent in early 2008. Meanwhile the male labor force continued to decline from 82 percent in 1948 to 68 percent during the same time period. It was not until 2008 during the US recession that both labor forces declined simultaneously, see chart 1. The chart also indicates the male and the female labor force projections from 2012 to 2024.[9]

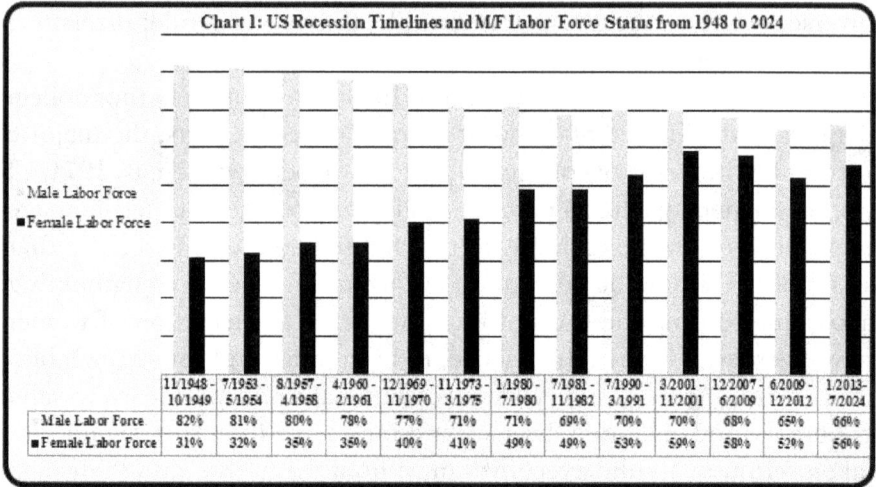

Chart 1: US Recession Timelines and M/F Labor Force Status from 1948 to 2024

	11/1948 - 10/1949	7/1953 - 5/1954	8/1957 - 4/1958	4/1960 - 2/1961	12/1969 - 11/1970	11/1973 - 3/1975	1/1980 - 7/1980	7/1981 - 11/1982	7/1990 - 3/1991	3/2001 - 11/2001	12/2007 - 6/2009	6/2009 - 12/2012	1/2013- 7/2024
Male Labor Force	82%	81%	80%	78%	77%	71%	71%	69%	70%	70%	68%	65%	66%
■ Female Labor Force	31%	32%	35%	35%	40%	41%	49%	49%	53%	59%	58%	52%	56%

Male Labor Force
■ Female Labor Force

Another reason to bring attention to D and I and the succession development planning process is to ensure future successors for key leadership positions are diversely and inclusively competent. This effort should commence at the C-suite executive level of the organization. C-suite executives and other leaders who are committed to changing the culture of their organization must enhance their welcome greetings and ensure that D and I becomes an attractant for future successors, according to Brady and Helmich. This phenomenon of including diversity in the workplace will also continue to be associated with the demanding US labor market and the limited amount of people with the required technical skills to do the work. Cynthia McCauley, Russ Moxley, and Ellen Van Velsor, authors of *The Center for Creative Leadership: Handbook of Leadership Development*, postulate that "for an organization to effectively develop diversity, the organization as a whole should get involved by using a strategy that encompasses elements of enforcement, education and exposure."[10] To ensure diversity practices are adhered to, enforcement is necessary. If women and minorities are to be developed for leadership positions, C-suite executives and managers must be held accountable for how they distribute challenging assignments, support their employees, and reward them accordingly via an incentive compensation system. All people have strengths and weaknesses; therefore, senior leaders across the organization must take the time to learn social and cultural elements about their employees.

In contrast, there are disadvantages to workforce diversity and inclusion. James Kouzes and Barry Posner, authors of *The Leadership Challenge: How to Keep Getting Extraordinary Things Done in Organizations*, argue that seeking out diverse opinions from a homogenous group is one thing, but involving culturally diverse groups in problem solving and decision making can present significant challenges to a leader.[11] Researchers who have completed studies on cultural diversity in the workplace also indicated that it took time to reach high levels of performance from culturally diverse groups, because homogenous groups were more likely to significantly outperform culturally diverse groups on measures of problem identification, quality of solutions, and overall performance in the initial weeks of a task. In addition, they indicated that during the initial phase of the project, homogenous groups were better at group processes than mixed groups. Nevertheless, seventeen weeks into the study, the researchers acknowledged the differences in overall performance or group process disappeared, and as time elapsed, both types of groups improved. The diverse groups, however, improved more, and their performance converged.

Nonetheless, according to Frances Hesselbein, Marshall Goldsmith, and Richard Beckhard, editors of *The Drucker Foundation: The Leaders of the Future: New Visions, Strategies and Practices for the Next Era*, in addition to race, ethnicity, and gender, workplaces should expect increasing diversity of religious beliefs and practices, ages, and lifestyles as an increased number of potential employees with physical disabilities join the workforce.[12] In essence, senior leaders must become more educated and aware of the social and cultural differences within their organization, what I call the "social and cultural intelligences." Karl Albrecht, author of *Social Intelligence: The New Science of Success*, defines "social intelligence" (SI) as the "ability to get along well with others and to get them to cooperate with you. It is about seeking human social effectiveness at a level beyond simple formulas—beyond saying 'please' and 'thank you.' It is about seeking to understand how highly effective employees navigate complex social relationships and environments."[13] According to M. Y. Ganaie and Hafiz Mudasir, authors of *A Study of Social Intelligence and Academic Achievement of College Students of District Srinagar, J&K, India*, Australian social scientist Ross Honeywill defines social intelligence as being "an aggregated measure of self- and social awareness, evolved social beliefs and attitudes, and a capacity and appetite to manage complex social change."[14] Psychologist Nicholas Humphrey argues that it is social intelligence, rather than quantitative intelligence, that defines humans. On the other hand, cultural intelligence is about having the capability to relate and work effectively in culturally diverse situations. It goes beyond existing notions of cultural sensitivity and awareness to highlight a theoretically based set of capabilities needed to successfully and respectfully accomplish work objectives in culturally diverse settings, according to the Wikipedia website.[15] Furthermore, David Livermore, author of *The Cultural Intelligence Difference*, defines cultural intelligence (CI) as "having the capability to function effectively in a variety of cultural contexts—including national, ethnic, organizational and generational. CI deals with the awareness of employees' values, emotions, ethnicity and behavior and how each transforms their beliefs."[16]

Moreover, as the cerebral processes of knowledge workers continue to outpace the need for physical capacities and as diverse work teams become more universal, changes in the human dimensions of the workplace will continue. Similarly, just as the global marketplace continues to develop, with these changes better intercultural and interpersonal communication will greatly impact productivity. Hesselbein, Goldsmith, and Beckhard contend true leaders of the future must be willing to accept five fundamental challenges.[17] Future leaders must

1. be willing to become more sensitive and understanding with respect to the ethnic, cultural, and gender differences within the workplace and to demonstrate that sensitivity and understanding;
2. have a vision for the workplace that ultimately results in a significant broadening of corporate and human cultures and workplace environments;
3. be willing to craft and implement new and different employment and communication processes to enhance and promote perceptions of fairness and equity;

4. be willing to bring full and unquestioned commitment to the effective utilization of a diverse workforce; and

5. be the linchpins between their organization and the larger community, to establish the organization as a place where people want to work and be productive, and to develop new markets and maintain existing ones.

Likewise, an organization's diversity and inclusion (D and I) policy should include manager-and supervisor-to-employee ratios. For a simple way of measuring how diversified and inclusive your organization is, develop a matrix that identifies the ratio of employees to managers and supervisors. An example of a ratio might be 10:1 or 20:1. This means for every ten Hispanic employees, there should be one Hispanic manager or supervisor, or for every twenty Hispanic employees, there should be one Hispanic manager or supervisor working in the organization. Having a manager or supervisor who has the same ethnicity and culture as his or her employees will lead to better communication, collaboration, and connection.

Because employees are hesitant to change or modify their thoughts, behaviors, or perception about others, a twenty-first-century survey of the workplace should commence with a discussion about workforce diversity and inclusion. A classical scenario concerning diversity and inclusion can be linked to the events of the twentieth century. The functional roles of black, Hispanic, and Asian people in the workplace have changed drastically. For instance, in the early twentieth century, nearly 90 percent of the black population who lived in the southern United States either worked in private homes as servants or on the land as sharecroppers and farmers. Under the administration of President Woodrow Wilson, around 1917 during World War I, when the first wave of the American Expeditionary Forces arrived in France, most blacks in the United States began their migration in great numbers to the north and west. As a result, today less than one-third of the black population resides in the south. During this movement, black migrants found few employment opportunities in the new areas; about 90 percent of the women found jobs as domestics, while the men occupied service and common day-labor positions. Only during and after World War II did black employment grow in the industrial workforce, and this came to a screeching halt when the Industrial Revolution began to decline.

The greater presence of blacks in the workplace is another part of the story of the changing demography of the workplace. Blacks, Asians, and Hispanics were not the only ones who were needed for succession; white women and children were also needed to work in the textile factories. These women and children were drawn from the poorest farm families. They received less pay than the white men and were found to be more obedient. Because their small hands provided easy access into the narrow slots of the machines, they were hired. They worked twelve to thirteen hours each day, rarely seeing the sun or their families, according to Winthrop D. Jordan, Leon F. Litwack, Richard Hofstadter, William Miller, and Daniel Aaron, authors of *The United States: Conquering a Continent*.[18]

Nonetheless, Jean Lipman-Blumen, author of *The Connective Edge: Leading in an Interdependent World*, argues, "The time-worn foundations of authoritarian, competitive, and ruggedly individualistic leadership are eroding." She admits that "it is a time marked by two contradictory forces, interdependence and diversity, pulling in opposite directions."[19] The tension of these twin forces will be rapidly rendering traditional leadership behaviors obsolete. Lipman-Blumen discusses a three-stage approach to connective leadership: the physical era, the geopolitical era, and the connective era. "The challenge of leadership succession bedevils many organizations," she contends. "Succession issues have traditionally centered either on new, younger leaders to replacing retiring chiefs, or avoiding the loss of enterprising stars who might move on to greener pastures."[20]

According to "Social and Demographic Trends: Breadwinner Moms," a May 29, 2013 online article by Wendy Wang, Kim Parker, and Paul Taylor, in today's households, 40 percent of females are the breadwinners, as compared to only 11 percent in the 1960s. These breadwinner moms are divided into two distinctly different groups. Approximately 5.1 million (37 percent) are married, and 8.6 million (63 percent) are unmarried. Women also make up 47 percent of the US workforce. They are well educated. In 2015, for example, 30.2 percent of women held a bachelor's degree, as compared to only 29.9 percent of men. Ten years earlier, men were the degree winners, with a rating of 28.5 percent, as compared to women at 26 percent. Between the ages of twenty-five and thirty-four, 37.5 percent of women hold a bachelor's degree or higher, as compared to men of the same age group at 29.5 percent.[21]

Keep in mind that during the early years of the twentieth century, less than one-fourth of all adult women in the United States worked outside their home, and only 10 percent of all women forty years of age worked during this same time period. Today, this number has increased to over 55 percent. According to a December 14, 2015 "US News & World" online report "US Job Market: Good, but Not Great" by Andrew Soergel, the US labor market generated approximately thirteen million new jobs since 2010. However, due to the Great Recession, the longest since World War II, which lasted from December 2007 to June 2009, the country missed out on six million additional new jobs, bringing the American employment total to over 149.3 million.[22] In addition, he acknowledged the labor market would not be fully recovered until the year 2020. If this is the case, the question executives should be asking is do we have a diversified workforce of employees with the right competencies (e.g., education, experience, skills, knowledge, aptitude, certifications, licenses, leadership, etc.) to compete in the twenty-first century?

To focus additional light on gender diversity, according to a 2007 online National Center for Education Statistics report "Digest of Education Statistics," in 1971, of the approximately 839,730 bachelor's degrees awarded, 475,594 were earned by males (57 percent) and 364,136 to females (43 percent), respectively. By 2006, this number climbed to 1,485,242 bachelor's degrees being awarded; 630,600 males (42.4 percent) and 854,642 females (57.5 percent), respectively.[23] Similarly, in 2006, US colleges and universities awarded approximately 594,065 graduate-level degrees, of which 60 percent (356,169) were earned by females.

However, women are not necessarily gaining ground in the science, technology, engineering, art, and math (STEAM) fields. According to a December 2013 online US Census Bureau Current Population Survey, data indicated there were approximately 216.6 million men and women between the ages of eighteen and seventy-four. Of this total population, 29.43 percent were granted high-school diplomas, 18.98 percent were granted bachelor's degrees, and 9.86 percent earned advanced degrees. [24] According to an online report, "12 Stats About Working Women," by Mark DeWolf of the US Bureau of Labor Statistics, women make up 47 percent of the total US workforce but are much less represented in science and engineering occupations. Women make up only 39 percent of material scientists and chemists, 28 percent of environmental scientists and geoscientists, 16 percent of chemical engineers, and just 12 percent of civil engineers. Overall, about 20 percent of undergraduate engineering degrees are awarded to women, but only 13 percent of the engineering workforce is female.[25]

On December 22, 2015, an online news article "A New Year's Resolution for the Boardroom" by Steve Odland of CNBC reported that women

- make up the majority of the United States' population;
- make up nearly half of the workforce;
- earn more college degrees than men;
- make 85 percent of consumer decisions; and
- control over half of all US wealth.[26]

Moreover, the age group eighteen to forty-nine reflected major differences. According to Camille L. Ryan and Kurt Bauman, authors of *Educational Attainment in the United States: 2015*, the male population with a high-school diploma and college degree(s) was 37.059 million as compared to the female population of 37.142 million. The male population for high-school graduates indicated 19.917 million (53.7 percent) as compared to female high-school graduates of 16.687 million (44.9 percent). The graduation percentage favored the female population as it pertained to bachelor's degrees. For females graduating with a bachelor's degree, the number was 14.2 million (38.27 percent) as compared to males at 11.99 million (32.37 percent). The female population outranked males in the advanced-degree category too. Over 6.24 million females (16.80 percent) obtained an advanced degree, compared to the male population of 5.145 million (13.88 percent).[27]

As organizations in the United States become more knowledge-based, female succession will become even more highly desirable. They will obtain a college education to assist organizations in being more competitive in the twenty-first century and will be highly sought after, not only in the United States but also globally. I am not knocking people who do not have a college education; however, the statistical data indicates that people with college degrees will be more highly desired and will make two to three times more in income over their life span. Because executives will not respect the status quo and will be seeking potential employees with higher education, succession development planning can be used as an important tool for hiring and promoting more women and minorities into the executive ranks of an organization.

Senior leaders who make diversity and inclusion part of their organization's business culture understand the composition of a diverse team and dictate its potential for success by allowing everyone the opportunity to contribute different points of view based on their exposure and experience. The United States' DNA, for example, was made up of this when immigrants immigrated here hundreds of years ago. More importantly, if organizations want to remain competitive in this global economy, they must establish business relationships with people who are from diverse backgrounds (religions, races, age, ethnicity, and gender). Executives, managers, supervisors, and employees alike will be required to understand other aspects of the human factor such as social, relationship, cultural, personal, and multigenerational intelligences. Today's leaders must learn to value coherence and celebrate diversity and inclusion.

As organizations progress competitively through the twenty-first century, succession development planning must take center stage in their business strategy efforts. Moreover, effective leadership will require senior leaders to proactively establish real accountability for results on diversity and inclusion with their direct reports. This accountability should include establishing diversity policies, guidelines, and performance reports, and diversity using integrated measurement systems for quantitative matrix purposes such as predictive analytics. In addition, consensus among experts on succession planning such as Taylor Cox Jr., Gene Brady, and Donald Helmich agree that attracting, retaining, and effectively training and developing a diversified workforce will be top priorities of leaders in all organizations, from high-tech firms to universities and from government agencies to heavy-manufacturing firms. For an organization to have a successful D and I program, it should include implementing the fourteen strategies listed below.

1. Establish a D and I taskforce or charter, to be led by a senior executive.
2. Identify and remove equal employment opportunity (EEO) barriers.
3. To adjust mind-sets, provide managing D and I training to managers and executives.
4. Establish a D and I committee that reports directly to the CEO of the organization.
5. Adopt best business practices to help promote D and I.
6. Establish policies and procedures that focus on recruiting, hiring, developing, and retaining a D and I workforce to include hiring veterans and people with disabilities.
7. Establish internal and external job announcements that include D and I representation.
8. Establish a D and I ratio initiative (e.g., for every forty Hispanic employees, there will be at least one Hispanic director or manager, for a ratio of forty to one).
9. Establish a policy to ensure all hiring panels are diversified (race, gender, age, etc.).
10. Integrate D and I into the organization's new hires and current employee orientation initiative.
11. Cultivate a D and I culture that encourages equality, flexibility, and teamwork.
12. Ensure the organization's leadership development program includes D and I.
13. Establish a D and I dashboard measurement and tracking system.
14. Establish mandatory monthly D and I dashboard-measurement meetings to include C-suite executive participation.

Diversity and Inclusion Scenario

Take this scenario, for example: What would you think if every person with a driver's license drove an identical car model and color? This would not be very appealing to most, correct? I think you would want to see a diversity of cars in various colors. Let's transition this thought into humans. Take China, for example: today, of the 184 countries around the globe, China's one-dimensional race population, approximately 1.388 billion, represents 19.48 percent of the world's total population, with India the world's second-largest country in close pursuit with a population just over 1.342 billion. Meanwhile, the United States—the third-largest country, with a population of approximately 326.47 million—is the most racially and ethnically diverse of the 184 countries. Between 2014 and 2060, US ethnicity will change gradually, Black/African American (increase from 12.4 to 13 percent), Native American/Alaska Native (decline from 0.7 to 0.6 percent), Asian American (increase from 5.2 to 9.1 percent), White (non-Hispanic (decline from 62.6 percent to 43.6 percent), Hispanic/ Latino (increase from 17.4 to 28.6 percent), and biracial groups/others (increase from 2 to 4.9 percent), respectively.[28]

Meanwhile, because of China's one-child policy, the country has aged significantly. Between 1978 and 2015, the one-child policy prevented 400 million new births from occurring. A country with a median age of 37.3 years, it has a soaring baby boomer retirement growth rate, which may lead to major economic consequences and a negative impact to the United States' global standing. With no succession development planning in sight, in 2015, China's working-age population decreased by 4.87 million people due to baby boomers retiring. To make matters worse, China's workforce ratio today is 5:1, which means for every five workers, one has met his or her retirement age. By 2040, however, this ratio will change drastically to a ratio of 1.6:1. By 2050, China's baby boomer age will be sixty-five, which indicates approximately 329 million employees will be retiring, according to Laurie Burkitt's online article, "China's Working-Age Population Sees Biggest-Ever Decline."[29] To resolve its workforce problem, China may seek to hire US workers and top executives to support its workforce shortfall, which will lead to a more diversified workplace.

What impact will this have on the United States? As China's workforce decreases due to baby boomers retiring, the US workforce will increase by 31 percent by 2050, which will positively impact economic growth, the Social Security system, workforce income, and its tax base.

The United States will continue to have a positive growth population, due to its immigration laws. According to an online Pew Research Center report by Mark Hugo Lopez, Jeffrey Passel, and Molly Rohal, "Modern Immigration Wave Brings 59 Million to US, Driving Population Growth and Change Through 2065," immigrants and their children and grandchildren will account for 88 percent of the US population growth by 2065.[30] Meanwhile, to replenish its workforce, China will seek to hire top-notch candidates from outside of its borders, which may impact the American workforce population. Millennials have surpassed baby boomers as the nation's largest living generation, according to Richard Fry, author of "Millennials Overtake Baby Boomers as America's Largest Generation." In 2015, millennials (those between the ages of eighteen and thirty-four) now number 75.4 million, surpassing the 74.9 million baby boomers (those between the ages of fifty-one and sixty-nine). And in 2015, generation X (those between the ages of thirty-five and fifty) was projected to pass the boomers in population by 2028. The millennial generation continues to grow as young immigrants expand its ranks. Boomers, whose generation was defined by the "boom" in US births following World War II, are older. Their numbers continue to decline as the rate of death exceeds the number of older immigrants arriving in the country.[31]

In today's world, where diversity signifies a multitude of organizational forms, succession development planning means building a cadre of leaders who can head a dynamic and diverse workforce. During their careers, however, this new group of leaders will be expected to lead various organizational structures, from short-term alliances to more stable partnerships and joint ventures. In other words, current and future organizations must exercise their leadership authority and hold senior executives, managers, and employees accountable for monitoring and developing employees at all levels of the organizations. Employees must also be held accountable for their own training and career development. This may require them to attend training classes and career-development workshops on their own time. Moreover, David Giber, Louis Carter, and Marshall Goldsmith, authors of *Linkage Inc's: Best Practices in Leadership Development Handbook*, assert that "leaders are not developed in a classroom. Even though they may be stimulated by discussion, the real learning comes from applying new tools and techniques such as action learning."[32] The characteristics of a typical action-learning experience, for example, may include

- an emphasis on learning by doing;
- team performances;
- actual and substantive organizational issues that put employees into problem-solver roles; and
- team decisions that are formalized into presentations.

The authors conducted a study on action learning of a Canadian company called Imasco Limited. Imasco Limited is a $10 billion (CAD) diversified company that focuses its business practices on providing consumer goods and services in North America. The company competes in the financial services, tobacco, drugstore, and land-development industries. In early 2000, the company was faced with the challenge of allocating its human-resources personnel to train and develop its decentralized group of general managers. To resolve this problem, Imasco used action learning to help develop its general managers during the succession development planning process.

According to the authors, through a careful selection of projects and experiences, action learning created for midlevel managers a condensed experience of the strategic and organizational leadership issues that senior management faced. Their study concluded that action learning depended on three critical success variables:

1. As a whole, the organization needed to be fully committed to the process in terms of time, resources, and candor.
2. Team diversity directly affected the quality of project outcome.
3. Facilitators played an essential role—far more than they originally had imagined.

They also acknowledged that the biggest contributing factor to the success of their study was the organization's team-dynamic culture. Teams that developed strong norms around candor and diversity of perspectives, for example, produced more insightful and more creative project recommendations. However, where a single individual or perspective dominated, teams tended to be far less innovative and effective in their presentations. The results of their study indicated that "a participant led other participants to believe that he had superior knowledge, and in turn, his recommendations constituted the majority of the team's proposals and produced a report that supported essentially the status quo and showed limited insight."[33]

Likewise, when creating a multicultural work environment, C-suite executives and senior managers must include the leveraging of employee diversity in the workplace to remain competitive in the future. The term "diversity" should not be limited to race; it must also include ethnicity, gender, religion, age, lifestyles, people with physical disabilities, and so on. As changes in human dimensions of the workplace develop, the concept and the reality of a global marketplace must also continue to develop. Implicit requirements for intercultural and interpersonal communication and workforce productivity will become functions more of the intellectual process of knowledge workers than of physical capacities. In essence, tomorrow's leaders must be willing to face fundamental challenges. They must align their D and I initiatives with organizational goals and implement business-analytic strategies to solve recruiting and succession development planning–related issues.

As a reminder, the maturity of a diversity and inclusion program will take time. A D and I mission statement should be established to include goals that are provided by C-suite executives from across the organization. Any organization with focused and mature diversity and inclusion policies and strategies will have a higher probability of retaining high-potential employees, improving its bottom line, attracting top talent, and improving retention rates. Establishing benchmarks and measurements are key components to ensuring a successful diversity and inclusion strategy. By using metrics and integrated HR systems to track workforce demographics, executives and managers can successfully make the case for culture change. In addition, D and I leadership accountability and yearly incentive statements should be included in the performance goals and objectives for executives and managers. These initiatives are key drivers to a more creative, innovative, and engaged workforce. Although the succession development planning process is the responsibility of the managers, the D and I process is the responsibility of the human resources office. In addition, the HRO is accountable for integrating D and I into talent acquisition, learning and development, employee engagement, and compliance.

Chapter Six

THE SUCCESSION DEVELOPMENT PLANNING PROCESS

> If you want to make enemies, try to change something.
> —WOODROW WILSON, TWENTY-EIGHTH
> PRESIDENT OF THE UNITED STATES

The Future State

If the United States wants to remain the world's multipolar superpower, many C-suite executives must alter their mind-sets, which now appear to be trapped in prehistoric times when it comes to succession development planning. The global success of the United States is greatly dependent on their ability to develop and grow the country's next generation of top leaders and high performers. The time has come for these leaders to catch up with the way great executives operate and how they see their role in tomorrow's workplace. Traditionally, chief financial officers have argued that the primary purpose of business is to make money. After all, the more they make, the higher their yearly bonus. This conveniently narrow image, deeply embedded in traditional corporate CFOs, constrains them to only focus on short-term profits. Their decisions are expressed in financial terms and not in employee career development and growth. On the other hand, nontraditional CFOs are those who think long-term and are most likely to care about workforce training, development, retention, and building an enduring organization. Moreover, the nontraditional CFO believes in succession development planning and the importance of investing in the organization's future by building a twenty-first-century knowledge-based workforce. Additionally, they are living in a future state mind-set. They see succession development planning as a choice, not a desperate obligation.

An organization's method of developing a competent workforce is one of the pillars of its overall business strategy. By the year 2024, approximately 40 percent of the US labor force will meet retirement eligibility, thereby resulting in a paucity of talent for many organizations. To make matters worse, the population between the ages of fifty-five and sixty-four will increase by 52 percent, according to the US Department of Labor Statistics.[1] Implementing a workforce succession development plan allows organizations the luxury of future-proofing their workforce, thereby ensuring employee competencies do not become obsolete. Succession development planning is like designing the new iPhone of the future. If the iPhone becomes obsolete, no one will buy it. Likewise, if employee competencies become obsolete, no one will contract your services; therefore, the organization would become obsolete. Equally important, the succession development plan can be used to establish a sense of urgency by reinvigorating the workforce in thinking the organization is a start-up. The difference between now and then as a start-up is that in the past, senior leaders focused on hiring technical workers instead of knowledge-based workers of the future. In fact, in 1979, when economist Theodore Schultz won the Nobel Prize, he argued that knowledge is the key to improving the welfare of people. Jac Fitz-enz, author of *The ROI of Human Capital: Measuring the Economic Value of Employee Performance*, also acknowledges that one of the key drivers to fulfillment is knowledge, which leads to an increase in employee job satisfaction. He asserts that as the United States shifts to a knowledge-based workforce, it will affect all aspects of organizational management, operating efficiency, marketing, organizational structure, and human-capital investment, which may directly or indirectly hinge on an understanding of the ability of people to cope with unforeseen, massive, and usually hurried change.[2]

Indeed, as the demand for knowledge-based and highly skilled workers (e.g., engineers, doctors, nurses, PhD/EdD holders, researchers, information-technology specialists, cybersecurity experts, technical/vocational, and administrators) continues to grow, organizations will be challenged with recruiting and hiring their next generation of knowledge-based workers. To fill this void, could migrants be the next generation of highly skilled workers in the United States? A 2013 United Nations Population Fund and International Organization for Migration report "International Migration and Development Recommendation of the International System" indicated that in 1990, migrant inventors were the most skilled and college educated, constituting 4.91 percent of patent applications.[3] By 2010, that percentage increased almost twofold to 9.83 percent.

Moreover, succession development planning leads to a more robust talent pool of employees who are available to succeed leaders and/or high performers who are retiring or departing the organization. It also allows for enhanced career development and cost savings from not having to rehire, train, and develop new employees. In addition, it allows workforce knowledge transfer to occur, saving HR specialists time from having to search for and recruit new hires. Succession planning helps organizations in establishing stronger bench strength, accelerated career development, and higher workforce performance. It helps to develop employees more fairly to meet the changing requirements of the organization's business strategy. In addition, trilateral cooperation among employees, managers, and top executives will be critical in the succession development planning process. The following questions can be used to stimulate conversations about the future competitiveness of your organization:

1. How does your organization identify internal candidates who may be ready to step into key roles today?
2. How does your organization ensure employees are training the right employees for the leadership roles and measuring them accordingly?
3. What would happen if a key contributor or member of the executive team departed unexpectedly?
4. What is the average age of your employees?
5. What percentage of your employee base is retiring within the next five years?
6. What is your current process for identifying employees with a high potential to take on leadership roles?

Is your workforce well equipped with the required competencies to meet your organization's current and future business demands? According to an online presentation by Kandeh K. Yumkella and Jeremy Rifkin, the five pillars of the Third Industrial Revolution will create thousands of small- and medium-sized businesses, as well as millions of jobs. At the same time, the TIR will change human relationships from hierarchical to lateral power, thereby impacting education, business, society, and civic life engagement.[4]

1. The first pillar reflects the migration to renewable energy.
2. The second pillar indicates that every continent will transform buildings into green micropower plants to collect on-site renewable energies.
3. The third pillar involves deploying hydrogen and other storage technologies in every building and throughout the infrastructure to store intermittent energies.
4. The fourth pillar projects that Internet technology will be used to transform the power grid of every continent into an energy Internet that performs like the Internet, as millions of buildings generate small amounts of renewable energy, which will be sold as surplus green electricity back to the electric power-grid.
5. The fifth and final pillar involves transitioning the transport fleet to electric plug-in and fuel-cell vehicles that can buy and sell green electricity on a smart, continental, interactive power grid, thereby creating an economic paradigm that will transform the world.

There are two additional pillars that should be included in Yumkella and Rifkin's presentation, those that are associated with "Big Data" and the "Internet of Things." You may ask, how is "Big Data" defined? It is defined as a diversified group of large datasets being produced that can be manipulated using data analytical tools to produce matrices used to proactively forecast outcomes. According to an online article "TechTarget: IoT Agenda" by Margaret Rouse, the term "Internet of Things (IoT)" is defined as "a system of interrelated computing devices, mechanical and digital machines, objects, animals, or people that are provided with unique identifiers and the ability to transfer data over a network without requiring human-to-human or human-to-computer interaction. The word 'thing' is defined as 'any object with embedded electronics that can transfer data over a network—without any human interaction.'"[5]

Are your employees' competencies updated to meet these new business opportunities? Is your organization future-proof? These are questions all C-suite executives and senior managers should be asking themselves. A successful succession development plan should include a combination of exotic ingredients. It should be the strategy used for future-proofing your workforce. According to a Wikipedia article, the term "future-proofing" is defined as "having the ability of something to continue to be value into the distant future; and that the item does not become obsolete."[6]

What is the first thing you do when you get out of bed in the morning? Most likely you would stretch to get your muscles loose so that you can become more flexible and ready to take on the day's challenges. In other words, you are future-proofing your muscles by making them more flexible. So why not future-proof your career by constantly stretching yourself professionally? Karie Willyerd and Barbara Mistick, the authors of *Stretch: How to Future-Proof Yourself for Tomorrow's Workplace*, state that "stretching" means having the ability to

- reach beyond your capabilities of today to be ready for tomorrow;
- expand your viewpoints and skills beyond your current state; and
- be relentlessly resourceful in pursuing your career dreams.

Willyerd and Mistick also associate future-proofing with three stretch imperatives for not becoming obsolete in the workforce:

- It's all on you (so learn on the fly and be open).
- You need options (build diverse networks and be greedy about experiences).
- You have dreams (bounce forward).[7]

In order to be competitive in the job marketplace, employees must keep their skills and abilities fresh. Succession development planning also serves as a means for ensuring organizations are proactively prepared to handle both unexpected and expected service disruptions due to workforce promotions or departures. The plan helps C-suite executives and managers proactively identify competencies required to support current and future job positions. The succession development plan also helps to reduce workforce stress and surprises relating to unexpected job vacancies. The following milestones will assist C-suite executives, directors, and managers in developing their own succession plans.

- It is very important for an organization to first establish a pilot program that will allow you to evaluate and test the succession development plan.
- It is highly recommended for you to select two to three different departments and their executives to participate in the pilot study.
- You should repeat the pilot study until all departments have participated.
- Once the pilot study is completed, you should share your results with all C-suite executives, managers, and staff members.
- Because the pilot is a living process, it is recommended that all changes be included in the database tracking system.

Both domestically and internationally, leadership supply remains a vital element in the life of any organization. In human-resource-management (HRM) terms, succession development planning involves

- staffing the organization by ensuring it has the right people in position with the right competencies (technical and nontechnical) to do the job;
- implementing performance-management and performance-appraisal systems to ensure the job is done well;
- training, developing, and planning for succession by supporting employee efforts to achieve organizational goals and promotions; and
- having an updated succession development plan to help navigate through these new and challenging times.

The appointment of unqualified individuals to leadership positions within any organization has profound implications, not only for your C-suite executives but also for those who are seeking promotion opportunities. Implementing a succession development plan will help your organization to resolve these issues proactively when selecting a candidate. At the same time, according to Rosabeth Moss Kanter, author of *Men and Women of the Corporation,* when leadership continuity planning is informal and unplanned, job incumbents tend to identify and groom successors who have similar habits, appearances, backgrounds, and values that are based on a "bureaucratic-kinship system."[8] This is a system in which C-suite executives and managers look for social similarities. This structure, however, sets in motion forces that can lead to the replication of managers as the same kind of social individuals. As a result, men and women who manage will be more likely to reproduce themselves in kind.

Time and time again, research has shown that males tend to pick other males as successors. This mind-set continues to be a major reason why organizations fail. It is also linked to the days when kings wanted to pick their unqualified and inexperienced sons as their successors. This practice also perpetuates such problems as employment discrimination, low employee morale, and unexpected departures. These problems, however, can be avoided by promoting diversity, inclusion, and multiculturalism in the workplace. Organizations are advised to use a systematic approach when identifying and grooming the best successors for key positions, in order to avoid hiring just those who resemble the present key job incumbent. Therefore, to ensure the coherence and coordination needed for implementing a successful succession development plan, C-suite executives should link individual and organizational demands both conceptually and procedurally to the succession development process. Goals should be defined and measured to support the justification of the plan. An example of the defined goals should include efforts to identify and track employees who

- have met all training and developmental requirements;
- are at the four professional levels (entry, intermediate, advanced, and expert);
- are ready to fill leadership positions; and

- have completed self-developmental and off-the-job training (OTJ), such as certification, license, vocational, and formal education.

Succession Development Planning Framework

As indicated in diagram 1, the Succession Development Planning Framework (SDPF) consists of a comprehensive fourteen-stage process that will help guide executives and managers in future-proofing their workforce.

Diagram 1: Succession Development Planning Framework

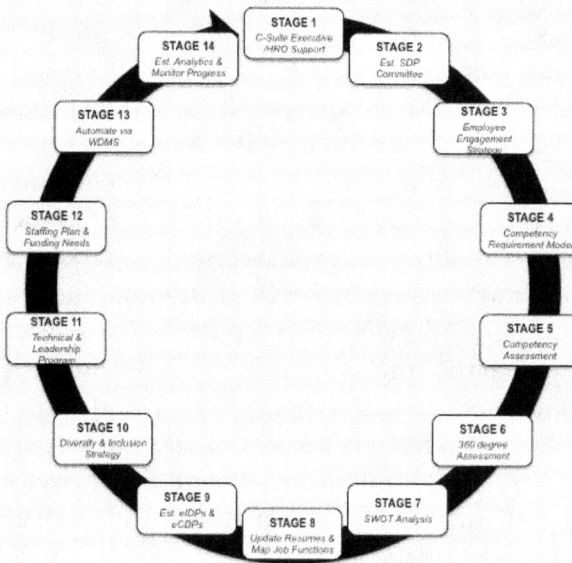

Stage 1: Obtain C-Suite Executive/HRO Support

Most managers make the cardinal sin of needing preapproval from their CEO when implementing an SDP. Succession development planning is the department manager's responsibility, not the CEO's. The CEO may understand the importance of implementing a succession development plan because it keeps the organization competitive in a tough and constantly changing global environment. On the other hand, he or she may not see the need and therefore may think a succession development plan is not necessary. Your CEO may also feel that SDPs require a great deal of energy to produce. Experts suggest that without CEO support and involvement, even the best succession development plan would fail. It is not uncharacteristic for the CEO to show little interest in the SDP process. It is very important, however, for you to keep the CEO and others abreast of your progress. Even though the CEO may not understand or know much about succession development planning, you should not take it personally, because most likely, he or she is more focused on other important and urgent matters and goals impacting the organization holistically.

Moreover, it is recommended that the succession development plan be marketed as a pilot project. This would allow greater support from other C-suite executives and human resources officers who may be curious and therefore be willing to sponsor the SDP pilot project. Along with HROs, these executives can help establish a sense of urgency by actively participating and showing commitment to the pilot plan. Garnering their support and commitment would also ensure the succession development plan has visibility and is taken seriously. Marketing the SDP as a pilot would be a more successful business strategy. These executives can ensure the succession development plan is being well communicated and collaborated across the organization. HRO can assist in developing business analytics, strategies, policies, and guidelines to help guide the process. Keep in mind the owners of the succession development planning process are the middle managers and directors, not HRO. Directors can lend the vital element of objectivity as well as ensuring the CEO does not procrastinate.

The HRO should only serve as facilitators and/or gatekeepers. Those in the HRO can also become your marketing and branding representatives. They can assist in establishing a sense of urgency among those C-suite executives who may be skeptical or uninterested. In addition, leveraging support from senior-level personnel who carry the title of senior vice president, vice president, or senior manager would be critical. They can help ensure each department's succession development plan is aligned with the organization's human-capital and business-strategy plans. Because each organization is different, your succession development plan should support your organization's vision, mission, and human-capital strategic plan, and not that of another company. I also recommend developing an SDP marketing strategy. For example, you should list your current and future business priorities, starting with the highest one. The priorities should be quantifiable. Now evaluate each to determine the most impact to the organization's business needs. For example, implementing a SDP will help improve employee retention rate and reduce workforce-training complaints.

A representative from each department should be actively involved in the succession development plan. Roles and responsibilities should be clearly defined. Although middle management and directors have ownership of the process and are accountable for identifying and developing talent for succession and cross-pollination, human-resources personnel should facilitate the process by providing technical expertise, functional support, and access to succession development planning tools. HR representatives must avoid taking ownership of the succession development process or creating the perception that they own the process. They should serve as catalysts who actively interact, stimulate, and push the process along, while remaining neutral. Moreover, middle management and directors should make the majority of succession development planning decisions. This would reduce the management layers, which leads to more effective communication and feedback.

Fixed Mind-set versus Growth Mind-set

On occasion, you may encounter executives and managers who resent the need to implement a succession development plan. If this is the case, their fixed mind-set may be polluted with organic cognitive bias. They may think that succession development planning is just a cognitive illusion to their immediate and future workforce and organizational needs. Carol Dweck, author of *Mindset: The New Psychology of Success*, discusses two types of mind-sets: fixed mind-set and growth mind-set. She states that executives who possess a *fixed mind-set* believe some people are superior and others are inferior. As a result, their organizations are a reflection of their own superiority. The fixed mind-set makes you concerned with how you will be judged. These types of leaders ignore the importance of building robust and collaborative teams, because they see themselves as geniuses who only need helpers to implement their ideas. The disappointing aspects to this type of mind-set are that it discourages creativity and limits growth throughout an organization.

Executives who have a *growth mind-set* are always focusing on how they can stretch themselves and their organizations by seeking new challenges or learning opportunities. They are more likely to promote similar mind-sets among their managers and employees, which encourages engagement, teamwork, higher productivity, and innovation. These executives believe in the growth of intellect and talent that inspires their employees to learn.[9] People with a growth mind-set are generally happier and healthier, and they are less prone to be depressed or suffer the impact of stress. Table 1 compares the two types of mind-sets.[10]

Table 1: Fixed versus Growth Mind-set	
Fixed Mind-set	**Growth Mind-set**
Intelligence is static	Intelligence can be developed
Wants to look smart	Wants to continually learn and grow
Challenges: avoids challenges	**Challenges**: embraces challenges
Obstacles: gives up easily	**Obstacles**: persists in the face of setbacks
Effort: sees effort as fruitless or worse	**Effort**: sees effort as the path to mastery
Criticism: ignores useful negative feedback	**Criticism**: learns from criticism
Success of Others: is threatened by the success of others	**Success of Others**: learns and finds inspiration in the success of others
As a result, they may plateau early and achieve less than their full potential, which confirms their deterministic view of the world	**As a result**, they reach ever-higher levels of achievement, which gives them a greater sense of free will

According to Karen Huffman, author of *Psychology in Action*, cognitive science has shown us that information processing help employees learn new ways of acting and thinking.[11] Because employees are key to an organization's success, how well executives and managers interact with them is very important. This is why it is critical for executives and managers to understand how perceptions, attitudes, and personality influence employees' emotion, behavior, engagement, learning, and decision making. We all know that the brain is an incredible and powerful tool. It provides us our ability to see, remember, learn, hear, perceive, think, understand, and feel. For my disclaimer, I must admit that I did not find any scientific data to support the Need to (Nt), Got to (Gt), Have to (Ht), Want to (Wt) mind-set transformation process. It was designed from the results of hundreds of focus group sessions, college classroom lectures, and business meetings that I have either facilitated or participated in over the past twenty-five years. The mind-set transformation process will not make you an expert on how employees may think or feel, but it can be used to help lead to beneficial outcomes for both the employees and the organization. It can be used as a tool to improve management practices for effectively interacting with and influencing employees to attain organizational goals. When garnering consensus, it can give you a different perspective on how an employee may mentally transition from a no vote to a yes vote. In the following scenarios, I will share with you my experiences in trying to garner support for two of my programs.

Scenario 1: As a former Regional Contracting Officer's Representative (RCOR) with the Marine Corps Systems Command in Quantico, VA., I was hired to transition over forty thousand users in the Southwest region onto the Department of the Navy's multibillion dollar information technology (IT) contract called "Navy Marine Corps Intranet (NMCI)." The contract provided Internet connectivity, computer, and software support to civilian and military personnel. As the RCOR, one of my primary duties included resolving IT-related contract disputes between the government and contractor. To improve IT services, I traveled throughout the Southwest region and held group meetings to capture users' feedback. One afternoon, I was contacted by the major general's assistant and asked to provide a NMCI transition status presentation to 150 senior officers and enlisted personnel. I was excited to support his request. After introductions, an officer at the rank of colonel slowly raised his hand to speak. He briskly stood up and stated in a high-pitched voice, "I hate this d–ned NMCI program. Why can't we keep the network system we already have?" Before he could finish his statements, participants throughout the room began applauding him with praise and support. They were all in agreement with his statements. Before I responded, I waited a few seconds for everyone to settle down. I then proceeded by asking him two questions: 1. What was the condition of his marines' computer systems? and, 2. What impact did these computer systems have on their warfighting mission? He could not give a comprehensive answer to the questions. I began to explain that seven months prior to this conference, I had visited his marines to identify their IT requirements. What I had uncovered was his marines were departing for war with antiquated computer systems that would greatly impede their warfighting mission. I informed him that within a three-month period, my team and I had acquired over twenty-three thousand new computer systems, inventoried and shipped them to their warfighting location overseas. I then asked him another simple question. Did the commandant of the marine corps give you your marching orders? "Absolutely," he responded with his high-pitched voice. I then stated to him that the commandant had also given me my marching orders, which was to transition the Southwest region marines onto the new NMCI network. The room went silent, and no other hands were raised to dispute the NMCI transition or my position. As I departed the room, I looked over to address the major general. He smiled and gave me two-thumbs up. It was obvious the colonel and the other marines in the room possessed great dislike for the NMCI program; however, they all reluctantly agreed to support the program. It would be dishonest of me to say that I changed everyone's mind-set from *need-to* to *want-to* in support of the NMCI program. I can say they showed a more positive attitude toward the NMCI program.

Scenario 2: As the former deputy chief information officer for TRICARE Region Nine, my chief information officer, a US Air Force Colonel and medical doctor and I were tasked with implementing a state-of-the-art technology program called "telemedicine." The program included interactive video teleconferencing, store-and-forward of medical information, and web-based technologies for thirty disperse medical hospitals and clinics. It was designed to save over $300,000 in medical costs and $220,000 in travel costs, which equated to saving over 2,257 workdays annually. The program offered continued medical education (CME) units to medical professionals across the region. The telemedicine program included medical services such as telepsychiatry, teledermatology, teleENT, teleradiology, and so on. The task included working with four of the five military branches—air force, navy, army, and marine corps. As we began to establish our board of directors, we failed to receive support from an air force medical doctor who possessed the rank of colonel. During our midweek teleconference sessions, we made several attempts to garner his support, but were unsuccessful. We could not understand why he refused to support the program. One day I decided to make the 240-mile round trip up and down the heavily populated I-5 freeway to the Los Angeles Air Force Base to meet with him face-to-face. When I arrived, he greeted me with a stern facial expression and a firm handshake. I began to explain to him how important it was for the board to receive his support. As I listened to his reasoning for not supporting the program, I realized that he was power stricken. His authority had been revoked as compared to his last command where he was in charge of a major medical clinic and had major authority over the decision-making process. But when he arrived at his current command, his decision-making authority and power were limited. As we continued to talk, I asked him would he be willing to become a regional board member. His demeanor changed instantly. He responded with an overwhelming yes. He became more relaxed and conversational. At the end, the colonel no longer felt he was being forced to support the telemedicine program. He wanted to support the program.

Mind-set Transformation Process

I recommend developing a communications strategy to help simplify the language and meaning of succession development planning for your organization. Using various influencing techniques can also help transform their mind-set. But before implementing the influencing framework, you should understand the mind-set people experience when adapting to new ideas or changes. For example, if a baseball or softball player hits a home run, he or she cannot run from home plate to first base and back to score; he or she must go from first to second to third and *then* to home plate to score the run. Similarly, when driving a four-speed manual vehicle, you do not go from first gear to fourth gear. It requires shifting from first gear to second gear to third gear and *then* to fourth gear. This is a similar process the mind may experience when transitioning from the *Need to, Got to, Have to,* and *Want to* (or Nt-Gt-Ht-Wt; see below). Diagram 2 depicts the four stages people may experience when acclimatizing to new ideas or changes. The first stage is called the Need to (*Nt*); the second, the Got to (*Gt*); the third, Have to (*Ht*); and the final stage is Want to (*Wt*). An example of a mind-set transformation survey is located in appendix C.

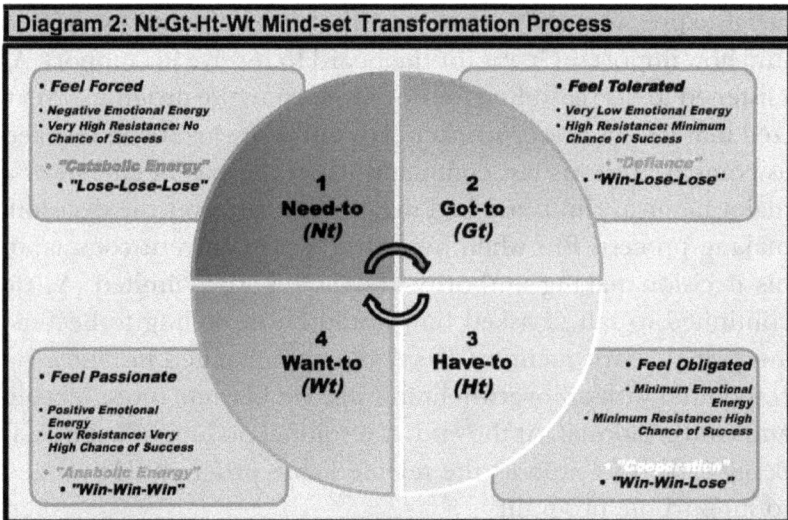

Diagram 2: Nt-Gt-Ht-Wt Mind-set Transformation Process

- **Feel Forced**
  - Negative Emotional Energy
  - Very High Resistance: No Chance of Success
  - "Catabolic Energy"
  - "Lose-Lose-Lose"

- **Feel Tolerated**
  - Very Low Emotional Energy
  - High Resistance: Minimum Chance of Success
  - "Defiance"
  - "Win-Lose-Lose"

- **Feel Passionate**
  - Positive Emotional Energy
  - Low Resistance: Very High Chance of Success
  - "Anabolic Energy"
  - "Win-Win-Win"

- **Feel Obligated**
  - Minimum Emotional Energy
  - Minimum Resistance: High Chance of Success
  - "Cooperation"
  - "Win-Win-Lose"

1 Need-to (Nt)   2 Got-to (Gt)   3 Have-to (Ht)   4 Want-to (Wt)

Phase 1: Need to *(Nt):* When a person's mind-set is wandering in the Need to (*Nt*) phase, he or she is grounded in high negative emotional energy or catabolic energy and may feel forced to participate in teamwork activities such as succession development planning. This is identified as a fixed mind-set. This is considered "lose-lose-lose" behavior, meaning the organization loses, the customer loses, and the employee loses. In this phase, there is a direct conflict between employees or people who support and who do not support organizational change, which will probably mean do-or-die energy for the change effort. Those who see change as a *need-to* often find it difficult to believe how far those against change will go to try to halt the change process. As a note, larger organizations may have the most difficulty implementing change as compared to smaller organizations. Bruce Schneider is the author of *Energy Leadership: Transforming Your Workplace and Your Life from the Core*, and he is founder of the Institute of Professional Excellence in Coaching (iPEC). Schneider describes *anabolic energy* as constructive, expanding, fueling, healing, and growth oriented. Anabolic energy helps to achieve positive, long-term, successful results, and is useful in leading others in the same direction. Meanwhile, *catabolic energy* is draining, resisting, and contracting energy. It is distracting and may deliver short-term benefits.[12] However, when used on a long-term basis, it imparts a mental, emotional, and physical toll that may be destructive to an organization. People with this mind-set have very high resistance to change, which leads to no chance for success.

Phase 2: Got to *(Gt)***:** Here, the person may feel he or she must tolerate being part of the team activities, such as succession development planning. This person may display very low emotional energy. He or she may exhibit defiance by not participating. As a result, financially the organization wins, the customer loses, and the employee loses. In this phase, employees or people who resist new ideas or changes are in smaller numbers, and the actual conflict is more restrained when compared to adversaries in the Need-to mind-set phase. In addition, people with this mind-set display high resistance to change and have minimum chance for success. Regardless of how much resistance they may show toward change, they will slowly begin to adapt.

Phase 3: Have to *(Ht)***:** In phase 3, people either feel obligated to accept new ideas or change or participate in workforce activities. While they are willing to cooperate, they are not fully supportive of teamwork activities such as succession development planning. They show a higher level of emotional energy as compared to the aforementioned phases. They may also feel they have to participate or risk being seen as nonteam players. In this phase, the organization wins, the customer wins, but the employee loses. As the understanding for change begins to inspire positive behavior, the negative mind-set toward change will begin to dissipate. When change is discussed in a positive form, people better understand the purpose for change. Even though the greater understanding may reduce their perceived threat regarding change, as time evolves, the uniqueness and incongruity of change will begin to slowly vanish. In addition, wisdom will be required when dealing with nonbelievers in change. They will only fully accept change when they are convinced of its benefits, leading to a high chance for success.

Phase 4: Want to *(Wt)***:** The HRO can serve as a major advocate by facilitating focus-group sessions to help executives, directors, middle managers, and employees transition into the Want-to (*Wt*) phase. It is a growth mind-set in which employees of all hierarchal levels of the organization generate positive anabolic energy. They become passionate about succession development planning. They want to be team members. Having anabolic energy will help move them forward to achieve positive, long-term growth and successful results. It is used for leading others in the same direction. In the Want-to phase, everyone wins—the organization, the customers, and the employees. When most of the employees or people witness change happening in a more positive way, nonsupporters will become less stubborn and will begin to transition toward the *Want to* mind-set.

Nevertheless, some C-suite executives, managers, and employees may still not share the same interests when it comes to succession development planning.

- C-suite executives may see things in a strategic perspective.
- Managers may see things in an accomplishment perspective.
- Employees may see things in an executable perspective.

Because change is very difficult for some people, it can lead them to become disgruntled. Change on an employee level, for example, may be linked to modifications of behavior, job skills, work procedures, or work relationships. For an executive or manager, change may be linked to policies, procedures, organization structures, or work processes. So how do you influence executives, managers, and employees in seeing things through the same lens? How can you influence the nonbelievers?

According to B. Kim Barnes, author of *Exercising Influence: A Guide for Making Things Happen at Work, at Home, and in Your Community,* using skillful influencing behavior activities such as expressive influence and receptive influence can help you to transform the mind-set of your workforce. Expressive influence, for example, is associated with sending innovative ideas to help generate anabolic energy. Expressive influence stimulates the thought process and inspires others in believing they can accomplish anything. It leads people to take positive action. If used correctly, expressive influence can communicate to employees that you are serious about your organization's business strategies, which helps you to accomplish your goal in implementing a successful succession development plan. Barnes acknowledges that skillful influencing can lead to increased flexibility in dealing with people from diverse professional and cultural backgrounds, as well those who differ from you in gender, generation, experience, and personality.[13]

Using receptive influence will help in the mind-set transformation process. Barnes associates receptive influence with inviting ideas and stimulating action. It allows employees to contribute ideas and information, so they can experience a sincere commitment to action. Receptive influence allows for receptive behavior to occur, which can be used to guide employees and others toward consensus and positive solutions for all parties involved. In opposition, she argues, organizations in which employees feel they have little influence over matters that affect them may become "cultures of compliant," leading to less engagement and negative energy, which is associated with catabolic energy. Schneider identifies catabolic energy as draining, resisting, and contracting. Although it might have short-term benefits, when used long term, catabolic energy imparts a mental, emotional, and physical toll that is destructive to all involved. It will lead to contumacious behavior among employees across the organization, leaving management to contend with employees who are rebellious and resistant to future organizational changes.

I am not a neuroscientist, and am I not attempting to portray one here, but when using constructive psychosomatic influencing (CPI) techniques to persuade others to support your cause, you should be aware of what parts of the brain are associated with a person's emotions. CPI stimulates positive emotion that leads to positive energy, which in turn inspires positive outcomes. Both positive and negative emotions can affect a person's decision making. Daniel G. Amen, MD, author of *Unleash the Power of the Female Brain: Supercharging Yours for Better Health, Energy, Mood, Focus, and Sex*, states that the brain is comprised of three critical parts:

- Forebrain (the cerebrum, thalamus, and hypothalamus)
- Midbrain (tectum and tegmentum)
- Hindbrain (cerebellum, pons, and medulla); commonly identified as the brainstem.

The cerebrum (cortex) is the largest part of the brain and is associated with higher brain functions such as action and thought. It is divided into four lobes:

- The *frontal lobe* is associated with planning, reasoning, speech, movement, emotions, and problem solving.
- The *parietal lobe* is linked with movement, orientation, recognition, and stimuli (motivation, incentive, and encouragement).
- The *occipital lobe* is associated with visual processing.
- The *temporal lobe* is associated with perception and recognition of auditory stimuli, memory, and speech.

Therefore, when attempting to use the influence framework, you should be aware of what part of the human brain you will be dealing with in the transformation process.[14] Using influencing behavior allows managers to use their sources of power to help transform the mind-set of their employees in the direction toward making conscious choices or commitments that support the organization's overall mission. According to B. Kim Barnes, using influence versus direct power shows respect for others, thereby resulting in positive and voluntary actions among the employees. With this in mind, C-suite executives and managers should practice using skillful influencing strategically and appropriately when implementing change across their organizations. Barnes associates "power" with having the ability, strength, and authority to transform the mind-set of others: "It is something you have." Influence is associated with having the ability to sway or induce another to take action: "Influence is something you do." Barnes uses a four-element influence framework model to help influence the mind-set transformational process. When using the influence framework, I recommend you assess the various generations across your organization. Why is this important? As previously stated, there are four generational groups in the workforce (traditionalists, baby boomers, generation Xers, and millennials), and each group's communication culture is different. I would highly recommend for your organization to assess how each group wants to be mentored, coached, and communicated with. I would also assess each group's learning and training methods and career-development aspirations. Barnes's four-element influence framework model consists of the following:

1. **Results:** What are you hoping to accomplish through influencing the workforce?
2. **Relationship:** What kind of influence relationship do you currently have with your workforce?
3. **Context:** What individual, organizational, or cultural issues might affect the results?
4. **Approach:** What influence tactics and behaviors are most likely to help you accomplish your goals?

Stage 2: Establish a SDP Leadership Committee (SLC)

Contributing to the implementation of the organization's strategic business plan is a succession development plan (SDP). With help from the HRO, the second milestone requires the establishment of a succession development planning leadership committee (SLC). As a reminder, the SDP should not be conducted in a vacuum. Rather, it should be linked to and supported by the organization's strategic business plan, human-capital strategic plan, and other organizational human-capital planning activities. The organization's strategic business plan is the document by which the organization chooses how it will survive and compete. It involves formulating and implementing a long-term plan by which the organization can take maximum advantage of its internal strengths and external opportunities, while minimizing the effects of internal organizational weaknesses and external threats. Many researchers and authors who have written on the topic of succession planning argue that the plan should receive support from top executives. However, in today's business environment, I recommend that the SLC use a T.E.A.M. approach in which members are chosen from across the organization. Each department should have at least one senior or midlevel representative participating on the SLC.

- *T: Top executives*—Human-resources executives, vice presidents, senior vice presidents, presidents, or chief executive officers. Executives are accountable for overseeing the work of managers.
- *E: Employees*—Nonmanager and/or nonsupervisory employees at all levels in the organization.
- *A: Administrators*—Senior employees who provide both clerical and administrative support to executives and managers. Administrators are key players, because they ensure committee members are well informed about current and future events of the organization.
- *M: Managers*—Nonexecutive leaders who are accountable for overseeing the work of supervisors. Supervisors are accountable for supervising and assigning employee tasks; defining purpose; organizing employees to maximize efficiency; nurturing employee skills, abilities, knowledge, and experience; inspiring results; focusing on structure and systems; and developing workforce talent.

The SLC team should be diversified and inclusive. There should be diversity in team member personality traits (e.g., open, extrovert, conscientious, neurotic, agreeable, introvert, ambivert, etc.). Having members with different personality traits will greatly enhance team dynamics. According to James S. Nairne author of, *"Psychology: The Adaptive Mind,"* there are several types of personality traits executives and managers should be aware of such as:

- **Open** personalities tend to be artistic, inventive, and curious.
- **Extroverts** are full of energy, outgoing, and impulsive.
- **Conscientious** individuals live with a purpose, and are dedicated, focused, and ambitious.
- **Neurotic** personalities tend to be very nervous, worrisome, and on edge.
- **Agreeable** people are cooperative, compassionate, and very accepting.
- **Introverts** are shy and enjoy being alone.
- **Ambiverts** reside in the middle between introverts and extroverts; they get along with most personality types, are equally comfortable in any situation, are risk takers, and have winning personalities. [15]

These traits can also directly affect a person's overall quality of life and can even affect how his or her body overcomes illness. For example, Susan Cain, author of *Quiet: The Power of Introverts in a World That Can't Stop Talking*, acknowledges that both introvert and extrovert personality types appear in the Bible and in the writings of Greek and Roman physicians. She argues that many introverts hide from themselves by living in a value system called the "extrovert ideal," which is the omnipresent belief that the ideal self is gregarious, alpha, and comfortable in the spotlight. According to Susan, introverts dislike conflict, while extroverts are comfortable with conflict. Introverts enjoy devoting their social energies to close friends, colleagues, and family members. They prefer listening over talking and thinking before speaking, which is in contrast to extroverts, who talk, rather than listen. Introverts prefer to focus on a single task rather than multitask, as compared to extroverts. More importantly, introverts prefer to express themselves in writing, as compared to extroverts, who prefer to express themselves in conversations. [16]

Using personality traits to help build collaborative teams and enhance relationships among employees, managers, and executives will become a new art in building team dynamics. Since the mid-1920s, Japan and Korea have used personality traits (e.g., blood type and human behavior) in relationship building and teambuilding, according to Wendy Watson, author of *Personality and Blood Type: A Guide to Love, Work and Friendships*. Watson identifies four blood types (see table 2).[17] Organizations must embrace both vocational and nonvocational training and career-development opportunities in their succession development plan. For example, in the next decade, the FIR will broaden professional careers by giving rise to vocational careers such as those in information technology, cybersecurity, or computer programming. The need for paralegals, massage therapists, medical assistants, respiratory therapists, licensed practical nurses, licensed vocational nurses, radiology technicians, automotive technicians, electrical technicians, pharmacy technicians, graphic designers, web-portal designers, radio technicians, dental-clinic assistants, certified professional coaches (e.g., business, executive, life, health, financial), and more will only increase.

Table 2: Personality Traits		
Blood Type	**General Attributes**	**Emotions**
O	Most flexible, easygoing, and open-minded; honest, bold, and brave; do not feel isolated; are selfless	Handle stress until the breaking point, and then they erupt
A	Calm, self-controlled, Zen-like personality; have subdued emotions; most responsible of the four groups; very discerning; indecisive and extremely careful; bold and daring; takes calculated risks	Have a little stress all the time; in a crisis, they are calm
B	Strong-minded, charming, and charismatic; passionate and self-assured; speak their mind; full of emotion; multitalented, passionate, and fearless risk-takers	Are up and down through the day and do not change with externals
AB	Intellectual, analytical, creative, compassionate people; friendly and loyal with a strong sense of social justice; great negotiators; joyful	Are unpredictable; can be calm or stressed throughout the day

Step 1: SLC establishes an integrated product team (IPT) for needs assessment and data analysis.
The SLC determines appropriate IPT members and clarifies IPT purpose, responsibilities, and project time line. The IPT is accountable for conducting workforce assessment studies pertaining to subjects as varied as competency-gap analyses, retirement, retention, workforce

engagement, new hires, workforce vacancies, and personnel staffing. Each department executive or his or her SLC representative is accountable for defining employee past, current, and future workforce competencies. This data will then be incorporated into the workforce development competency-gap analysis assessment tool (WDCGAAT) to be measured. The WDCGAAT would be used as a preventive measure by ensuring the organization remains proactive in deterring archaism. Past competencies should also be reviewed and measured to help resolve or ratify basic understanding of new technical problems.

Step 2: Establish communications strategies.
The SLC is accountable for developing and implementing a communications strategy that includes a marketing and branding strategy. The communications strategy will be critical to the succession development planning process. It will help alleviate obstructions that may negatively impact the development and implementation of a successful SDP. At the same time, department managers or directors should facilitate focus-group sessions to help garner support from their employees by listening, talking, communicating, collaborating, understanding, and connecting (LTCCUC) as to why succession development is important to them and the organization. Communicating why succession development is important will help. Overall, improved communication will

- provide C-suite executives, senior vice-presidents, managers, and employees with a better understanding of what will be expected;
- explain the benefits to both the organization and the employees;
- serve as a support and marketing strategy;
- establish focus-group and working-group sessions to discuss workforce training and developmental status;
- increase workforce morale;
- increase workforce productivity;
- increase workforce retention;
- reduce job vacancies; and
- reduce costs for new hires.

Step 3: Develop policies, procedures, guidelines, and vision.

Along with support from the HRO, the SLC should develop and establish workforce succession development planning policies, procedures, and guidelines that managers will be held accountable to follow and enforce. Employees will be held accountable for completing their required training, learning, and development activities. Training should also reflect what the organization is attempting to accomplish. Do you seek to explore improvements to health and safety, sexual harassment, discrimination, or teamwork? Learning and development are defined as what employees want to accomplish to help drive their own career development and growth. In addition, implementing training, learning, and development policies can be used as a set of principles all employees must follow. These policies will also help reflect the organization's fundamental philosophy and values, and they can be used as a basic system and management guide for all employees to follow.

Keep in mind that it is critical for C-suite executives to select a representative to champion and advocate on their behalf. During the CEO monthly meeting, the SLC can present the documents for review before they are signed into action. The CEO should then task other C-suites to help facilitate workshops to discuss all concerns, issues, or problems. This will also help reduce adversarial mind-set behavior. Note: Be aware of the pitfalls from nonsupporters who may not agree and may attempt to derail the succession development planning initiative. To help establish a sense of urgency, below are five future-proofing questions the SLC can ask its nonsupporters.

   a. Do the services and products we provide to our customers continue to add value to their businesses in the next three to five years?

   b. Are employee competencies (e.g., knowledge, skills, abilities, experiences, education, and/or certifications) becoming obsolete across our workforce?

   c. Are the job functions currently being performed across the organization at risk of becoming obsolete in the next two, three, or five years?

   d. Does the organization have a well-developed workforce with the right competencies to support and sustain future growth?

e. Does the organization have a well-diversified workforce to back-fill or support future job vacancies?

The SLC should align its vision and mission with the organization's over-all vision and mission, to help demonstrate an understanding of the appropriate staffing needed to achieve strategic goals and objectives. Keep in mind that if there is no vision, there are no employees, and when there are no employees, there is no need for succession develop-ment planning. The succession development plan can be used as an action-planning tool to help retain and recruit and to ensure your orga-nization has a talent pool with the right skills, experiences, and compe-tencies to meet its mission, goals, and challenges of the future.

> Where there is no vision, the people perish.
> —PROVERBS 29:18, KING JAMES BIBLE

Stage 3: Measure Employee Engagement Strategy
Research has shown there is a direct correlation between leadership energy level and employee engagement. When employee engagement is high, organizational performance outcomes such as employee produc-tivity, retention, and profitability increase. William A. Kahn, author of *Psychological Conditions of Personal Engagement and Disengagement at Work,* defines employee engagement as "the simultaneous employment and expression of a person's preferred self in task behaviors that promote connections to work and to others, personal presence (physical, cogni-tive, emotional) and active, full role performances."[18] Conducting a pilot employee-engagement assessment will help determine the degree to which employees are fully emotionally involved and committed to their daily work activities. Accountability for the development, distribution, and data collection of the employee-engagement assessment and feed-back should rest, however, on the shoulders of your HRO. Only one or two departments should participate in the pilot employee-engagement assessment. This will give the committee an opportunity to examine data results and provide feedback to the CEO and others. Boosting employee engagement levels is critical, because it can lead to a higher degree of loyalty, better customer service, and a higher competitive advantage. You

may ask, "Why is an employee engagement important to the succession development planning process?"

According to an online report by the US Bureau of National Affairs, companies lose approximately $11 billion annually due to employee turnover.[19] Meanwhile, 74 percent of the employees who departed cited a lack of employer or manager engagement as their principal reason for leaving, according to an online *Harvard Business Review* report.[20] A 2015 Gallup poll also reflected 67 percent of all employees were either disengaged or not fully engaged in their daily work activities, and only 33 percent indicated engagement across the workforce, which costs US organizations billions of dollars annually. In contrast, the higher the engagement rate among talented managers, the higher the engagement rate among employees, thereby leading to 147 percent higher earnings as compared to their competition.[21] An example of an employee engagement assessment is located in appendix B.

SAS (Statistical Analysis System) is a multinational developer of analytics software, based in Cary, North Carolina. According to Jenn Mann, SAS vice president, human resources, and James Goodnight and John Sall, SAS cofounders, their company understands the benefits of employee retention. To improve employee retention, they propose a relaxed work environment and an egalitarian culture. They provide employees daily on-site daycare services, free medical services, thirty-five-hour work weeks, free access to recreation and fitness centers, life-counseling service, on-site cafeterias and cafés, and free M&Ms. SAS also hosts summer camps for children. As a result, on average, the organization's annual turnover rate is between 3 and 5 percent, as compared to the software industry rate of 20 to 25 percent. This commitment to quality of experience saves the organization between $60 to $80 million annually in expenses related to employee turnover.[22]

Moreover, when employees are disengaged at work, they will eventually leave to find more satisfying opportunities elsewhere. These opportunities could be associated with a better work/life balance; leadership, supervisory, promotion, training, and development opportunities; and other reasons. In fact, the Gallup Organization reports that 68 percent of US employees are disengaged at work.[23] According to Leigh Branham, author of *The 7 Hidden Reasons Employees Leave,* there are seven major reasons employees may become disengaged and decide to leave an organization.[24] These seven reasons are identified below.

- Reason 1: Job or workplace was not as expected.
- Reason 2: A mismatch between job and person.
- Reason 3: Too little coaching and feedback.
- Reason 4: Too little growth and advancement opportunity.
- Reason 5: Feeling devalued and unrecognized.
- Reason 6: Stress from overwork and work/life imbalance.
- Reason 7: Loss of trust and confidence in senior leaders.

C-suite executives and managers are not the only ones accountable for ensuring employees remain engaged. Employees are also accountable for keeping themselves engaged. Employees must also be held accountable for training and developing their own careers; they must not depend exclusively on the organization to fulfill their training and developmental needs. They must transition out of the mind-set of an employee and become leaders of their own careers. Below are seven tips that will help employees.

Seven Tips to Becoming a Leader of Your Own Life and Career

1. Gradually Adjust Your Mind-set

Great leaders continually seek innovative and creative solutions to world problems. Instead of spontaneously changing their mind-set, they gradually adjust their mind-set. They are open-minded and flexible. They consistently cherish and invest in their strengths, as they also remain aware of their limitations. According to Tom Rath and Barry Conchie, authors of *Strengths-Based Leadership: Great Leaders, Teams, and Why People Follow,* great leaders have four distinct leadership strengths in common: executing, influencing, relationship building, and strategic thinking. What are your major strengths?

Moreover, they understand their purpose in life—and so should you. Great leaders are fearful of becoming obsolete; therefore, they gradually become lifelong learners who are always seeking ways to future-proof their professional and personal careers through the pursuit of new certifications, continuing-education opportunities, or leadership training. They are constantly challenging themselves. Basically, their business motto is "Either you grow—or you go!" In fact, when leaders focus more on employee strengths instead of their weaknesses, employees are more engaged at work and become more self-confident.[25]

2. Cherish Life and Family, not Work

You must learn to take control of your own life and learn to cherish it every day. If you don't, you may perish from the stressful workload growing upon your shoulders. Take time out of your busy work schedule to enjoy the many joyous offerings surrounding you and your family. Keep in mind your family creates lifelong memories; your coworkers don't. You only get one chance in life, so make the best of it.

3. Identify Your Inherited Potential

We all carry the *potential* gene. It doesn't matter if we inherited it; we have it. The question is, once you identify your potential, what are you going to do with it? You have a choice: are you going to expand upon your enormous potential, or will you allow it to stagnate? You should use this enormous potential to advance your career and life. We all have the capacity to become a prominent figure in the future. But do we all have the courage to take on this challenge?

4. Step Outside Your Domain

Great leaders understand the importance of stepping outside of their comfort zone or domain. This is when they learn the most. If you are an introvert, this may be somewhat difficult, but give it your best. If you are an extrovert, this may be easy for you to accomplish. And if you are an ambivert, you are always seeking ways you can best balance the situation. Moreover, the four greatest skills great leaders have in common are their abilities to listen, collaborate, understand, and connect with others. If you want to become a great leader, you must step outside of your comfort zone and connect with those outside of your domain.

5. Reinvent Yourself

Reinventing yourself in today's globally competitive environment will allow you to become a very valuable and marketable person. To accomplish this task, you must be excited about learning new ideas via research, formal education, or acquiring new certifications that are not necessarily related to your current job but support future opportunities in a different profession. In other words, you must ignore the antiquated stovepipe one-dimensional career-development model organizations continue to use and refocus your attention toward the new multidimensional career-development model in which you are empowered by learning a diverse set of competencies.

6. Develop Your Personal Marketing and Branding Strategies

Your personal marketing or branding strategy is for you to select a primary goal in life. Whether it is improving your family relationship or getting a better job, you should develop a marketing strategy. This strategy should help you identify your strengths and weaknesses as they help you define a road map as to how you will accomplish your goals. Developing your personal marketing strategy will require some research, but you can do it. To start, develop a slogan that reflects your goals.

7. Build Connections

Building life connections is a key element to life success. How does someone build connections? Jeffrey Gitomer, author of *Little Black Book of Connections: 6.5 Assets for Networking Your Way to RICH Relationships,* states that building connections is about building stronger relationships with customers, bosses, coworkers, vendors, friends, and family. It is about how to maximize your connections so that others benefit from you and more importantly, you benefit from others. Do you have someone listed in your *Little Black Book* whom you can call early in the morning without upsetting him or her? If so, you are on track to building your own portfolio of connections. The more people are attracted to your slogan, the more connected you will become. Gitomer acknowledges, "There is power in who you know. Not just connection power. Success power. Even fulfillment power." In other words, the more people you know and connect with, the more you grow.[26]

Stage 4: Establish a Competency Requirement Model (CRM)
Each department's SLC representative is accountable for working with his or her executive to determine these requirements. Once data is received from each department, the SLC is accountable for developing and standardizing a basic enterprise CRM. A flexible and modifiable CRM can be used to help determine employee competency requirements. The CRM can also help to

- determine what critical competencies are needed for effective performance and to succeed in the workplace;
- shift mind-sets from focusing on workplace activity to workplace results;
- mitigate obsolete competencies;
- identify work-related competencies throughout the organization;
- identify both high and low performers;
- identify both technical and nontechnical competencies;
- serve as a possible promotional decision tool;
- identify success factors for excellent performance;
- identify employees' past, current, and future job experiences;
- identify knowledge, skills, experiences, aptitude, education, and certification of all positions;
- identify external recruitment requirements to fill hard-to-fill vacancies;
- ensure the organization becomes a multidimensional workforce versus a one-dimensional workforce; and
- monitor geographical business trends and analyses for both internal and external changes (e.g., workforce demographics, reduction in force, work/life balance, mergers, etc.).

To ensure a fair and effective process, decisions should be based on systematic analyses such as job requirements (both current and projected) of upper-level and middle-level positions, current performance rating and potential of individual employees, based on their educational background and vocational skills, for example. Because an effective succession development plan is based on well-defined competencies and reliable information about current performances and potential of employees, key positions should be identified, and requirements for these positions should be defined. Job analyses should be used to identify competencies for key positions in highly technical and stable organizations. In flexible organizations, however, competencies that are more general should be established. In addition, competency assessments for key positions should be obtained using a variety of methods, such as merging a list of generic management leadership competencies, for example, along with organization-specific competencies to create a successful executive profile. Because most organizations are continuously changing, the focus of succession development planning should not only be on competencies for current jobs but also focus on determining how jobs and organizational roles might change in the future. Once that is established, the task becomes to define the competencies needed to meet these changes. Competency profiles should also be based on an estimate of what positions in the organization will look like both currently and in the future.

Stage 5: Conduct Workforce Competency Gap Analysis Assessment
Succession development planning involves clearly defining the requirements and requisite competencies (e.g., knowledge, skills, aptitude, education, certification, licenses, etc.) for all positions and then identifying employees to fill future positions, therefore future-proofing the organization to ensure it maintains its competitiveness and longevity. A workforce competency gap analysis assessment must be conducted. Department executives, managers, and HRO work in concert to develop and administer the workforce competency gap analysis assessment survey. The survey should be easily modified to support various departmental job functions and competency requirements. Once consensus is met concerning a standardized assessment tool, it should be used to measure each employee's past, current, and future competencies (knowledge, skills, abilities, experiences, education, certifications, etc.). The data would then be incorporated into a workforce development competency gap analysis assessment tool and distributed to employees who are slated to participate in the pilot study. The assessment would be used as a preventive measure by ensuring the organization remains proactive in deterring archaism. Note: Past competencies should also be reviewed

and measured to help resolve or ratify a basic understanding or misunderstanding of new technical problems. The following scenario explains why past competencies should be measured.

Scenario: Your organization just acquired a new software application that must be configured and installed on 750 computers that are geographically dispersed. If this task were outsourced, it would cost the organization more than two million dollars. The project manager decided to assemble a team of in-house experts to help with this critical task. The problem is she is unaware of any employees who have the necessary skills to do this type of work.

However, because the organization just completed its workforce competency gap analysis assessment, she decided to review the survey results. She then learned that the organization had three employees with past experience in software installation and configuration. Even though the three employees are doing engineering design work for other departments located in various geographical locations, they all agreed to support the task. As a result, she saved the organization approximately two million dollars. Including past workforce competencies in the assessment can help in future-proofing your organization. At the same time, current and future competencies should be identified and included in the assessment. The assessment will also help

- identify early funding requirements;
- enhance workforce morale and job challenges;
- identify what competencies are needed to succeed in today's and tomorrow's workforces;
- create employee individual and career development plans;
- proactively identify jobs that are becoming obsolete;
- enhance employee recruitment and selection; and
- proactively identify future job requirements

Each department executive or representative should modify the tool to meet departmental past, current, and future competency requirements in support of their goals, programs, projects, and objectives. However, survey questions or statements pertaining to age, race, gender, time in position, employment time in the organization, work/life balance, and so on, should remain consistent. The assessment should include proactive succession risk assessment questions or statements, which will help determine if employees are seeking employment elsewhere. Moreover, managers and HRO should meet with their C-suite executives and capture their feedback on what future competencies may be required to support future workload requirements across the organization. Once the study is complete, the SLC can present the results to the CEO and other C-suite executives to confirm their support. Again, because each department is required to conduct certain job functions, each department manager should modify the workforce competency gap analysis survey tool to reflect his or her own department competency requirements.

To ensure the survey's validity and reliability, committee representatives will randomly select approximately twenty-five to thirty individuals from their departments to complete the assessment twice within seven business days. The survey should be distributed via a web link detailing the workforce competency gap analysis assessment location. Once the survey results are provided to both the manager and employee, the manager is accountable for meeting with each employee to discuss and provide feedback on the employee's results, career-development goals, and strategies. The discussion should include sharing and comparing the department's overall results via data matrices and discussing the employee's career-development goals and strategies. In addition, the manager and employee should work in concert to develop a plan to manage competency gaps, just in case an employee leaves or is promoted.

Stage 6: Conduct 360-Degree Assessments
As organizations focus more on leadership succession, 360-degree assessments would include collecting data on managers and high performers.

In other words, instead of identifying the right person for the right position at the right time, C-suite executives should seek to develop strong leadership teams for strategic tasks. Using a 360-degree assessment tool will help in this process. There are three key benefits to implementing 360-degree assessments:

1. It can improve the accuracy or comprehensiveness of an employee's views of him- or herself and how others view them. Each employee is presented with the views of other stakeholders such as subordinates, supervisors, customers, family members, community, and peers. Doing so will reflect shades of contrast and similarity to his or her own self-view.
2. It will lead to a meaningful experience that directs an employee toward understanding his or her own behavior from others.
3. A 360-degree assessment will provide a vehicle for delivering information on an employee's current leadership strengths and weaknesses and help him or her recognize what new skills exist. General Electric, for example, uses a 360-degree feedback assessment to support its workforce-development program.

To help identify high potential for succession development and their developmental needs, employees develop a perspective on their own management and leadership styles and competency deficiencies through feedback from senior leaders, managers, work teams, peers, and customers. To a high degree of predictability, the assessment would help identify future successors' promotability for C-suite executive-level positions. Experts Brian Becker, Mark Huselid, and Dave Ulrich, authors of *The HR Scorecard: Linking People, Strategy, and Performance,* advise that when assessing the link between candidates and future positions, management should consider the nature of competencies (knowledge, skills, abilities, or personality characteristics) required for successful performance in upper-level positions. The assessment of a C-suite executive match should involve comparing each potential executive's skills and competencies profile with the organization's requirements in terms of tasks, roles, culture, social, risk, feedback, technology, and so on. In addition, the authors recommend linking employee strategic focus to the organization's performance, which would help align organizational processes and support systems so employees can have a better understanding of the organization's overall business strategy. In turn, this would encourage and motivate more positive and strategic behaviors among managers and employees.[27]

Stage 7: Develop Competency SWOT Analysis
Matrices using strengths, weaknesses, opportunities, and threats (SWOT) analysis should be developed from the results of the competency gap analysis data. The data will help the SLC to determine workforce strengths, define weaknesses, exploit opportunities, and minimize threats. After completing the matrices, it is critical for managers to meet with their employees to discuss and capture their feedback. This is an opportunity for both managers and employees to share their concerns. At the same time, managers can acquire a better understanding of the career desires of their employees. Diagram 3 reflects an example of a workforce competency analysis SWOT matrix. Internal competencies are associated with strengths and weaknesses. External competencies are associated with opportunities and threats. Below are several other critical reasons for using a competency SWOT analysis. The matrix can be used to

- help future-proof and bring your organization's workforce competencies into balance with your competitors;
- ensure these competencies remain balanced in the future;
- help explore and enhance employees' soft and hard skills;
- identify workforce competency deficiencies via quantitative data by sorting the data into four categories: strengths, weaknesses, opportunities, and threats (SWOT)
- determine what external competencies are required to meet project goals;
- support predictive analytics and modeling when creating or analyzing future succession development requirements;
- assist in developing a competitor profile chart; and
- help monitor job vacancy trends to help forecast the number of employees departing the organization monthly, quarterly, and yearly.

Diagram 3: Workforce Competency SWOT Analysis Matrix

INTERNAL COMPETENCIES

STRENGTHS
What percentage of the workforce competencies being used to promote outstanding organizational performance, cost, and productivity?

WEAKNESSES
What percentage of current workforce competencies could be used to increase productivity and performance and help your organization reach its full potential?

EXTERNAL COMPETENCIES

OPPORTUNITIES
What percentage of current and new workforce competencies could be used to promote new business opportunnities, reduce cost, increase performance, and productivity?

THREATS
What percentage of workforce competencies are needed in the future to help reduce business vulnerabilities that may negatively impact productivity, cost, and performance?

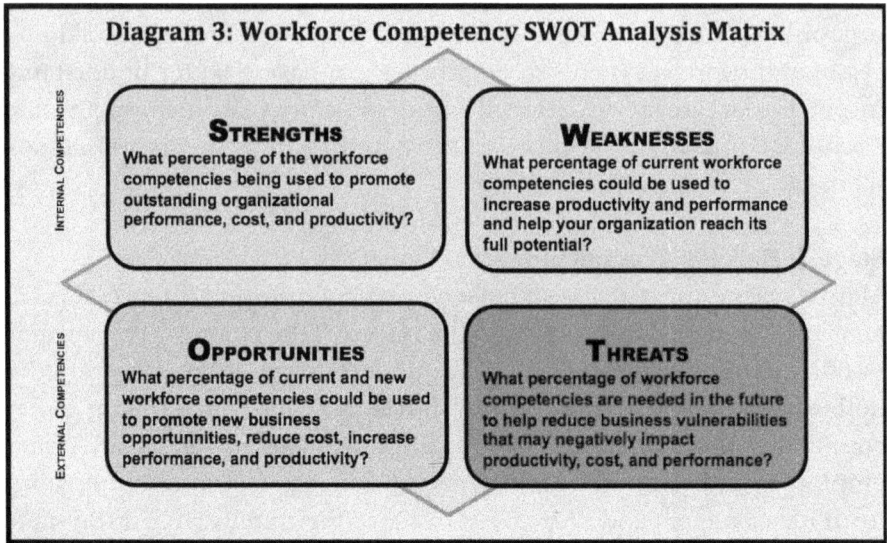

Stage 8: Update Employee Résumés, Job Descriptions, and Map Job Functions

This stage requires updating employee résumés, mapping their job functions, and updating their job descriptions. Updating these items will help deflect any potential Equal Employment Opportunity–related problems or complaints. Department executives, managers, and employees are accountable for ensuring these items are updated and entered into the workforce development management system.

Step 1: Update Résumés

According to researchers, there are a limited number of high-performing and high-potential employees on the horizon (as compared to past generations). Therefore, it will be critical for executives and managers to invest in their current workforce's career development. Department executives and managers should work in concert with their direct reports to ensure employee résumés are updated. Employee résumés should reflect past and current job experiences. This should also include nonwork-related experiences such as mentoring, coaching, leadership positions, community-outreach services, or self-development activities that were conducted on personal time. The SLC is not accountable for this task.

Step 2: Update Job Descriptions

Updating employee job descriptions can be a very daunting task. However, having updated job descriptions can help in the development of employee compensation plans. Department executives are accountable for ensuring that employee job descriptions are updated and uploaded into the workforce development management system (WDMS). This effort may require support from your HR department. Updated job descriptions can be used to

- ensure legal compliance with local, state, and federal laws and unemployment claims;
- communicate expectations and performance appraisal;
- help employees better understand their responsibilities and duties;
- define employee job functions to ensure employees meet job performance expectations;
- assist managers in ensuring employee duties align with the organization's vision;
- help define education and training requirements; and
- serve as a communication tool for the purpose of relaying job requirements to employees.

Step 3: Map Job Functions

Job functions should be mapped to reflect daily services being provided and supported. Managers should work in concert with their employees to ensure job functions, roles, and responsibilities are properly mapped to the services and products they provide to their customers. The functional workflow chart should show what job functions each employee supports across the organization. In addition, the workload/competency matrix will depict bottlenecks and workload excess of each employee.

Stage 9: Establish Employee eIDP and eCDP

Establishing employee electronic individual development plans (eIDP) and electronic career development plans (eCDP) are critical components for aligning their short- and long-term training and career-development activities to the organization's mission, goals, and objectives. Establishing eIDPs is also a critical point of any well-defined succession development plan. Department executives, managers, and employees are responsible for ensuring their eIDPs and/or eCDPs are updated and uploaded into the WDMS. In addition, when establishing a sense of urgency, both eIDPs and eCDPs should contain specific time frames and action plans and should also clearly delineate who is accountable for the implementation of specific developmental plans. The eIDP and eCDP can be used to

- assist managers in developing a better understanding of their employees' individual and career goals, strengths, developmental needs, and opportunities;
- increase communication and interaction between managers and employees;
- evaluate usefulness of training and developmental experiences; and
- help enhance workforce satisfaction.

Stage 10: Implement a Diversity and Inclusion Strategy

Barriers to diversity and inclusion can be associated with differences in social class, ethnicity, education, language, gender, cultural background, age, and so on. As stated in chapter five, managing diversity and inclusion are critical components to future business success and succession development planning. An organization of the future will foster a diverse and inclusive work environment. It will inspire creativity and innovation and allow for a 360-degree perspective to encourage employee knowledge, skills, backgrounds, and experiences to flourish. D and I are also very important to the diverse communities and customers an organization serves. They also serve as a catalyst for ensuring an organization remains competitive. Meanwhile, most C-suite executives are no longer talking about the need for diversity and inclusion; they are taking critical steps toward ensuring their workforces reflect their organization's customers and communities. Why are they thinking proactively?

Here are several reasons. As the US population more than doubled from 152.3 million in 1950 to 324 million in 2016, the labor force has also grown from 62 million to 159.5 million. By the year 2030, nearly 37 million (or 23 percent) of this population will be fifty-five and older. According to a June 2008 *Population Bulletin*, "US Labor Force Trends," in 2005, 70 percent of the US labor force was non-Hispanic white. This number, however, is expected to change dramatically by 2050, because Hispanics and Asians are the fastest-growing populations in the workforce. The Hispanic and Asian labor forces, for example, will reach 24 percent and 8 percent, respectively. Meanwhile, the African American labor force is expected to have a small increase of 3 percent (from 11 to 14 percent). At the same time, the white non-Hispanic labor force will decrease nearly 18 percent by 2050.[28] In addition, implementing diversity and inclusion strategies will help mitigate litigation-related issues. To ensure their organization remain competitive, many executives whom I have spoken with are no longer talking about the need for diversity and inclusion. Now, they are taking critical steps toward ensuring their workforces reflect their organization's customers and communities.

Stage 11: Establish Learning, Technical Leadership Development Programs
Establishing an in-house learning and technical development program (LTDP) will help employees solidify their reason for remaining devoted to the organization. The LTDP can also improve recruitment trends and employee retention. The programs can also be used to

- develop workforce technical competencies;
- develop workforce soft-skill competencies (leadership, emotional intelligence, social intelligence, culture intelligence, etc.);
- plan for workforce and leadership successions; and
- proactively future-proof the workforce to ensure the organization remains competitive.

Action learning can be used to deliver a learning experience that is tailored to both the organization's needs and the employee's own career development, according to Robert Fulmer and Jay Conger, authors of

Growing Your Company's Leaders: How Great Organizations Use Succession Management to Sustain Competitive Advantage.[29] Companies such as Arthur Andersen, Dow Chemical, General Electric (GE), Bank of America, and Dell Computer are just a few organizations that incorporate action learning into their leadership development programs. Arthur Andersen, for example, uses many problem-solving activities with small groups in its leadership development activities. Other learning techniques include case methods, simulations, experiential learning, and executive coaching. General Electric's action-learning techniques are incorporated into its leadership-development core curriculum, which is designed to help provide leadership direction for the organization—from both a regional strategic and a global organizational standpoint.

GE's former chairman and CEO Jack Welch personally chose action learning topics for each of the organization's quarterly business-management courses (BMC) and each annual executive-development course (EDC), according to Robert Fulmer and Marshall Goldsmith, authors of *The Leadership Investment: How the World's Best Organizations Gain Strategic Advantage through Leadership Development.* As a result, according to Fulmer and Goldsmith, when GE's employees heard that a certain initiative was a recommendation from the BMC or EDC, they made every effort to ensure the initiative became a reality by ensuring their recommendations were implemented. Keep in mind that in addition to knowledge, action learning is the goal of leadership development. When preparing their leaders for making critical decisions, senior management must do more than simply provide their high-potential employees with knowledge and information. The right knowledge can build a strong foundation, but action learning can equip employees with the skills, qualities, and techniques to apply that knowledge in ambiguous situations. For example, managers can incorporate employee input by initiating best-practice partnering. Best-practice partnering emphasizes the use of action learning—the use of real-time business issues for learning and development, according to Fulmer and Goldsmith.[30]

Furthermore, Johnson & Johnson (J&J) uses technology strategies in its action-learning program. For instance, part of J&J's strategy was to create an organization of ninety thousand leaders. C-suite executives and senior managers realized they could not put ninety thousand employees through its top development programs. They could, however, provide computer technology for their employees around the world, to interact and learn from one another. In this case, technology was a potential bridge between senior management and employees within the organization. An example of the technology initiative was used during GE's Executive Conference II (one of J&J's first formal corporate-development programs). The company challenged senior managers with several exercises requiring the use of laptop computers. The benefits were two-fold. The computers tabulated participant responses, data analysis, and information retrieval.

These exercises provided leaders inexperienced with computer applications with nonthreatening coaching and hands-on experience. Serendipitously, the exercises identified leaders with skill-base deficiencies that were required for them to move on to more sophisticated challenges. Management feedback and coaching are also key components of action-able learning. Lynn Slavenski and Marilyn Buckner, authors of *Career Development Programs in the Workplace*, assert that employees receiving coaching and mentoring during temporary assignments or promotions can be linked to action learning (on-the-job-training), which is useful for developing employee skills and knowledge critical for promotion potential.[31]

Peter M. Senge, author of *The Fifth Discipline: The Art and Practice of the Learning Organization*, suggests that because the most powerful learning comes from direct experience such as action learning, learning organizations must join adaptive learning and generative learning to enhance an employee's capacity to create and innovate.[32] Adaptive learning is about building and developing multidimensional competencies to help deal with ongoing changes in an organization and in an employee's professional career. Moreover, when implementing an action-learning approach, content cannot be sacrificed for simplistic solutions, and the answers cannot be found in the instructor's head or in the back of a book. Creative and realistic answers should be developed and implemented on the spot by the employees. In essence, it becomes the employees' responsibility to successfully implement their recommendations, thereby allowing managers a bird's-eye view of the employee's leadership skills and abilities. Listed below are other nontraditional ways by which to meet successor needs in key positions, according to William Rothwell.[33]

- **Temping:** The organization makes it a practice to hire individuals from outside on a short–term basis to fill in during a search for a successor. The temps become candidates for consideration. If they do not work out, however, the arrangement can be severed on short notice.
- **Job Sharing**: An experienced employee in a key position temporarily shares the job with another in order to provide on-the-job training or to assess how well the candidate can perform.
- **Part-time Employment:** Prospective candidates for key positions are brought in on a part-time basis. They are carefully assessed before employment offers are made.
- **Consulting:** Prospective candidates for key positions are brought in as consultants on projects related to the position duties. Their performance is carefully assessed before employment offers are made.
- **Overtime:** Prospective candidates from within the organization may be required to work in other capacities in addition to their current jobs. This represents overtime work. The employer then assesses how well the individuals can perform in the key positions, making allowances for the unusual pressure under which the individuals are functioning.
- **Job Rotation:** Prospective candidates for key positions can be developed from within by moving them, for an extended time, into another job or rotating them in a series of preparatory jobs.
- **Use of Retirees:** Hire retired individuals (annuitants) with proven track records to return to critical positions, either temporarily or permanently.
- **Integration:** Integrate the additional workload into other positions throughout the organization and abolish the position.
- **Temp-Promote:** Temporary promotions will help in the development of potential future leaders. It also increases workforce morale and productivity. A temp promotion should not exceed 120 days.

A succession development plan ensures there are qualified, engaged, and motivated employees who are able to take over when an executive or another employee departs the organization—or a means of recruiting them. It also demonstrates to C-suite executives and stakeholders (clients, founders, employees and volunteers) that the organization remains committed to providing excellent programs, products, and services at all times, including during times of transition. This greatly improves employee retention and can be used in the recruiting process. Every organization will lose employees to their competitors; it is unavoidable. Therefore, as employees depart and new ones assume their responsibilities, the SDP should be updated to identify the next person to be groomed for promotion or new position. For organizations that engage in an annual (or regular) human-capital strategy planning, SDP must be included in the discussion. The discussion should include various career or professional-development activities and plans such as formal education, training, workshops, focus groups, action learning, and seminars, as well as less-formal learning opportunities such as the chance to represent the organization at conferences. The developmental plans should be formalized and integrated into the workforce development management system (WDMS).

Stage 12: Develop a Staffing Plan and Identify Funding Needs
Department executives and managers are accountable for creating a staffing bench-strength plan to assess vacancy and retention risks. A staffing plan can help determine which positions will present the greatest recruiting and developmental needs for the next one to five years. It is a road map that defines and outlines both the department and the organization's staffing requirements in its current and future states. Each department is accountable for uploading staffing planning data into the WDMS. Having a staffing plan will provide each department the opportunity to deal with unexpected vacancies or respond to opportunities expeditiously. The plan will help alleviate emotional hiring driven by bad decision making, thereby allowing more focus on good staffing decisions. Implementation of a comprehensive staffing plan requires the establishment of a staffing planning integrated product team (SP-IPT), which reports to the department's SLC representative. Department

executives and managers should ensure their staffing requirements meet both their job vacancies and funding limitations. The plan would ensure each department has the correct number of employees with the right competencies to support daily business operations. You must also be aware of both your internal and external environments by ensuring the plan is integrated into the organization's overall human-capital strategy and business plan. Once the staffing plan is developed, the SP-IPT can be suspended. The following items should be included in a staffing plan:

- Identify both departmental and organizational missions, goals, and business needs.
- Identify departmental and organizational customers and their needs.
- Identify both critical and noncritical job functions.
- Review diversity, inclusion, and disability efforts, and policies to ensure equity screening of potential applicants and current employees.
- Develop and/or update job descriptions for current and future positions.

When an organization is in dire need, the first line of accounting to be cut is the training budget. During critical budget cuts, each department executive must remain proactive in identifying his or her training budget requirements. Below are additional reasons for measuring workforce competencies and, at the same time, the need to identify funding. It is also recommended for executives to use predictive-analytics data to solicit annual funding. Predictive-analytics data can

- be used to help determine annual training budget;
- help the organization establish and maintain a learning culture;
- show a return on investment (ROI) via an increase in workforce productivity; and
- help streamline workforce training and development activities.

Stage 13: Automation via WDMS

The succession development plan should not function as an isolated system but rather as an integral component of the overall human-capital strategy plan. Organizations should review other human-resources procedures and policies to determine how the SDP can integrate with other human-resources programs. This will permit the plan to be more effective when human-resources practices are reviewed and designed to facilitate rather than impede the SDP process. Walter Mahler and Stephen Drotter, authors of *The Succession Planning Handbook for the Chief Executive*, assert that the closer the link between the succession plan and other personnel systems and management programs, the more effective planning efforts will be.[34] Therefore, to automate the succession development process, the SLC should implement a workforce development management system (WDMS), which would include several individual modules (e.g., employee performance appraisal, rewards, résumé, coaching, training (both on and off the job), education, certification, licensing, vocational training, leadership training, executive leadership training, mentoring, new hires, potential retirement candidates, and the like. A business analytic module should also be incorporated into the WDMS to help track accomplishments of the workforce in education, vocational programs, certification, retraining, training, and career development. This will help identify accountability and foster memoranda of understanding among C-suite executives, managers, and employees. It would also improve accountability, trust, respect, retention, and cooperation.

The insight gained through the use of prospective diagnostic studies on good practices and capabilities have shown organizations attempting to manage workforce developmental activities are dismal, to say the least, but implementing a WDMS would help alleviate this problem. The WDMS allows for automation of management processes and workflows, thereby simplifying the gathering of data and information. It can also integrate information compiled from other HR talent management programs, such as employee performance review process and job vacancies. All reports and meeting records should be electronic, thereby making it easier to administer, complete, and share information. In addition, the WDMS aggregates and analyzes the data gathered, enabling managers and employees to make better business decisions, particularly about succession readiness and employee career development. In addition, it is recommended for the WDMS to be web-based for job vacancy postings and alerts. Implementing a WDMS can be a critical tool to help assist managers in tracking and monitoring the status of employee career-development activities, individual development plans, position descriptions, and staffing plans. It should be integrated onto the desktop computer as an icon. The icon would provide alerts to executives and managers when employee training and career-development requirements are either met or have become delinquent. Quantifiable data can be collected and displayed by way of an icon, which would flash green, for example, when all training requirements are met (100 percent); flash yellow when training requirements are partially met (75 percent), and flash red when training requirements are totally delinquent. It can also serve as a tool for

- proactively predicting vacancies;
- identifying training and development costs;
- identifying most qualified candidates to fill critical job vacancies;
- assisting new hires in finding and completing required job forms;
- storing employee résumés and job-performance documents;
- alleviating time-consuming work spent preparing training compliance reports;
- managing a central data repository; and
- data mining and data sharing across the organization.

The most effective succession development plans are closely integrated with and build upon available information from existing human-resources systems, such as performance appraisal, management development, education, certifications, training and development, compensation, equal employment and affirmative action functions, career planning, and recruitment. If these processes are not interwoven into an integrated human-resources system, the expended effort may not be fruitful.

Succession development planning is important for other reasons as well. It forms the basis for

- communicating employee career paths;
- establishing training and career-development plans;
- establishing individual job moves;
- communicating upward and laterally concerning organizational management status; and
- creating a more comprehensive human-resources planning system.

Furthermore, the WDMS can be used to help managers identify successors for jobs throughout the organization and track the development of their high performers' strengths and weaknesses. Another advantage to implementing a WDMS is that it provides all the relevant information in an easy-to-use and manipulative format. However, the system should avoid information overload and should not blur the attention of the users of the data. The system should have extensive data capacity and the ability to link the succession development plan to other management staffing and career-development systems. The data is not contingent on the proficiency of a sophisticated computer system, but rather on the quality and relevance of the information collected. Finally, implementing a WDMS to function on personal computers will accelerate executives' and managers' ability to keep pace with staffing needs and changes. In essence, succession development planning rests on intelligence, diligence, and insight.

Stage 14: Establish Business Analytics and Monitor Progress

For most business executives, data acquisition has become a major topic of discussion. Having the ability to proactively extract the required data to improve your business decision-making ability can be very cumbersome and time consuming, because the task requires extracting data from various database systems. There are various types of commercial off-the-shelf business analytics software applications that can be used to help manage, monitor, and track your succession development planning data. Business analytics software can be used as a data-mining tool to proactively explore new data patterns and relationships in employees' training and career-development activities, by way of predictive modeling to improve both business and financial decisions. Dashboards and reports can be exported from the tool to help depict problem areas, which can enhance executives' insight to determine innovative ways to automate and optimize competitive advantages and business processes. As these patterns and relationships in the data become exposed, executives would have the opportunity to ask probing questions to better understand unforeseen problems that may impact their tactical decision-making ability in real time. It provides an innovative perspective and an opportunity to see and respond to data disruptions in scalable and graphical formats.

Furthermore, business analytics can provide predictive solutions used for building analysis models and simulations to create real-time business-related scenarios. It provides organizations with the ability to apply analytics and statistical analyses during the data-mining process. The decision to use business analytics software should be based on the organization's business culture, because some may be opposed to using this type of analytical tool. Using business analytic tools to achieve competitive advantages may require major commitment from executives, managers, and IS administrators. This may include acclimatizing organizational behavior and culture. Using analytics to monitor and support business decision making would also require a strategic plan that aligns with the organization's overall business strategy. In addition, there are various business analytics software applications and tools for organizations to explore (e.g., COGNOS, Tanagra, Oracle, Weka, Fusion Tables, etc.).

Chapter Seven

WORKFORCE COMPETENCY GAP ANALYSIS CASE STUDY

Employees are your first priority; customers are your second priority.

Case Study

As many organizations continue to deny the need for workforce succession development planning, they will continue to be confronted with major increases in overhead costs associated with employees retiring and departing. These costs include training and developing new hires, salaries, benefits, recruitment, new workspace, technology equipment, geographical location expenses, and other related costs. According to Matt Thompson, author of *How Much Does It Cost to Hire a New Employee?*, organizations could spend up to 150 percent of a manager's salary to prepare an employee for a management position. Costs may be even higher depending on the profession. For example, a person working in the information-technology profession may earn $60,000 annually, but to backfill his or her position the cost could be approximately $150,000.[1] US companies will continue to face major challenges filling positions in the science, technology, engineering, arts, and mathematics (STEAM) fields. Companies will also pay dearly in the areas of lost productivity and knowledge, thereby leaving behind a heavy workload for those remaining. This may subsequently lead to a decrease in employee morale and an increase in work-related stress and absenteeism.

To make matters worse, as US colleges and universities continue to benefit financially from international students filling their classrooms, the US student population wanting to enroll in STEAM curricula will continue to decline. Sharon Witherell's Institute of International Education (November 11, 2016) online report indicated that the international student population increased by 10 percent in 2015, to a record number of approximately 975,000 as compared to 130,000 students in the 1998–99 school year. In contrast, the US student population studying abroad was only 289,408 in school year 2013–14.[2] On an economic scale, John Siegmund and Barb Rawdon, authors of *2016 Top Markets Report: Education*, reported that international students contributed nearly $31 billion to the US economy in the 2014 and 2015 school years. The two major participants were China, with an international student population of 31 percent of all US foreign students, and India, with nearly 14 percent. Keep in mind these students pay between three and five times more for college enrollment than US students do. They are also more likely to return to their native land to complete their professional careers. The following tables help to illustrate the impact of international students have on US education. The top ten US institutions with international student enrollment in 2015 were the following:

1. New York University: 13,178
2. University of Southern California: 12,334
3. Columbia University: 11,510
4. Arizona State University: 11,330
5. University of Illinois, Urbana-Champaign: 11,223
6. Northeastern University: 10,559
7. Purdue University, West Lafayette: 10,230
8. University of California, Los Angeles: 10,209
9. Michigan State University: 8,146
10. University of Washington: 8,035

Table 1 indicates international student population by field of study, and table 2 reflects international student population by country of origin. What impact does this have on US public and private businesses? Sixty-eight percent of the student population enrolled in the STEAM curriculum—international students—will be taking their educational experiences and skills back to their homelands and leaving educational and technical competency gaps in the US business environment.[3]

Table 1: International Student Academic Field of Study 2014–15		
Rank	Field of Study	Student Enrollment Population
1.	Engineering	197,000
2.	Math and Computer Science	113,000
3.	Business and Management	197,000
4.	Social Sciences	76,000
5.	Physical and Life Sciences	76,000
6.	Fine and Applied Arts	75,000
7.	Intensive English	49,000
8.	Health Professions	33,000
9.	Communications/Journalism	20,000
10.	Humanities	18,000
11.	Legal Studies/Law Enforcement	14,000
12.	Agriculture	12,000

Table 2: International Student Population by Country of Origin 2014–15		
Rank	Country of Origin	Student Enrollment Population
1.	China	304,000
2.	India	133,000
3.	South Korea	64,000
4.	Saudi Arabia	60,000
5.	Brazil	24,000
6.	Taiwan	21,000
7.	Japan	19,000
8.	Vietnam	19,000
9.	Mexico	17,000

In 2014, I served as the chief information officer (CIO) for a prominent federal government engineering organization. With this knowledge, I could proactively plan for leadership and workforce succession. I conducted a comprehensive workforce competency gap analysis study within my department. The study provided answers to the following questions:

- Is the CIO department workload being distributed equally?
- What are the deficiencies and proficiencies in employees' competency levels?
- How diversified are employee competencies?
- Where are the workload bottlenecks in customer-service delivery?

- What workforce developmental activities—on-the-job training, job shadowing, or rotational assignments—should be
  implemented?
- What amount of funding will be required to meet employee
  training and developmental needs for the next two years?
- Who requires additional training and development to do his or
  her job more efficiently and effectively?

According to Harvard University's online Competency Dictionary, "competencies" are defined in the most general terms as "things" that an individual must demonstrate to be effective in a job, role, function, task, or
duty. These "things" include:

- Job-relevant behavior (what a person says or does that results in
  good or poor performance)
- Motivation (how a person feels about a job, organization, or geographic location)
- Technical knowledge/skills (what a person knows/demonstrates
  regarding facts, technologies, a profession, procedures, a job, an
  organization, etc.)

Competencies are identified through the study of jobs and roles.[4]

As organizations transition toward a competency-based workforce,
C-suite executives and managers must become aware of the importance
of ensuring their employees' competencies are updated and correctly
aligned and mapped to support current and future business requirements. Competency-based alignment, modeling, and mapping (CMM)
were processes I used to help future-proof my workforce. Note: For this
chapter, an example of the IS division's competency gap analysis data
results is provided. The workforce competency gap analysis survey can
be taken at the following Website: www.fennerconsultinggroup.com. To
ensure anonymity, the assessment excluded race, gender, and age.

Competency-Based Alignment

Currently, many preeminent executives are preparing their recruitment
and retention strategies to solicit top talent to work in their organization.

They are developing and implementing state-of-the-art recruiting strategies, customizable training and development programs, benefit packages, and creative leadership and social-networking techniques. They are using competency modeling to align employee knowledge, skills, aptitude, or attributes to the organization's human-capital strategy, goals, and objectives. It will also help to determine the optimal number of employees needed for business success. A commonality among these executives is their ability to understand the criticality of preserving an efficient and high-performing labor force that is well prepared to execute the organization's mission.

However, to ensure a competency-based-aligned organization is successful, executives must first conduct a programmatic review of their employees' training, education, certification, learning, and developmental deficiencies and proficiencies. This can be accomplished by assessing employees' competency levels by way of a workforce development competency gap analysis assessment. Competencies are the foundation for employee selection and development. They are preparatory for decision making and identifying what to seek in both new hires and current employees. They are the basis for both succession development planning and career development planning, where potential strengths and weaknesses can be identified through assessment and comparison. Once the assessment is completed, a competency requirement model (CRM) can be developed and implemented to include professional training and development frameworks. Each department's CRM should reflect its own competency requirements, not those of another department. In addition, these competencies can be used for employee recruitment, selection, retention, training and development, performance and talent management, job profiling, succession planning, and rewards and recognition.

As the war for talent continues to be in the forefront for many organizations, a CRM can play a major role in recruitment and retention. It can be used as a framework for organizing, collecting, and measuring employees' knowledge, skills, behaviors, aptitudes, and personality traits. It describes what training, development, education, certification, or license employees may need to successfully execute their job assignments more efficiently and effectively. In addition, a CRM provides a road map for employee professional development and career planning.

It will assist employees in focusing on the critical requirements for improving their contribution to the organization's business success. At the same time, the CRM should be implemented strategically and not in a vacuum. Without the support of all leaders of the organization, it may fail. Other advanced and expert levels' additional requirements for a successful CRM should include relationship building, business analytics, management (i.e., coaching, delegation, performance management, project and process management, business acumen, human capital, etc.), and self-development (i.e., college degree, certification, etc.). Here are a few questions you should be asking yourself and others when assessing and establishing workforce competencies:

- What are the organization's current and future business strategies?
- What workforce competencies are required to support customers' and stakeholders' current and future business strategies and needs to ensure they remain competitive?
- How should the organization's business be aligned to these competencies?
- What impacts (financial, behavior, morale, culture, etc.) are there to the workforce?

Asking these strategic questions can help demystify potential criticism or delays. Both talent segments and job roles must first define essential workforce competencies. Depending on the job title, roles, and responsibilities, the competency requirement model should reflect five major competencies:

1. **General Competencies:** These competencies describe the combination of abilities, motivations, and traits required to perform effectively in a wide range of jobs within an organization. They are an integral part of on-the-job success in virtually every context and occupation. Examples of general competencies include interactive communication, social responsibility, and achievement orientation, according to the Human Resource Systems Group.[5] General competencies are the main strengths or strategic

advantages of a business, including the combination of pooled knowledge that allows an organization to remain competitive.

2. **Core/Functional Competencies:** These competencies are specific to a particular department or type of job and are not easily imitable. They are associated with the knowledge, skills, and abilities required to complete required job tasks, duties, or responsibilities. According to Susan Ward of The Balance, the more current definition of core competency would be the "key abilities or strengths that a company has developed that give it a competitive advantage over its peers and contribute to its long-term success."[6]

3. **Technical Competencies:** These competencies describe behaviors such as knowledge and skills needed to perform effectively in a specific job or group of jobs within the organization. These types of competencies are closely aligned with the knowledge and skills or know-how needed for successful performance. According to the Business Dictionary, technical competencies are defined as "knowledge of, and skill in the exercise of, practices required for successful accomplishment of a business, job, or task."[7]

4. **Management Competencies:** Management competencies are in contrast to leadership competencies. These competencies can be taught or developed over time. According to Gary Hamel and Bill Breen, authors of *The Future of Management*, management competencies may extend in the areas such as managing diversity and inclusion, risk taking, emotional awareness, financial management, strategic thinking, knowledge management, critical thinking, performance management, project management, conceptual and systematic thinking, analytical thinking, reward and recognition, talent development, mentoring and coaching, hiring, promoting, and retention.[8]

5. **Leadership Competencies**: These competencies are leadership skills and behaviors that contribute to superior performance, according to the Society for Human Resource Management (SHRM). By using a competency-based approach to leadership, organizations can better identify and develop their next

generation of leaders. In today's work environment, essential leadership competencies and attributes should include both domestic and international competencies, both of which would create competitive advantages. Keep in mind that future business trends and strategies should drive the development of new leadership competencies.[9]

Competency Modeling

According to Greg Sekowski of Human Resource Strategic Partners, Inc., competency modeling is a framework used to align the skills, knowledge, and abilities of employees with the organization's strategic goals and objectives.[10] It can assist leaders in defining what skills, knowledge, aptitude, experience, education, and certification are needed for successful job performance. CM is a proactive strategy to help organizations become more effective, competitive, and efficient in a twenty-first-century business environment. It can be used as a future-proofing tool to help C-suite executives determine if employees have the required competencies to meet the organization's strategic business goals. At the same time, CM can help managers identify employees' performance benchmarks, as well as retraining, training, and developmental deficiencies for the future. In addition, competency mapping can reduce the recruitment and hiring process by employing candidates who already have the required core competencies.

Competency Mapping

As organizations transition to a more competency-based workforce, leaders must be oriented on the importance of ensuring their employees' competencies are updated and correctly mapped to support future workload requirements. More importantly, as economic, social, and technological changes continue to drive business success, organizations populated with employees who possess multidimensional and relevant competencies will succeed and sustain a greater competitive advantage. Therefore, to remain indispensable to their customers, organizations must reevaluate their employees' competencies and update job descriptions and résumés on an annual basis. Reassessing employees' competencies can also be accomplished via the competency-mapping process.

For this book, competency mapping is defined as a process used to help leaders identify key competencies (skills, knowledge, aptitudes, and behaviors, etc.) needed to support both current and future job functions across their organization. These competencies may depend on various factors such as work environment, task assignments, leadership, or job functions. They may change depending on the position an employee is occupying. Moreover, competency mapping reinforces the organization's vision, mission, goals, hiring and selection, workforce culture, and business strategies. It can also be used for leveraging employee training, performance expectations, employee retention, recruitment, career development, job performance, job evaluation, team dynamics, and succession development planning. Competencies are associated with the knowledge, skills, aptitude, personality, education, or certification of an individual as applied to a role or job in the context of the present and future environment that accounts for sustained success within the framework of organizational values, vision, mission, and goals. Chart 1 indicates the competency mapping process, which may consist of, but is not limited to, the following steps.

Chart 1: Competency Mapping Process

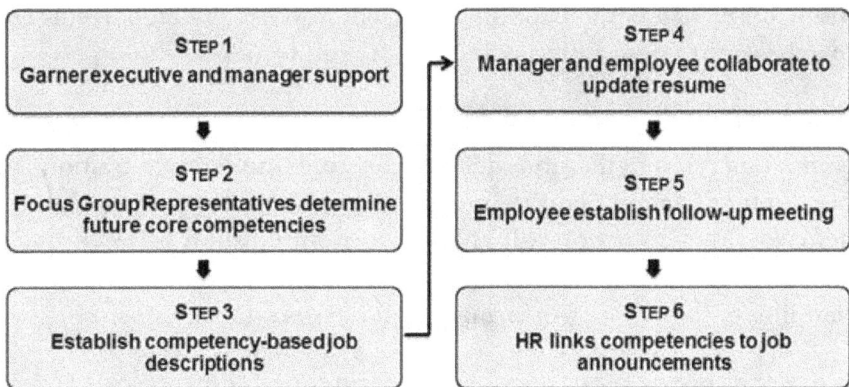

STEP 1 Garner executive and manager support	STEP 4 Manager and employee collaborate to update resume
STEP 2 Focus Group Representatives determine future core competencies	STEP 5 Employee establish follow-up meeting
STEP 3 Establish competency-based job descriptions	STEP 6 HR links competencies to job announcements

Step 1: Garner support from senior executives, human-resources office, and managers to discuss job positions and requirements.

Step 2: Establish focus-group sessions to include all levels across the organization or department (employees, supervisors, managers and executives) to help identify past, current, and future core competencies required to perform current and new job positions. HR representatives should facilitate focus-group sessions. It is recommended for focus-group members to discuss past competencies, because the organization may need team members who have foundational experience in past job functions.

> *Scenario:* Your organization is bidding on a multimillion-dollar information-technology contract. The contract requires computer repair service-level agreements. It has been several years since the organization has performed this type of work. Employees who were previously performing computer-repair work are currently assigned to different departments and conducting new task assignments. How would you determine if the organization still has this level of in-house IT expertise?

Step 3: The next step is for focus groups to develop new competency-based job descriptions. Focus groups should use performance appraisal forms, face-to-face interviews, survey questionnaires, HRO database tools, current job descriptions, and employees' updated résumés to match new job description competency requirements.

Step 4: Managers and employees should meet to discuss employees' competency strengths and deficiencies and implement training and development action plans to include objectives to help strengthen these deficiencies. This action will enhance communication between managers and employees. At the same time, employees will gain a better understanding of their work performance and expectations.

Step 5: Employees are accountable for establishing follow-up meetings to discuss their progress. This will give employees the opportunity to share their new skills and cross-training experiences with their manager, which could lead to promotional opportunities in the future.

Step 6: When hiring either inside or outside the organization, human-resources specialists and managers should work in concert to ensure core competencies are both properly identified in the job announcement and mapped to the skills potential candidates already have identified in their updated résumés. Having this information will reduce the résumé-reviewing process, thereby eliminating candidates who are not highly qualified for a position.

Competency modeling and mapping (CMM) are two of the most critical steps in the succession development planning process. They can be used as tools to help identify key core and technical competencies needed to support current and future job functions across an organization. CMM also reinforces the organization's vision, mission, goals, hiring and selection practices, workforce culture, and business strategies. It can aid in establishing performance expectations, employee retention, career development, job performance, and team dynamics. These competencies may depend on various factors such as work environment, task assignments, leadership, social intelligence, cultural intelligence, personal intelligence, job function, and so on. Keep in mind these competency requirements may change depending on an employee's job position.

The CMM will provide leaders with the opportunity to identify both soft and technical skill competencies necessary to support organizational goals to meet mission achievements. Future-proofing the workforce by assessing employees' past, current, and future competencies against workforce competency proficiency levels across the organization will help identify gaps where workforce retraining, training, and career development can be enhanced or modified. An analysis for workforce competency modeling and mapping involves two primary components: the selection of competencies to assess and the identification of current and future proficiency gaps in employees' ability to apply these competencies during job performance.

In August 2014, I was tasked with proactively identifying gaps in competencies across the department of the chief information office. In response, I conducted a comprehensive workforce competency gap analysis study. The primary objectives of the workforce competency gap analysis survey were to

1. reconnoiter the department's competency gaps across its core functional areas (information technology, information systems, telecommunications, industrial control systems, information assurance, cybersecurity, and resource management);
2. model and map employees' competency levels and deficiencies;
3. determine solutions to deal with recruitment and retention of professionals with expertise in the aforementioned areas;
4. deal with an aging workforce via cross-pollination;
5. identify employees' training and career-development shortfalls;
6. determine personnel bandwidth demands to support current and future workload requirements;
7. determine the gaps in employees' education and certifications; and
8. develop a succession-management framework and a performance-management system to preemptively identify, monitor, track, and support future workforce competency gaps, experience, behavioral, knowledge, skills, retirements, retentions, replacement, and workload distributions.

Methodology

The methodology included a three-phase approach:

- Phase 1 employed a multistep process to help determine experience levels (entry, intermediate, advanced, and expert) across each functional area.
- Phase 2 included validation of the survey statements.
- Phase 3 was comprised of two parts:

  o Part 1 required prioritizing workforce succession development (WSD) competency gaps.
  o Part 2 identified training and certification deficiencies. Employees' training, career development, and professional certifications needed to be extended beyond the

boundaries of their traditional technical skills. The gap assessment also included soft-skill competencies such as leadership competency, training, customer service, formal education, mentoring, coaching, teamwork, employment status, work area, and leadership-training programs.

Population Sample Data

The chief information office staff was the population of the study. The sample size consisted of thirty-five employees, twenty-four males and eleven females, including managers and supervisors.

Validity and Reliability

Thirty-five employees completed the survey, with an average mean score of 168.7. To ensure survey validity and reliability, fifteen employees (nine males and six females, both supervisors and nonsupervisors) retook the identical survey within seven days and received an average mean score of 168. Validity and reliability testing allowed for immediate clarification of ambiguous statements. In addition, of the 147 survey statements, ninety were rated using the following scoring system:

- Entry = one point
- Intermediate = two points
- Advanced = three points
- Expert = four points
  Note: The remaining fifty-seven statements were not rated.

Technical Data Results

The data were identified based on the results from the five core functional areas:

1. Information systems (IS)
2. Information technology (IT)

3. Information assurance (IA)
4. Resource management (RM)
5. Industrial control systems (ICS)

The workforce aggregate ratings of the overall survey results of the major competency gaps occurring across the core functional areas were:

- 41 percent at entry level
- 35 percent at intermediate level
- 19 percent at advanced level
- 5 percent at expert level

The workforce being reviewed at the 76 percent level (an aggregate of entry and intermediate levels) indicates a lack of training, retraining, experience, knowledge, skills, and abilities to perform at the advanced and expert levels.

Years of Experience in the Same Job Function

For this category, the study reflected 57 percent of the workforce having between twenty and thirty-plus years of experience in a particular job function. It also indicated this group of employees is nearing retirement age, which reflects an urgent need for succession development planning. The remaining 43 percent of the workforce has between one and nineteen years in a particular job function. The data indicate a one-dimensional workforce that will face major problems in the future as new job functions and workloads increase.

As managers in the IS division continue to focus on cost reductions and, at the same time, increase in work productivity, information systems (IS) workload will be a key component for ensuring the department and the organization remain competitive in both today's and tomorrow's global market. Because information systems are associated with data manipulation, software problem identification, application management, and operational controls, strategic planning and data transactional processing, leaders, employees, and customers alike will become more dependent on these functionalities for better decision making, business processes, and cost deliberations. Moreover, as information systems functional areas develop into an interdependent and evolving business environment, terms such as "big data" and "Internet of Things," for example, will continue to be a global conversation of interest. The commonality between big data and Internet of Things is linked to data collection and communication, which in turn is associated with information systems. Dave Evans, author of *The Internet of Things: How the Next Evolution of the Internet Is Changing Everything*, estimates that by 2020, IoTs will consist of over fifty billion objects and approximately one trillion sensors that will be installed on items ranging from cars to home appliances.[11] In addition, information systems can be used for keeping executives and managers aware of internal and external performances and, at the same time, they can remain conscious of external threats and opportunities. This is why the survey results of the department's IS division will be used as an example in this chapter.

An aggregate of all employees in the CIO department responding to the information systems functional area, 51 percent of acknowledged that their competency level is at entry level, while 30 percent thought they possessed intermediate level skills. Less than 19 percent of the employees believed they were proficient at the advanced and expert levels. More importantly, the CIO department faces major operational problems, with 81 percent of its employees identifying their competencies at entry and intermediate levels in this critical functional area. As a result, due to limited resources, training, retraining, and development opportunities, morale will continue to be impacted across the department. This will also impact their ability to execute their work more effectively and efficiently. The survey results were not achieved with strictly scientific controls and measures and therefore are, at best, a superficial representation of how they perceived their competency levels. What is important and cannot be refuted is the lack of confidence in the capabilities among the workforce.

Figure 1 represents the competency levels for only employees of the information systems division *(n=12)*. The bar chart indicates 41 percent of the employees believed their capabilities were at entry level, while 31 percent believed they met the intermediate level, with only 19 percent indicating they were at the advanced level, and 9 percent indicating they were at the expert level. The CIO department cannot reach its full IS functional and operational potential with 72 percent of its IS employees identifying their competencies at entry and intermediate levels. With limited resources in the information-systems workforce, coupled with the loss of trained workers who are not only feeling inadequate about their capabilities but are woefully behind the curve of software technology competencies.

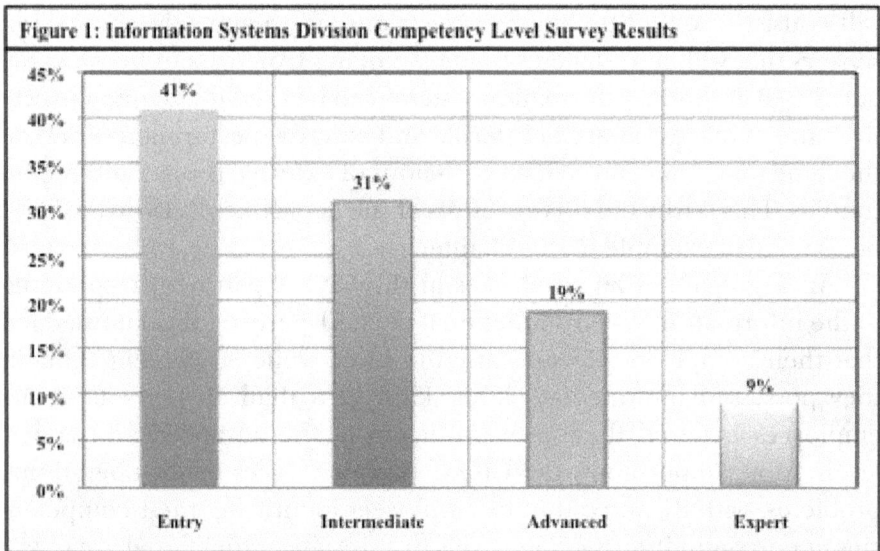

Figure 1: Information Systems Division Competency Level Survey Results

Table 3 is a snapshot of the information systems division's overall competency level rating of 2.2, required competency benchmark of 3.6, and gap/competency deficiencies of -1.4 respectively. Column two lists the number of current employees performing the daily job functions and the rating score of one through four. The third column represents the required number of employees needed to perform the daily tasks with the same rating score of one through four. Column four represents the gap in employees' competency level to perform the daily task assignments. It also maps employees' current and required competency levels.

Table 3: IS Technical and Soft-Skill Competency Gaps / Mapping Matrix			
Competency	Current Competency Level (Rating: 1–4)	Required Competency Level (Benchmark: 1–4)	Gap
Citrix Application	2	4	-2
Facilities Information System	2	4	-2
Environmental Waste Billing System	1	3	-2
Financial Management System	2	4	-2
Invoice One-Pay System	3	4	-1
Labor Management System	2	3	-1
Graymarc Logistics System	3	4	-1
Standard Financial Procurement System	3	3	0
Structured Query Language	3	4	-1
Motorola PDA Applications	4	4	0
Oracle Application Express	2	4	-2
Visual Basic Applications	3	4	-1
Circuits Data Integration	3	4	-1
Configuration Mgmt. System	1	3	-2
Wide Area Workflow System	3	4	-1
Building Alliance	2	3	-1
Business Acumen	1	3	-2
Solution Driven	2	4	-2
Leading Others	1	3	-2
Leading Change	1	3	-2
Rating	**2.2**	**3.6**	**−1.4**

Workload and Competency Comparative Analysis

Employee training and career development have become major vulnerabilities for many organizations. Because employees account for a major share of operating costs, their training and career-development activities are the first to be cut from the organization's overall budget. To mitigate this problem, subject-by-subject comparisons and competency comparative analyses (CCA) were conducted to determine employees' individual training, career development, education, and certification deficiencies. In the IS division, for example, each employee's individual survey results were compared to the CIO department's overall results. Division managers held individual meetings with each employee to compare his or her individual results with the department's overall results.

The comparative analysis indicated both similarities and differences in each employee's individual competency levels. The data reflected results from the CIO department's five core functional areas (information systems, information technology, information assurance, resource management, and industrial-control systems). The CIO department's workforce aggregate ratings indicated 41 percent at entry level, 35 percent at intermediate level, 19 percent at advanced level, and 5 percent at expert level. Similarly, the IS division's workforce survey results indicated 41 percent of the its employees' overall competency proficiencies were at entry level, 31 percent at intermediate level, and 28 percent indicating proficiency levels at advanced or expert. The department's overall workforce being viewed at the 76 and 72 percent levels, an aggregate of entry and intermediate levels between both groups, indicates a lack of training, retraining, experience, knowledge, skills, and abilities to perform at the advanced and expert levels. Moreover, the survey results were not achieved with strictly scientific controls and measures and, therefore, are at best a superficial representation of how they perceived their competency levels. What is important and cannot be refuted is the lack of confidence in the capabilities among the workforce. As a result, due to limited training, retraining, and development opportunities, morale is greatly impacted across the information systems division. This will lead to disabled and disempowered employees in an effort to execute their task assignments more effectively and efficiently. This also negatively impacts the CIO department holistically. At the same time, C-suite executives, managers, and employees alike should strive to attain self-sufficiency to meet their professional and personal competencies (training, career development, education, certification).

Why is succession development planning so important? It helps you to become proactive in future-proofing your workforce by detecting competency deficiencies at the infancy stage. If the competency deficiency problem is not detected, it could erode employee morale, reduce work productivity, cause employee burnout, and increase employees' stress levels. The following steps will help guide you in developing a workload matrix for your organization to alleviate these potential problems.

Step 1: Link Mission Statements
The first step in developing a workload matrix is to ensure the division's mission statement is linked to the department's mission statement and

the department's mission statement is linked to the organization's over-all mission statement.

Step 2: Identify Roles and Responsibilities

This step involves identifying the information systems division's roles and responsibilities and the types of services being provided to the cus-tomer (software programming, system maintenance, system integration, configuration management, etc.). Doing so will help reduce ambiguity and confusion. It will also show how each employee's job function sup-ports the organization's overall business needs.

Step 3: Identify Customers

This step involves identifying and knowing who your customers are (e.g., Departments A-G).

Step 4: Identify Types of Services

Once steps one through three are completed, the next step is to iden-tify the types of services and link the services to the customers receiving those services (Citrix application; facilities information systems, etc.).

Step 5: Assign Subject-Matter Experts

Step five involves assigning subject-matter experts who will be account-able for delivering the services. For example, in the lower section of the matrix, looking down the "Services" column, you will see a list of twelve software applications that the IS division is accountable for providing to its customers. Across the top is a list of departments (Department A, Department B, etc.) in which the services are being rendered. A check mark indicates what department should be receiving what type of software application support. The far-right column indicates what employee/subject-matter expert (Employee A, Employee B, etc.) is accountable for delivering software-application support.

Step 6: Identify New Requirements

Chart 2 reflects a breakdown of the current number ($n=12$) of IS divi-sion employees it has to support its five thousand direct customers' and two hundred fifty thousand indirect customers' business needs.

It also indicates three new service requirements, which are marked as "TBD." "N/R" indicates no service is required at this time. Service lines 13 through 15, marked "To Be Determined" or "TBD," indicate the IS

Chart 2: Division A—Information Systems Workload/Competency Comparative Matrix *(EXAMPLE)*

MISSION: Provide effective and reliable information-systems support, solutions, governance, and resources to empower customers and, at the same time, balance stewardship of software applications.

Software Programming Support and Information-Systems Maintenance:
Deliver system maintenance and programming support of business and corporate systems, interfaces, and tools. Enhance business-application systems to meet newly identified requirements in accordance with organizational policies and procedures.
- Provide requirements analysis and information systems engineering
- Systems specification gathering
- Database specifications, requirement analyses, and engineering
- Database modeling, diagram, and data dictionary
- Provide web portal content maintenance and management
- Develop application test plans, procedures, and analysis reports
- Establish system documentation and user guides
- Deliver information systems security testing and user-level access
- Provide application user training, deployment, and installation

System Integration:
Provide user support to ensure integration of current and future software applications are compliant; to include support in areas of software design evaluation, interface requirements, software upgrade studies, capacity planning, system integration with coordination of shared data, and user-friendly customer interface.

Configuration Management:
Provide document control and version-management support maintenance of program source code and documentation libraries for management information's under departmental control, according to organizational policies, procedures, and governance.

Services	Department A	Department B	Department C	Department D	Department E	Department F	Department G	# of Subject-Matter Expert(s)
Customer Application Support Services								
1. CITRIX Application	√	√	√	√	√	√	√	Employee A
2. Facilities information system	√	N/R	√	N/R	√	√	N/R	Employee B
3. Environmental Waste Billing System	√	N/R	√	N/R	√	N/R	√	Employee C
4. Financial Management System	N/R	√	√	√	N/R	√	N/R	Employee D
5. Invoice One-Pay S stem	N/R	√	N/R	√	√	N/R	√	Employee E
6. Labor Management System	√	N/R	√	√	N/R	√	N/R	Employee F
7. Graymarc Logistics System	√	N/R	√	√	√	N/R	√	Employees G&H
8. Standard Procurement System	N/R	√	√	N/R	√	√	√	Employee H
9. Structured Query Language	√	N/R	√	√	√	N/R	√	Employee I
10. Microsoft PDA Applications	N/R	√	√	√	N/R	√	√	Employee J
11. Oracle Application Express	√	√	√	√	√	√	√	Employee K
12. Visual Basic Applications	√	√	√	√	√	√	√	Employees L&J
13. CIRCUITS Data Integration	*NS	*NS	*NS	*NS	*NS	*NS	NS	**TBD
14. Configuration Management System	*NS	*NS	*NS	*NS	*NS	*S	*NS	* TBD
15. Wide Area Workflow System	*NS	*NS	*NS	*NS	*NS	*NS	*NS	**TBD
*NS = new services; **TBD = No employee with the competencies to perform this work *** N/R = Not Required								

division does not have the required personnel, nor does it have personnel with the necessary competencies to support the new requirements. The chart also reflects a bottleneck in its service delivery. For example, in some functional areas, the IS division has only one subject-matter expert (SME) to support multiple departments. This may lead to employee burnout and increased stress, which may result in employees seeking work in another organization. The chart depicts the employee(s) who provide software-application support service to the various departments throughout the organization. Currently, each employee in the IS division works eight hours daily. However, due to limited personnel and an untrained workforce, each employee (A, G, H, J, K, and L) on average works an additional forty hours of overtime per month, totaling 240 hours. Meanwhile, employees B, C, D, E, F, and I work zero overtime hours and have not been cross-trained or possess the certification requirements to help balance the workload of the aforementioned employees. As a result, employees A, G, H, J, K, and L were stressed, distressed, and seeking new employment. The cost-benefit analysis research indicated the average cost to retrain, train, and cross-train the twelve IS employees would be more cost effective than hiring ten additional employees. Employees across the IS division were therefore trained, retrained, and cross-trained to support a balanced workload for each employee to include supporting the CIO department's newly established application systems requirements.

Step 7: Assess Workforce and Workload Demand Gaps
Table 4 is a snapshot of the information systems division's current number of employees and required number of employees to perform daily task assignments and gaps. It also includes monthly overtime hours and subject-matter experts' support roles. For example, under the "Competency" column, the first line item is "Citrix Application," in which departments A through G require support; however, "Employee A" is the only subject-matter expert (SME) with the required competencies (knowledge, skills, experience, education, certification, etc.). On average, "Employee A" also works forty hours of overtime per month. In addition, Employees G, H, J, K, and L work an additional forty hours of overtime each month. This does not include supporting the three new

or "TBD" job functions. Holistically, these six employees work a total of 240 hours of overtime each month. If for some reason one or two of the employees depart the organization or become ill, the customers would be greatly impacted.

Table 4: IS Division Workforce/Workload Demand *(Example)*					
Competency	Current # of FTEs	Required # of FTEs	Workforce Demand Signal	SME(s)	Average Overtime Hours *(Monthly)*
Citrix Application	1	2	-1	Employee A	40
Facilities Information System	1	1	0	Employee B	0
Environmental Waste Billing System	1	1	-1	Employee C	0
Financial Management System	1	1.5	-.5	Employee D	0
Invoice One-Pay System	1	1.5	-.5	Employee E	0
Labor Management System	1	1.5	-.5	Employee F	0
Graymarc Logistics System	1.5	2	-.5	Employees G&H	40
Standard Financial Procurement System	.5	1	-.5	Employee H	40
Structured Query Language	1	2	-1	Employee I	0
Microsoft PDA Applications	.5	1	-.5	Employee J	40
Oracle Application Express	1	2	-1	Employee K	40
Visual Basic Applications	1.5	2	-.5	Employees L&J	40
Circuits Data Integration	0	1	*NS (1)	TBD	TBD
Configuration Mgmt. System	0	1	*NS (1)	TBD	TBD
Wide Area Workflow System	0	1	*NS (1)	TBD	TBD
FULL TIME EQUIVALENTS	**12**	**21.5**	**10.5**		**217**

Note: FTE = Full Time Equivalent, SME = Subject-Matter Expert

Certification Data Results

The data indicates that 94 percent of the IS division's workforce does not have a professional certification, with only 2 percent indicating they have a professional/technical certification. The security life cycle of the organization's information systems and data protection are critical due to cybersecurity threats. This amplifies the immediate need for additional personnel and training, retraining, and career-development activities to occur across the IS division.

Leadership Competency Data Results

Leadership competencies are critical to the mission of both the CIO department and the organization. Sixty-one percent of the IS division's workforce leadership competencies resonate at entry and intermediate levels. Only 39 percent are at or above the advanced level. In an effort for the CIO department to better leverage employees' knowledge across the IS division, it must create a dynamic and contextual learning environment by ensuring critical leadership training, retraining, and development activities are being provided.

Education

In reference to formal education across the IS division, 100 percent had a bachelor's degree and 60 percent had master's degrees. The desired outcome is for all IS employees to obtain a master's degree. Nevertheless, the results indicate the IS branch workforce has met its formal education requirements.

IS Professional Competency Requirement Model (CRM)

Table 5 depicts an example of an information-systems professional competency requirement model. The CRM should consist of four competency levels (entry, intermediate, advanced, and expert), according to Timothy Logan, Margaret Barton, and Anne Holloway-Lundy, authors of *Workforce and Succession Planning for Mission Critical Occupations.*[12] Keep in mind the various levels do not guarantee a promotion, and experience should not necessarily be a nexus to a position title or grade level. Below are the definitions for each proficiency level.

- **Level 1—Entry:** At this level, employees are expected to apply basic knowledge to somewhat difficult situations. Requires frequent guidance. Demonstrates familiarity with concepts and processes.
- **Level 2—Intermediate:** At this level, employees are expected to apply the competency in difficult situations. Requires occasional guidance. Demonstrates understanding of concepts and processes.
- **Level 3—Advanced:** At this level, employees are expected to apply the competency in considerably difficult situations. Generally requires little or no guidance. Demonstrates broad understanding of concepts and processes.

- **Level 4—Expert:** At this level, employees are expected to apply the competency in exceptionally difficult situations. Serves as a key resource and advises others. Demonstrates comprehensive and expert understanding of concepts and processes.

Table 5: Information Systems Professional CRM *(EXAMPLE)*

Competency Level	Assignments and Experiences	Knowledge, Skills, Abilities, Educations and Certification	Leadership Proficiencies
Entry Level This stage is the most basic developmental level. It generally applies to individuals who are new to a department and are capable of performing well with close supervision. Efforts at this stage involve applying basic concepts and principles with significant support from others.	> Experience in applying principles of basic software application and programming. > Experience demonstrates written and verbal communication skills, problem analysis and solving, research, customer orientation, basic organization awareness, and interpersonal/team skills.	> Bachelor's degree (desired) and 2–3 years of commensurate work experience. > Basic knowledge of various programming languages. > Ability to use basic business and application tools. > Oracle APEX, C and C++ Cert, and so on.	> Self-development > Cooperation and teamwork > Oral and written communication > Have understanding of social, cultural, and multigenerational intelligences. > Basic leadership skills > Relationship building skills
Intermediate Level This stage represents individuals who have gained capability within a competency area. They generally begin to operate independently in a wide range of efforts, and may begin taking on responsibility for delivery within a team structure or for leading team efforts.	> Demonstrate ability to identify and apply current enterprise application principles and practices. > Describe and apply basic software application evaluation theories. > Design and administer software applications programs. > Identify training needs; conduct annual assessments of software requirements. > Evaluate customer application data and trends.	> Bachelor's or master's degree desired and 3–5 years of relevant experience. > Completed at least two software application certifications. > Gained and applied knowledge of enterprise software applications. > Obtain a Certified Secure Software Lifecycle Professional Certification. > All requirements of the entry level apply.	> Accountability > Creativity and innovation > Problem solving > Situational leadership > Teambuilding > Diversity and inclusion intelligence > All requirements of the entry level apply
Advanced Level This stage represents those individuals who are capable of leading and mentoring multiple teams and/or large groups. They may perform interaction with Enterprise level counterparts	> Experience in exercising senior supervisory, lead, and program-management responsibilities in the areas of software application support, development, and training. > Have a strong understanding of enterprise application programs and principles. > Extensive knowledge applying statutes, regulations, affecting enterprise software application development and training issues.	> Master's degree (desired) in related field or 5–10 years of increasing difficult in software programming or IS. > Ability and skills in developing in-house software applications to substantive customer concerns. > Ability to lead teams and meet established objectives. > MCSD Application Builder Certification, and so on. > All requirements of the intermediate level apply.	> Management > Self-development > Relationship building > Leading others > Entrepreneurship > Customer focus > Human-capital mgmt. > Managing diversity > Advanced leadership skills > All requirements of Intermediate level apply
Expert Level This is the highest level of development within the CRM. At this stage, employees are sought out for consultation and assistance in their particular area of expertise. They generally develop policies and strategies and interface with C-suite executives in other departments and organizations.	> Serves as the expert on computer and IT systems. > SME for HD and SW installation and upgrades. > Demonstrates strategic vision and strategic planning, influencing, and negotiating skills. > Lead organizational HW/SW polices and standardized practices development. > SME in developing of private intranet and public Internet websites.	> Master's degree (desired) in related field or 5–10 years of increasing difficulty in software programming or IS. > Mastery of software development and programming principles, concepts, and practice gained through formal education, training, and certifications. > SME on implementing and programming of computer networks and upgrades. > All requirements of the advanced level apply.	> Formal management and executive leadership training > Influencing and negotiating skills > Partnering and political savvy > Strategic thinking and vision > Excellent social, cultural, executive, multigenerational and emotional intelligences > Diversity and inclusion savvy intelligence > All requirements of the advanced level apply.

Workforce Economy of Scale

An information systems workforce economy of scale (WEoS) was used to help determine the financial cost for developing the workforce to become multidimensional via retraining, training, formal education, and certificating the CIO workforce. It was also used to determine whether or not there was a need to hire additional employees to meet the organization's current and future business demands. Moreover, as technical service demands increase, there is a higher probability for an increase in service delivery, which leads to greater quality of service and quicker response to customer service calls. The reverse side of the WEoS is the workforce diseconomy of scale (WDS), in which maintaining the level of service and at the same time supporting newly established technical service requirements may exceed the savings gained from developing a multidimensional workforce via training, retraining, education, and certification. Business case analyses were conducted to help determine cost-effective measures pertaining to employee development and hiring ten additional new hires to support the CIO department's current and future workload requirements. For example, initially, the IS division's true workforce demand was ten additional new hires, totaling twenty-two; see chart 3.

However, after investing in the IS division workforce training and retraining efforts, that human-capital demand was reduced by 50 percent, from ten down to five. The IS division's WEoS depicts a reduction in service delivery time from seven hours to two hours. Let's assume, for example, that the cost of training twelve information-systems employees on new software applications is $300,000 versus hiring ten additional employees at a total annual salary of $1,000,000 (ten employees x $100,000 yearly salary). As a result of this training, only five additional new hires were required, resulting in $500,000 in overhead cost savings. To determine the ROI, the cost benefit of $500,000 was divided by the training cost ($300,000), which yielded a cost benefit ratio of 1.67 to 1. Multiplying the result 1.67 by 100, the cost benefit was 166.67 percent. At the same time, service delivery timeframe increased by 350 percent (7 hours divided by 2 hours (3.5) times 100 resulted in a 350 percent increase in service delivery). Moreover, for every dollar spent on employee training, there was a cost reduction of $1.67. These cost

savings do not include customers being unable to complete task assignments due to service delivery or technical problems, which would reflect
an even higher ROI. These cost savings were a direct result of having a
well-trained multidimensional workforce.

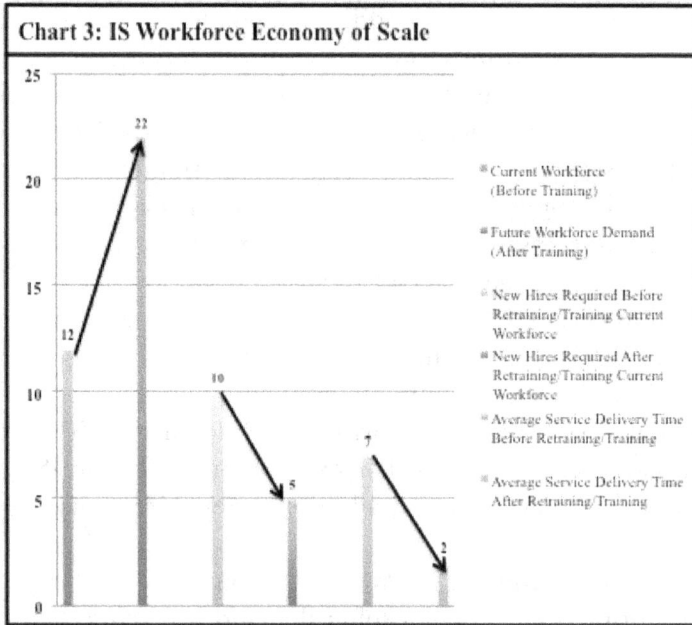

Chart 3: IS Workforce Economy of Scale

Training Cost Demand

As a result of this comprehensive study, the CIO department conducted
an inclusive research study to determine the funding requirements
needed to meet its training and developmental needs. The department's
resource manager met with numerous training organizations from
across the country to help determine the most cost-effective training
courses. Table 6 reflects an example of the IS workforce fiscal years 2014
and 2015 technical and soft-skill training and development demands of
$300,003. The study provided a comprehensive strategy for averting the
workforce shortage and offers a framework upon which an organization
can focus on prioritizing, improving, and bridging competency gaps.
Because the security life cycle of software applications is critical due to

cybersecurity threats, this study amplifies the immediate need for workforce training and development.

As technology continues to evolve, technical certifications will become even more critical for managing core functional areas such as information technology, information systems, cybersecurity, information assurance, and industrial control systems. In addition, the workforce competency gap analysis survey tool (WCGAST) allows the department to conform to the policies, instructions, and directives established by the organization and the federal government.

Table 6: Training and Development Demands *(EXAMPLE)*					
Course/Certification	Ave. Cost Per Course	1st Qtr FY14	1st Qtr FY15	# of Employees	Total Cost
Technical Skill Training Demands					
Citrix Application	$3,147	4	4	8	$25,176
Building Management Information System	$1,097	6	6	12	$13,164
Environmental Waste Billing System	$747.50	6	6	12	$8,970
Financial Management System	$1,097	6	6	12	$13,164
Invoice One-Pay System	$1,100	2	2	4	$4,400
Labor Management System	$2,000	3	3	6	$12,000
Graymare Logistics System	$2,500	2	2	4	$10,000
Standard Financial Procurement System	$1,500	6	6	12	$18,000
Structured Query Language	$1,800	2	2	4	$7,200
Microsoft PDA Applications	$2,210	4	4	8	$17,680
Oracle Application Express	$2,500	3	3	6	$15,000
Visual Basic Applications	$2,500	3	3	6	$15,000
IS service management, service level agreements (SLA)	$1,097	6	6	12	$13,164
Software Architecture	$747.50	6	6	12	$8,970
ITIL v3 (Service Management)	$1,712	6	6	12	$20,544
Lifecycle Management	$597	6	6	12	$7,164
Portfolio Management	$597	3	2	5	$2,985
Networks and Cybersecurity Threats	$1,795	6	6	12	$21,540
Project Management	$2,600	6	6	12	$31,200
Cloud, iCloud and/or Private Cloud Technology	$715	4	4	8	$5,720
Circuits Data Integration	$1,200	1	1	2	$2,400
Configuration Mgmt. System	$597	1	1	2	$1,194
Wide Area Workflow System	$1,500	1	1	2	$3,000
Knowledge Management	$1,300	3	3	6	$7,800
Estimated Total Cost		$143,010	$142,425		$285,435
Soft-Skill Training Demands					
Conflict Management	$319	6	6	12	$3,828
Situational Leadership	$570	6	6	12	$6,840
Customer Service Training	$325	6	6	12	$3,900
Estimated Total Cost		$7,284	$7,284		$14,568
Grand Total Required		$150,294	$149,709		**$300,003**

Summary

As organizations transition toward a competency-based workforce, C-suite executives and managers must become aware of the importance of ensuring their employees' competencies are updated and correctly aligned and mapped to support current and future business demands. It does not matter whether you plan to build your employees (promote internally) or buy them (hire externally); succession development planning should be a key pillar in your business strategy plan. Succession development planning galvanizes visionary thinking. It inspires the need for current and future planning, mitigates expected and unexpected job vacancies, and alleviates unanticipated overhead costs associated with employees departing. According to Matt Thompson, author of *How Much Does It Cost to Hire a New Employee*, for example, organizations could spend up to 150 percent of a manager's salary to prepare an employee for a management position. These costs are associated with training and developing new hires, salaries, benefits, recruitment, new workspace, technology equipment, geographical location expenses, and other related costs. To make matters worse, those departing will take with them a high degree of technical, managerial, and leadership competencies and experiences. For those remaining, this may subsequently lead to a decrease in their morale and an increase in work-related stress and absenteeism.

One of the first steps in implementing a *successful* succession development plan is to establish a workforce competency baseline. A competency baseline review can be accomplished via a comprehensive workforce competency gap analysis study. This helped determine the chief information office department employees' competency gaps and deficiencies. For this case study, thirty-five employees participated in the workforce competency gap analysis survey. Of the thirty-five employees, twelve worked in the IS division. The methodology included a three-phase approach. Phase 1 employed a multistep process to help determine experience levels (entry, intermediate, advanced, and expert). Phase 2 included validation of the survey statements in which fifteen employees retook the identical survey within seven business days to ensure survey statements' validity and reliability. Finally, phase 3 was composed of two parts: Part 1 required prioritizing training and development activities to mitigate competency gaps. Part 2 identified training and certification deficiencies. The study also captured the number of years employees worked in a particular job function. The information systems division data was used as an example. The results of workforce competency gap analysis survey results identified four major problems: (1) major deficiencies in employees' competencies (technical and soft skills); (2) shortfalls in employees' training and career development; (3) shortfalls in human capital to meet current and future workload demands; (4) gaps and deficiencies in employees' technical certifications. Moreover, the study indicated that 57 percent of the total workforce worked in the same job function for twenty to thirty-plus years. It also indicated this group of employees was nearing retirement age. The remaining 43 percent of the workforce had between one and nineteen years in a particular job function. Equally important, the data indicated 51 percent of the workforce acknowledged their competency level was at entry level, while 30 percent thought they possessed intermediate level skills. Less than 19 percent of the employees believed they were proficient at the advanced and expert levels. Overall, 81 percent of the employees identified their competencies at entry and intermediate levels in the IS functional area.

A comparative analysis (CA) review was conducted, which reflected both similarities and differences in each employee's individual competency levels. For instance, the data reflected results from the CIO department's five core functional areas (information systems (IS), information technology/telecommunications (IT/telecom), information assurance/cybersecurity (IA/CS), resource management (RM), and industrial control systems (ICS). As indicated in chart 4, the expected competency level for employees with fifteen or more years in a particular job function would range between advanced and expert level. My assumptions were wrong. The red line shows a downward correlation between experience-level percentage and the years in job function. Based on their experience level and years in the job function, it should show a reverse correlation. The CIO department's workforce aggregate ratings, for example, indicated 41 percent at entry level, 35 percent at intermediate level, and 24 percent at advanced or expert levels. In comparison, the IS division's workforce survey results indicated 41 percent at entry level, 31 percent at intermediate level, and 28 percent at advanced or expert levels. Nevertheless, the CIO department's overall workforce being viewed at the 76 percent (72 percent level for IS workforce), an aggregate of entry and intermediate levels, indicates a lack of training, retraining, cross-training, experience, knowledge, skills, and abilities to perform at the advanced and expert levels.

The IS workforce overall competency level rating of 2.2 did not meet the competency benchmark of 3.6 and reflected a -1.4 in competency deficiencies. In addition, the study indicated there were additional requirements for five new hires to support current and future work-load demands. The study also indicated that 94 percent of the IS division's employees did not have the required professional certifications. Moreover, employees' leadership competencies fell short, with only 61 percent of the employees' leadership competencies resonating at entry and intermediate levels and 39 percent being at or above the advanced level. Employees' formal education indicated the highest rating of 100 percent. All employees had at least a bachelor's degree, and 60 percent had master's degrees. In addition, with limited human capital, coupled with the loss of trained workers who were feeling inadequate about their capabilities, the IS division employees were woefully behind the curve in their technical and soft-skill competencies.

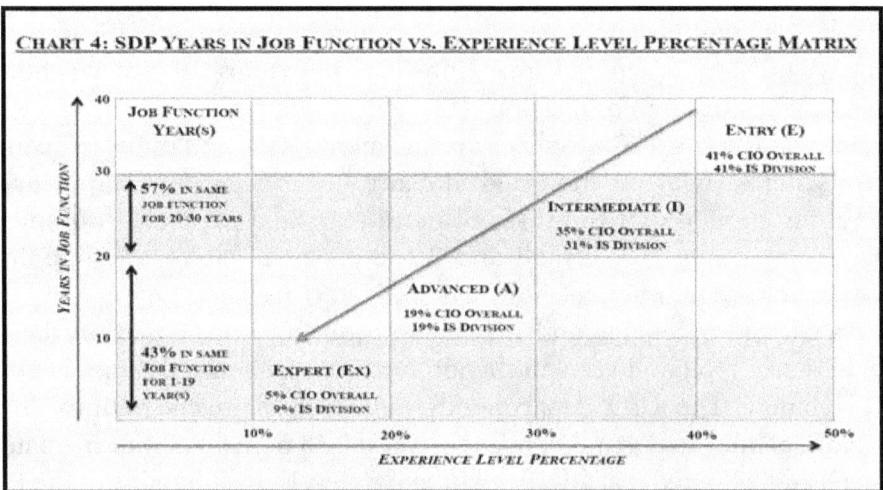

CHART 4: SDP YEARS IN JOB FUNCTION VS. EXPERIENCE LEVEL PERCENTAGE MATRIX

A workforce economy of scale (WEoS) was implemented to help determine the financial costs associated with converting a one-dimensional information-systems workforce into a multidimensional workforce via cross-pollination, retraining, training, education, and certification.

The WEoS was also used to determine whether or not there is a need to hire additional employees to meet the organization's current and future business demands. The reverse side of the WEoS was the workforce dis-economy of scale (WDS), in which maintaining the level of service and at the same time supporting newly established technical-service demands would exceed the savings gained from developing a multidimensional workforce. Business case analyses were therefore conducted to help determine cost-effective measures pertaining to employee development and hiring ten additional new hires to support the CIO department's current and future workload requirements. Initially, the IS Division's true workforce demand was ten additional new hires, totaling twenty-two. However, after investing in the IS division workforce training and retraining efforts, that human capital demand was reduced by 50 per-cent, from ten down to five. The training and career-development initia-tives reflected a reduction in service delivery time from seven hours to two hours.

Two critical steps in the succession development planning process were competency modeling and mapping (CMM). A CMM process helped identify key technical competencies needed to support current and future job functions. The CMM reinforced the CIO department's vision, mission, and goals. Competency-modeling (CM) techniques were used to align employees' knowledge, skills, aptitude, or attributes to the organization's overall human-capital strategy, goals, and objectives. The CM was used as a proactive strategy to help the CIO department overall become more effective and efficient. It was used as a workforce future-proofing tool to help managers determine whether or not their employ-ees have the required competencies to meet the department and the organization's strategic business demands and, at the same time, help managers identify employees' performance benchmarks, retraining, training, and developmental deficiencies for the future. Once compe-tency modeling and mapping (CMM) were completed, a competency requirement model (CRM) was established to reflect professional train-ing and career-developmental frameworks. The CRM was used for employee recruitment, selection, retention, training, development, per-formance and talent management, job profiling, succession planning, and rewards and recognition.

Finally, the case study concluded with a training and career-development cost benefit analysis (CBA). The CBA provided a systematic approach for estimating training and career-development weaknesses, strengths, and overall funding requirements. After meeting with numerous training organizations from across the country to help determine the most cost-effective training courses, the IS workforce fiscal years 2014 and 2015 technical and soft-skill training and career-development funding costs were approximately $300,003. The study provided a comprehensive strategy for averting the workforce shortage and offered a framework upon which an organization can focus on prioritizing, improving, and bridging competency gaps. Because the security life cycle of software applications is critical due to cybersecurity threats, this study amplifies the immediate need for additional cybersecurity training and development.

Moreover, as technology continues to evolve, technical certifications will become even more critical for managing core functional areas such as information technology, information systems, cybersecurity, information assurance, industrial control systems, and smart grid technology. In addition, the workforce competency gap analysis survey tool (WCGAST) allows the department to conform to the policies, instructions, and directives established by the organization and the federal government. The case study amplified an immediate need for workforce training, retraining, cross-training, and career development in the areas of both soft and technical skills. The study should serve as a guide for maximizing the CIO department's ability to ensure it has a pool of qualified candidates to fill both current and future job vacancies and at the same time support emerging technology and customer demands. As technology continues to evolve, technical certifications and education will become even more critical for managing core functional areas in the information systems (IS) profession. Managers must therefore work in concert with their employees to establish training matrices to help determine training course and certification costs. Smart autonomy is to include employees at all levels (C-suite executives, managers, and employees) of the organization to develop a succession development plan.

APPENDIX A
SUCCESSION DEVELOPMENT PLANNING ASSESSMENT

This succession development planning assessment should take about twenty-five minutes. Please use the following directions to complete the assessment. Be sure to read each statement carefully and indicate the extent to which you agree or disagree with each of the following statements by using the scale below. Once completed, score and interpret the results using the instructions appearing at the end of the assessment questionnaire. When scoring your assessment, use the following point system:

- Strongly Disagree = 1 point
- Disagree = 2 points
- Unsure = 3 points
- Agree = 4 points
- Strongly Agree = 5 points

In your opinion, what is your perception as to why succession development planning is important to your organization? If your aggregate score is between 144 and 180, top executives are great supporters of the organization's succession development planning efforts, and the organization remains competitive in the twenty-first century. If your aggregate score is between 109 and 143, your organization is on the right course, and succession development planning is being handled effectively. If your score is between 73 and 108, you should continue to dedicate time to integrate innovative succession development planning ideas and practices. In other words, it really deserves more attention. If your aggregate score is between 36 and 72, your organization succession development planning efforts require much improvement and deserve immediate attention. Executives must establish a sense of urgency and implement a succession-planning program. This score indicates it is highly unlikely successors for critical positions have been identified and developed.

Succession Development Planning Assessment					
	Statement	Strongly Disagree	Disagree	Unsure	Agree	Strongly Agree
1.	Can be viewed by top executives as a phenomenon that occurs only at the top of the organization					
2.	Will establish accountability for top executive participations and support					
3.	Can be used as an incentive program for developing employees at all levels					
4.	Should be used for ensuring cadres of qualified employees are available to fill both critical and noncritical job vacancies					
5.	Sensitizes executives to an obligation to identify and prepare future successors					
6.	Helps to mitigate high workforce turnover					
7.	Prompts the organization to conduct workforce competency assessments					
8.	Stimulates high morale in the organization					
9.	Encourages cross-departmental sharing of both information and employees					
10.	Helps support equal employment opportunity					
11.	Helps improve communication across a multigenerational workforce					
12.	Assists in a crisis mode when unexpected key vacancies arise					
13.	Brings awareness of the costs for training and developing new hires					
14.	Is linked to the organization's human-capital strategic plan					
15.	During a crisis, can ensure it has the right person in the right job at the right time					
16.	Has encouraged a clear policy favoring job promotion from within					
17.	Is used to help establish workforce training and developmental policies					
18.	Ensures a cadre of top management talent is available to fill top executive ranks from within					
19.	Helps to ensure a succession development planning committee is established					
20.	Ensures a cadre of middle-management talent is available to fill top-management ranks from within					
21.	Helps to increase employee loyalty					
22.	Reinforces top executive decision to reward managers for promoting high-potential employees					
23.	Is viewed by top executives as an HRO function					
24.	Is viewed by top executives as too much paperwork and time					
25.	Ensures a cadre of employee talent is available to fill middle management ranks from within					
26.	Is used to deal with organizational downsizing					
27.	Has encouraged the organization to implement a coaching program for executives, managers, and employees					
28.	Ensures a cadre of internal talent is available to fill critical jobs from within					
29.	Can help managers and top executives avoid the pitfall of mirroring each other in values, appearance, and behavior					
30.	Encourages the organization to establish a multidimensional workforce that is diversified in various competencies to perform different job functions					
31.	Prompts the organization to establish a mentoring program					
32.	Has prompted the organization to invest in employee training					
33.	Encourages top executives to possess a balanced workforce of college-educated and certificated (technical) workers					
34.	Encourages and acknowledges workforce diversity and inclusion					
35.	Is guided by a climate assessment survey that is distributed to the workforce every two years					
36.	Prompt top executives to assess the aging (maturing) of their workforce					
	TOTAL SCORES					
	YOUR AGGREGATE SCORE					

If your score is
Between 36–72

Your organization is in danger; the high costs of losing, recruiting, retaining, and training employees will seriously damage your bottom line, if they have not already.

Between 73–108

You are typical of most organizations. Though you are doing some good things, you must make major improvements to your work environment if you are going to survive and thrive in today's competitive market.

Between 109–143

You're on the right track! Your turnover is probably lower than the industry average; you are doing a good job, but there is room for improvement.

Between 144–180

Congratulations! Not only is turnover lower than the average for your industry, but the work atmosphere you have created is so attractive to employees that recruiting nearly takes care of itself. Great job!

APPENDIX B
WORKFORCE ENGAGEMENT SURVEY

Employee engagement is critical to an organization's business success. The following questionnaire asks for your response to a series of statements. There are twelve sections, supported by three statements. Be sure to read each statement carefully and indicate the extent to which you disagree or agree with each of the following statements by using the scale below. Once completed, score and calculate the results using the instructions appearing at the end of the assessment questionnaire. When scoring your assessment, use the following point system.

- Strongly Disagree = 1 point
- Disagree = 2 points
- Unsure = 3 points
- Agree = 4 points
- Strongly Agree = 5 points

In your opinion, what is your perception of employee engagement culture in your organization? If your aggregate score is between 144 and 180, top executives are great supporters of their employees and, in turn, the organization remains competitive in the twenty-first century. If your aggregate score is between 109 and 143, your organization is on the right course and workforce engagement is being handled effectively. If your score is between 73 and 108, you should continue to dedicate time to ensure workforce engagement ideas and tools are enforced. In other words, it really deserves more attention. Finally, if your aggregate score is between 36 and 72, your organization's workforce engagement practices are ineffective and require immediate attention. This score indicates employees may be seeking employment with a competitor.

Workforce Engagement Survey Statements	Strongly Disagree	Disagree	Unsure	Agree	Strongly Agree
1. Workplace Satisfaction					
My job is stimulating and energizing.					
I am happy working in this organization.					
If I received a 10 percent raise from another company, I would accept it.					
2. Feeling Valued and Appreciated					
I feel valued and appreciated in this organization.					
Leaders take employees' feedback seriously.					
Employees are allowed to make decisions affecting their work.					
3. Satisfaction with Coworkers					
Employees have a personal connection with their peers.					
Employees treat each other with respect.					
Employees trust each other in this organization.					
4. Satisfaction with Supervisors					
My supervisor's performance is good.					
My supervisor supports the use of social-networking tools.					
My supervisor is trustworthy.					
5. Career Growth/Promotion Opportunities					
I have opportunities for professional growth in the organization.					
The employee performance review process and feedback are good.					
I have the tools and resources to do my job well.					
6. Organizational Pride					
I would recommend my organization's products and services to friends.					
This organization services its customers well.					
I would recommend this organization as great place to work.					
7. Work/Life Balance					
Work/life balance is good in this organization.					
Working remotely is encouraged in this organization.					
This organization supports flexible work schedules.					
8. Workforce Retention					
I feel I can reach my full potential here.					
I can see myself working here for the next two years.					
This organization seldom conducts a ninety-day interview with its new hires.					
9. Organizational Culture					
Employees can recite the organization's values and goals.					
There is modest bureaucracy and red tape here.					
The work atmosphere could be described as relaxed and informal.					
10. Support and Appreciate Employee Differences					
Leadership promotes and participates in diversity events.					
Leadership supports and appreciates employee differences.					
Leadership believes a diverse workforce positively impacts productivity.					
11. Training & Career Development					
I am satisfied with the investment the organization is making in my training and development.					
My organization has a training and development policy applicable to all employees.					
Supervisors give employees the chance to use their training on the job.					
12. WORK COMPENSATION					
I am satisfied with the compensation as compared to the local market.					
Recognition and rewards are given when employees go above and beyond their regular job assignments.					
The organization's benefits are fair and competitive.					
Total Scores					
Aggregate Score					

If your score is
Between 36–72

Your organization is in danger; the high costs of losing, recruiting, retaining, and training employees will seriously damage your bottom line, if they have not already.

Between 73–108

You are typical of most organizations. Though you are doing some good things, you must make major improvements to your work environment if you are going to survive and thrive in today's competitive market.

Between 109–143

Your turnover is probably lower than the industry average; you are doing a good job, but there is room for improvement.

Between 144–180

Congratulations! Not only is turnover lower than the average for your industry, but the work atmosphere you have created is so attractive to employees that recruiting nearly takes care of itself. Great job!

APPENDIX C
MIND-SET TRANSFORMATION SURVEY

Quite often C-suite executives fail to understand the emotional mind-set managers and employees may experience while at work, which may range from feeling forced to participate in workforce activities to feeling passionate about participating in them. Having low energy levels and passion could lead to low work productivity, performance, and morale. How much does each statement apply to your mind-set? How much does each statement apply to your leaders' mind-set? Read each statement carefully before making the best selection. From the guide below, score each statement by circling the appropriate number that best support your mind-set. Please follow the same process when measuring your leaders' mind-set. Each statement can only receive one score. For this survey the term "leaders" is associated with all levels of management from C-suite executives to supervisory positions. The term "employees" is associated with nonsupervisory positions.

←			→
1	**2**	**3**	**4**
Need to	**Got to**	**Have to**	**Want to**
(Feel Forced)	*(Feel Tolerated)*	*(Feel Obligated)*	*(Feel Passionate)*

First, compare your aggregate score with the below individual scores to determine your mind-set about leaders in your organization. Now, compare your leaders' score with the below scores to determine their mind-set in your organization. Once completed, develop a plan of action to help improve your mind-set.

1 = Need to ~ 2 = Got to ~ 3 = Have to ~ 4 = Want to	Need to 1 (pt)	Got to 2 (pts)	Have to 3 (pts)	Want to 4 (pts)
MEASURE YOURSELF				
1 I ____ be able to stand apart from my thoughts and feelings and examine them.	1	2	3	4
2 I ____ increase my emotional energy level in order to deliver high-quality customer service.	1	2	3	4
3 I ____ value working toward goals, even if it strains personal relationships with my coworkers.	1	2	3	4
4 I ____ be open and candid in dealings with team members.	1	2	3	4
5 I ____ better understand how to describe my feelings.	1	2	3	4
6 I ____ meet other employees and get to know what makes them tick.	1	2	3	4
7 I ____ recognize when I am stressed.	1	2	3	4
8 I ____ learn how to see things from my leaders' viewpoint.	1	2	3	4
9 I ____ learn how to reframe bad situations much more quickly.	1	2	3	4
10 I ____ learn how to consciously alter my frame of mind or mood during challenging times.	1	2	3	4
11 I ____ consider the impact of my decisions on my coworkers.	1	2	3	4
12 I ____ build solid relationships with my coworkers.	1	2	3	4
13 I ____ know what it will take for me to be successful in my organization.	1	2	3	4
SCORE				
MEASURE YOUR LEADER				
1 In order for this organization to be successful in the future, leaders ____ think more innovatively.	1	2	3	4
2 Leaders ____ demonstrate patience when it comes to discussing employees' performance appraisals.	1	2	3	4
3 Leaders ____ be able to stand apart from their thoughts and feelings and examine them.	1	2	3	4
4 Leaders ____ recognize when they are stressed.	1	2	3	4
5 Leaders ____ see things from the employees' viewpoint.	1	2	3	4
6 Leaders ____ consciously alter their frame of mind or mood during challenging times.	1	2	3	4
7 Leaders ____ consider the impact of their decisions on their employees.	1	2	3	4
8 Leaders ____ value and use employees' different competencies.	1	2	3	4
9 Leaders ____ learn how to be more empathetic to their employees.	1	2	3	4
10 Leaders ____ learn how to deal with the stresses of adjusting to a diversified and inclusive workforce.	1	2	3	4
11 Leaders ____ develop action plans when interacting with employees from a different culture.	1	2	3	4
12 Leaders ____ understand that past methods for problem solving are not relevant for solving today's work-related problems.	1	2	3	4
13 Leaders ____ communicate to their employees that they appreciate their knowledge, skills, and abilities.	1	2	3	4
SCORE				
AGGREGATE SCORE				

Score	Status	Action
1–13	Feel Forced	(*Nt*) Requires urgent attention and development.
14–26	Feel Tolerated (*Gt*)	Requires attention and development.
27–39	Feel Obligated (*Ht*)	Consider strengthening.
40–52	Feel Passionate (*Wt*)	Use as leverage to develop yourself or others.

Phase 1: Need to *(Nt)*. When a person's mind-set is wandering in the Need to (*Nt*) area, he or she is grounded in negative emotional energy or catabolic energy and may feel forced to participate in teamwork activities such as succession planning. This is identified as a fixed mind-set. This is considered "*lose-lose-lose*" behavior, meaning the organization loses, the customer loses, and the employee loses.

Phase 2: Got to *(Gt)*. Here the person may feel he or she must tolerate being part of the team activities such as succession planning and may display low emotional energy. He or she may feel defiance in not participating. As a result, the organization wins, the customer loses, and the employee loses [*win-lose-lose*].

Phase 3: Have to *(Ht)*. Phase 3 depicts people as feeling obligated to accept new ideas or change or to participate in workforce activities. They are willing to cooperate but not fully supportive of teamwork activities such as succession development planning. They show higher level of emotional energy as compared to the aforementioned phases. They may also feel they have to participate or risk not being seen as a team player. In this phase, the organization wins, the customer wins, but the employee loses [*win-win-lose*].

Phase 4: Want to *(Wt)*. The HRO can serve as a major advocate by facilitating focus-group sessions to help senior leaders transition into the Want-to (*Wt*) phase. It is a growth mind-set. This is where employees of all hierarchal levels of the organization generate positive energy. They become passionate about succession development planning. They want to be a team player. In this phase, the organization wins, the customer wins, and the employee wins [*win-win-win*].

NOTES

Chapter One: Historical Perspective on Succession Development Planning

1. Gene F. Brady and Donald L. Helmich, *Executive Succession: Toward Excellence in Corporate Leadership* (Englewood Cliffs, NJ: Prentice-Hall, 1984).

2. Shawn Tully, "Step One: Save a 204-Year-Old Financial Icon, Step Two: Bow Out Gracefully," *University of San Diego Magazine* Fall (2014): 20.

3. Robert K. Greenleaf, "The Servant as Leader," accessed July 9, 2015, www.benning.army.mil/infantry/199th/ocs/content/pdf/The%20 Servant%20Leader.pdf.

4. Roger Collins, *Palgrave History of Europe: Early Medieval Europe 300–1000*, 3rd ed. (New York: Palgrave MacMillan, 2010).

5. Katherine Fischer Drew, *The Laws of the Salian Franks* (Philadelphia: University of Pennsylvania Press, 1991).

6. *British Dictionary*, s.v. "succession," accessed March 2, 2015, http:// www.dictionary.com/browse/succession.

7. Craig Taylor, ed., *Debating the Hundred Years' War: Pour ce que Plusieurs (La Loy Salique) and a Declaration of the Trew and Dewe Title of Henrie VIII*, Vol. 29, 5th series. (Cambridge: Press Syndicate of the University of Cambridge, 2006).

8. National Constitution Center, *The Constitution of the United States*, accessed August 14, 2016, https://constitutioncenter.org/media/ files/constitution.pdf.

9. James Falkner, *The War of the Spanish Succession, 1701–1714* (South Yorkshire: Pen and Sword Military, 2016).

10. Taylor, *Debating the Hundred Year's War*, 32–49.

Chapter Two: Slaves and Immigrants Succession in North America

1. Barry Lewis, Robert Jurmain, and Lynn Kilgore, *Understanding Humans: Introduction to Physical Anthropology and Archaeology*, 10th ed. (Belmont: Wadsworth Cengage Learning, 2010).

2. Winthrop D. Jordan and Leon F. Litwack, *The United States: Conquering a Continent*, Vol. 1, 6th ed. (Englewood Cliffs, NJ: Prentice Hall, 1987).

3. Bernard Grun, *The Timetables of History: A Horizontal Linkage of People and Events* (New York: Simon and Schuster, 1991).

4. Toby Lester, *The Fourth Part of the World: An Astonishing Epic of Global Discovery, Imperial Ambition, and the Birth of America* (New York: Free Press, 2009).

5. Gerry Spence, *Give Me Liberty!: Freeing Ourselves in the Twenty-First Century* (New York: St. Martin's Press, 1998).

6. Walter Johnson, *River of Dark Dreams: Slavery and Empire in the Cotton Kingdom* (Cambridge, MA: Belknap Press of Harvard University, 2013).

7. Rebecca Brooks Gruver, *An American History. Vol. 1: to 1877*, 3rd ed. (Menlo Park, CA: Addison-Wesley Publishing Company, 1981).

8. Grun, *The Timetables of History*, 191.

9. John Hope Franklin and Alfred A. Moss, Jr., *From Slavery to Freedom: A History of African Americans*, 7th ed. (New York: McGraw-Hill, 1994).

10. Leon L. Bram and Norma H. Dickey, eds., *Funk and Wagnalls. New Encyclopedia, Vol. 1, A to American Elk* (Seattle, WA: Funk & Wagnalls Corporation, 1971).

11. Robin D. G. Kelly and Earl Lewis, *To Make Our World Anew: The History of African Americans* (New York: Oxford University Press, 2000).

12. Doris Kearns Goodwin, *Team of Rivals: The Political Genius of Abraham Lincoln* (New York: Simon & Schuster, 2005).

13. Julian E. Zelizer, *The American Congress: The Building of Democracy* (New York: Houghton Mifflin Company, 2004).

14. Ibid.

15. Adele Logan Alexander, *Homelands and Waterways: The American Journey of the Bond Family, 1846–1926* (New York: Pantheon Books, 1999).

16. *Wikipedia*, s.v. "Irish immigrants to the United States," accessed January 2, 2017, en.wikipedia.org/wiki/Irish_Americans.

17. John Mack Faragher, Daniel Czitrom, Mari Jo Buhle, and Susan H. Armitage, *Out of Many: A History of the American People*, 5th ed. (Englewood Cliffs, NJ: Prentice Hall, 2006).

18. Ibid.

19. Lawrence M. Friedman, *A History of American Law*, 3rd ed. (New York: Simon & Schuster, 2005).

20. Faragher et al., *Out of Many*, 504.

21. "United States Immigration since 1965," *The Immigration and Naturalization Act of 1965*, accessed October 12, 2016, www.history.com/topics/us-immigration-since-1965.

22. Laurie Mercier, "Japanese Americans in the Columbia River Basin: Historical Overview," accessed February 12, 2016, http://archive.vancouver.wsu.edu/crbeha/ja/ja.htm.

23. David G. Gutierrez, "American Latino Theme Study: The Making of America," accessed April 7, 2016, www.nps.gov/heritageinitiatives/latino/latinothemestudy/immigration.htm.

24. Renee Stepler and Anna Brown, "Statistical Portrait of Hispanics in the United States," Pew Research Center, created April 19, 2016, accessed July 3, 2016, www.pewhispanic.org/2016/04/19/statistical-portrait-of-hispanics-in-the-united-states-key-charts/.

25. Ron Haskins, "Economic Mobility of Immigrants in the United States," created June 7, 2016, accessed February 12, 2017, https://www.brookings.edu/wp-content/uploads/2016/06/07useconomics_haskins.pdf.

26. Camille L. Ryan and Kurt Bauman, "Educational Attainment in the United States: 2015," United States Census Bureau, created March 2016, accessed June 23, 2016, https://www.census.gov/content/dam/Census/library/publications/2016/demo/p20-578.pdf.

DOUGLAS E. FENNER, ED.D., CPC, ELI-MP, EQP

Chapter Three: The Coming of the Fourth Industrial Revolution

1. Frederick W. Taylor, *Scientific Management* (New York: Harper and Brothers, 1947).

2. Irwin Gray, *General and Industrial Management* (New York: IEEE Engineering Management Society, 1984).

3. Walter R. Mahler and William F. Wrightnour, *Executive Continuity: How to Build and Retain an Effective Management Team* (Chicago: Dow Jones-Irwin, 1973).

4. Cynthia D. McCauley, Russ Moxley, and Ellen Van Velsor, eds., *The Center for Creative Leadership: Handbook of Leadership Development* (San Francisco: Jossey-Bass Publishers, 1998).

5. Robert A. Levit and Christina Gikakis, eds., *Shared Wisdom: Best Practice in Development & Succession Planning* (New York: Princeton Academic Press, 1994), 13.

6. Jeremy Rifkin, *The Third Industrial Revolution: How Lateral Power Is Transforming Energy, the Economy, and the World* (New York: Palgrave Macmillan, 2001).

7. Rebecca Luhn Wolfe, *Systematic Succession Planning: Building Leadership from Within* (Menlo Park, CA: Crisp Publications, 1996).

8. William J. Rothwell, *Effective Succession Planning, Ensuring Leadership Continuity and Building Talent from Within*, 2nd ed. (New York: American Management Association, 2001).

9. Klaus Schwab, "The Fourth Industrial Revolution: What It Means, How to Respond," created January 4, 2016, accessed May 27, 2017,

https://www.weforum.org/agenda/2016/01/the-fourth-industrial-revolution-what-it-means-and-how-to-respond.

10. Jeffrey Sparshott, "The US Occupations at Great Risk of a Labor Shortage," created April 19, 2016, accessed October 23, 2016, http://blogs.wsj.com/elaborconomics/2016/04/19/the-u-s-occupations-at-greatest-risk-of-a-labor-shortage.

11. Hilda L. Solis, "Employment Outlook: 2010–2020," Bureau of Labor Statistics, *Monthly Labor Review*, created January 2012, Vol. 135, Number 1, accessed January 2, 2017, https://www.bls.gov/opub/mlr/201201.pdf.

12. Tableau Corporation, "The Top Ten Big Data Trends for 2017," accessed March 3, 2017, https://www.tableau.com/sites/default/files/media/Whitepaper/whitepaper_top_10_big_data_trends_2017.pdf.

13. Harold L. Sirkin, Michael Zinser, and Douglas Hohner, "Made in America, Again: Why Manufacturing Will Return to the US," The Boston Consulting Group, created August 2011, accessed December 12, 2016, https://www.bcg.com/documents/file84471.pdf.

14. Allan Schweyer, "Generations in the Workforce & Marketplace: Preferences in Rewards, Recognition & Incentives," created July 21, 2015, accessed March 3, 2017, http://theirf.org/research/generations-in-the-workforce-marketplacepreferences-in-rewards-recognition-incentives/1427/.

15. Bruce Tulgan, "The Great Generation Shift: The Emerging Post-Boomer Workforce," created November 2013, accessed April 4, 2017, http://www.rainmakerthinking.com/assets/uploads/2013/10/Gen-Z-Whitepaper.pdf.

16. Don Tapscott, *Grown Up Digital: How the Net Generation Is Changing Your World* (New York: McGraw Hill, 2009).

17. Susan Gregory Thomas, "The Divorce Generation," *Wall Street Journal,* created July 9, 2011, accessed April 2, 2016, https://www.wsj.com/articles/SB10001424052702303544604576430341393583056.

18. Christina Merhar, "Employee Retention—The Real Cost of Losing an Employee," created February 4, 2016, accessed March 12, 2017, https://www.zanebenefits.com/blog/bid/312123/employee-retention-the-real-cost-of-losing-an-employee.

19. Amy Adkins, "Millennials: The Job-Hopping Generation," created May 12, 2016, accessed January 12, 2017, www.gallup.com/business-journal/191459/millennials-job-hopping-generation.aspx.

20. Amy Adkins, "Employee Engagement in US Stagnant in 2015," created January 13, 2016, accessed July 14, 2016, www.gallup.com/poll/188144/employee-engagement-stagnant-2015.aspx.

21. Karie Willyerd and Barbara Mistick, *Stretch: How to Future-Proof Yourself for Tomorrow's Workplace* (Hoboken, NJ: John Wiley & Sons, 2016).

22. Joshua Freedom, *At the Heart of Leadership: How to Get Results with Emotional Intelligence* (Freedom, CA: SixSeconds Emotional Intelligence Press, 2012).

23. Carol P. Harvey and M. June Allard, *Understanding and Managing Diversity: Readings, Cases, and Exercises*, 5th ed. (Upper Saddle River, NJ: Prentice Hall, 2012).

24. Eric Klein and John B. Izzo, *Awakening Corporate Soul: Four Paths to Unleash the Power of People at Work*, 2nd ed. (British Columbia: Fair Winds Press, 1999).

25. Ibid.

26. Thomas R. Roosevelt Jr., *Building on the Promise of Diversity: How We Can Move to the Next Level in Our Workplaces, Our Communities, and Our Society* (New York: American Management Association, 2006).

27. Anna Davies, Devin Fidler, and Marina Gorbi, "Future Work Skills 2020," University of Phoenix Research Institute, created 2011, accessed March 11, 2015, http://www.iftf.org/uploads/media/ SR-1382A_UPRI_future_work_skills_sm.pdf/.

28. Robert E. Scott, "Manufacturing Job Loss: Trade, Not Productivity, Is the Culprit," Economic Policy Institute, created August 11, 2015, accessed April 28, 2017, www.epi.org/publication/manufacturing-job-loss-trade-not-productivity-is-the-culprit.

29. Tom Worstall, "The US Lost 7 Million Manufacturing Jobs—and Added 33 Million Higher-Paying Service Jobs," *Forbes*, created October 19, 2016, accessed March 2, 2017, https://www.forbes.com/sites/tim-worstall/2016/10/19/the-us-lost-7-million-manufacturing-jobs-and-added-33-million-higher-paying-service-jobs/#10d480734a20.

30. Patrick Gillespie, "US Manufacturing Job Openings at 2007 Levels," created December 21, 2016, accessed March 3, 2017, http://money.cnn.com/2016/12/21/news/economy/job-openings-manufacturing-trump/.

31. David Langdon and Rebecca Lehrman, "The Benefits of Manufacturing Jobs," Created May 9, 2012, accessed May 5, 2015, www.esa.doc.gov/sites/default/files/1thebenefitsofmanufacturingj obsfinal5912.pdf.

32. Michael Sauter and Samuel B. Stebbins, "Manufacturers Bringing the Most Jobs Back to America," *USA Today*, created April 19, 2016, accessed February 3, 2017, http://www.usatoday.com/story/money/ business/2016/04/23/24-7-wallst-economy-manufacturers-jobs-out-sourcing/83406518/.

Chapter Four: The Importance of Succession Development Planning

1. Richard Fry, "Millennials Overtake Baby Boomers as America's Largest Generation," created April 25, 2016, accessed November 11, 2016, http://www.pewresearch.org/fact-tank/2016/04/25/millennials-overtake-baby-boomers/.

2. Roman Friedrich, Michael Peterson, Alex Koster, and Sebastian Blum, "The Rise of Generation C: Implications for the World of 2020," Strategy&, PWC, Booz & Company, created 2010, accessed February 3, 2017, www.strategyand.pwc.com/media/file/Startegyand_Rise-of-generation-C.pdf.pdf.

3. Alexa Mantell and Barbara Brynko, "Dealing with Hyperconnectivity." *Information Today Magazine*, created June 2012, accessed April 14, 2017, https://www.questia.com/.../dealing-with-hyperconnectivity.

4. Douglas Coupland, *Generation X: Tales for an Accelerated Culture*, 1st ed. (New York: St. Martin's Press, 1991).

5. Marlene A. Lee and Mark Mather, "US Labor Force Trends," Population Reference Bureau, Population Bulletin, created June 2008, accessed March 1, 2014, www.prb.org/pdf08/63.2uslabor.pdf.

6. Intuit 2020 Report, "Twenty Trends That Will Shape the Next Decade," created October 2010, accessed March 3, 2017, http-download.Intuit.com/http.intuit/CMO/intuit/futureofsmallbusiness/intuit_2020_report.pdf.

7. Congressional Research Service, "What Does the Gig Economy Mean for Workers?," created February 5, 2016, accessed March 30, 2017, https://www.fas.org/sgp/crs/misc/R44365.pdf.

8. Camille L. Ryan and Kurt Bauman, "Educational Attainment in the United States: 2015 Current Population Reports," created March

2016, accessed April 5, 2017, http://www.census.gov/content/dam/Census/library/publications/2016/demo/p20-578.pdf.

9. Lawrence F. Katz and Alan B. Krueger, "The Rise and Nature of Alternative Work Arrangement in the United States, 1995–2015," created March 29, 2016, accessed January 2, 2017, www.kruger.princeton.edu/sites/default/files/akrueger/files/katz_krueger_cws_-_march_29_20165.pdf.

10. John Egan, "The Top 14 Self-Employment Hubs in America," created November 23, 2016, accessed January 12, 2017, https://www.lawnstarter.com/blog/city-rankings/top-metros-for-self-employment/.

11. Rosabeth Moss Kanter, *Men and Women of the Corporation* (New York: BasicBooks, 1977).

12. William J. Rothwell, *Effective Succession Planning, Ensuring Leadership Continuity and Building Talent from Within,* 2nd ed. (New York: American Management Association, 2011).

13. Bureau of Labor Statistics. "Monthly Labor Review Industry Employment and Output Projections to 2024," created December 12, 2015, accessed February 3, 2017, www.bls.gov/opub/mlr/2015/article/pdf/industry-employment-and-output-projectinos-to-2024.pdf.

14. Antonia Cusumano, "The Connected Workforce Is Talking SMAC. Are You Ready?," created March 2015, accessed March 27, 2017, https://www.pwc.com/us/en/people.../connected-workforce.pdf.

15. Thiederman, Sondra, *The Diversity and Inclusion Handbook* (Bedford: Walk the Talk, 2012).

16. Robert Goldenkoff, "Federal Workforce: Recent Trends in Federal Civilian Employment and Compensation," created January 2014, accessed April 2, 2017, www.gao.gov/assets/670/660449.pdf.

17. Susannah Zak Figura, *"Leadership Void,"* *Government Executive Magazine*, created September 1, 1999, accessed June 2, 2016, www.govexec.com/magazine/1999/09/leadership-void/6106/.

18. William J. Hussar, "Projection of Education Statistics to 2020, 39th edition," created September 2011, accessed October 3, 2015, https://nces.ed.gov/pubs2011/2011026.pdf.

19. Scott Bronstein and Drew Griffin, "A Fatal Wait: Veterans Languish and Die on a VA Hospital's Secret List," CNN, AC 360°, created April 23, 2014, accessed April 3, 2015, www.cnn.com/2014/04/23/health/veterans-dying-health-care-delays/index.html.

20. Partnership for Public Service, Agency Report, Department of Veterans Affairs, "2013 Best Places to Work in the Federal Government," created 2016, accessed April 21, 2017, http://www.bestplacetowork.org/BPTW/rankings/detail/VA00.

21. Robert A. Pretzel, "Interim Workforce and Succession Strategic Plan, 2014," accessed March 5, 2017, http://vaww.succession.va.gov/Workforce_Planning/default.aspx.

22. US Department of Veterans Affairs, "Surface Transportation and Veterans Health Care Choice Improvement Act of 2015," created October 30, 2015, accessed February 5, 2017, www.va.gov/opa/publications/VA_Community_Care-Report_11_03_2015.pdf.

23. Eric Klein and John B. Izzo, *Awakening Corporate Soul: Four Paths to Unleash the Power of People at Work*, 2nd ed. (British Columbia: Fair Winds Press, 1999).

24. Douglas E. Fenner, "Linking Succession Planning to Employee Training: A Study of Federal Employees," EdD diss., University of San Diego, 2005.

25. Office of Personnel Management, "Supervisors in the Federal Government: A Wake-Up Call," accessed February 2, 2017, https://www.opm.gov/policy-data-oversight/performance-management/performance-management-cycle/monitoring/supervisorsin-the-federal-government/.

26. Rothwell, *Effective Succession Planning*.

27. Ibid., 70.

28. Walter R. Mahler and Stephen J. Drotter, *The Succession Planning Handbook for the Chief Executive* (Midland Park, NJ: Mahler Publishing Company, 1986).

29. Rothwell, *Effective Succession Planning*, 99.

30. Robert Fulmer and Marshall Goldsmith, *The Leadership Investment: How the World's Best Organizations Gain Strategic Advantage through Leadership Development* (New York: AMACOM, 2001).

31. Josh Bersin, Dimple, Bill Pelster, and Jeff Schwartz, "Global Human Capital Trends 2015: Leading in the New World of Work," Deloitte University Press, created 2015, accessed August 3, 2016, https://www2.deloitte.com/content/dam/deloitte/es/documents/human-capital/deloitte_es_human_capital_humancapitaltrends2015.pdf.

**Chapter Five: Diversity and Inclusion in the Fourth
Industrial Revolution**

1. Equal Employment Opportunity Commission, "Charge Statistics FY 1997 Through FY 2016," accessed October 5, 2016, www.eeoc.gov/eeoc/statistics/enforcement/charges.cfm.

2. Taylor Cox Jr., *Creating the Multicultural Organization: A Strategy for Capturing the Power of Diversity* (San Francisco: Jossey-Bass, 2001).

3. Sandy Sparks, "What Is Unconscious Bias: Considerations and Top Tips," Created June 2, 2014, accessed April 7, 2017, https://www2.warwick.ac.uk/services/ldc/researchers/opportunities/development_support/e_and_d/unconscious_bias/unconscious_bias_-2_june.pdf.

4. Marlene A. Lee and Mark Mather, "US Labor Force Trends, Population Bulletin," created June 2008, accessed September 9, 2016, www.prb.org/pdf08/63.2uslabor.pdf.

5. Conner Forrest, "Diversity Stats: Ten Tech Companies That Have Come Clean," created August 28, 2014, accessed April 2, 2016, http://www.techrepublic.com/article/diversity-stats-10-tech-companies-that-have-come-clean/.

6. Aileen Lee, "Welcome to the Unicorn Club, 2015: Learning from Billion-Dollar Companies," created July 18, 2015, accessed December 12, 2016, https://techcrunch.com/2015/07/18/welcome-to-the-unicorn-club-2015-learning-from-billion-dollar-companies/.

7. Cox, *Creating the Multicultural Organization*, 2.

8. Economic Cycle Research Institute, "Women's Labor Force Participation Down, Capping Jobs & Economic Growth," created February 1, 2017, accessed April 5, 2017, https://www.businesscycle.com/ecri-news-events/news-details/economic-cycle-research-ecri-

women-s-labor-force-participation-down-capping-jobs-economic-growth.

9. United States Department of Labor, Bureau of Labor Statistics, "Women in the Labor Force: A Databook," created April 2017, accessed August 4, 2017, https://www.bls.gov/opub/reports/womens-databook/2016/home.htm

10. Cynthia McCauley, Russ Moxley, and Ellen Van Velsor, *The Center for Creative Leadership: Handbook of Leadership Development* (San Francisco: Jossey-Bass Publishers, 1998).

11. James Kouzes and Barry Posner, *The Leadership Challenge: How to Keep Getting Extraordinary Things Done in Organizations* (San Francisco: Jossey-Bass Publishers, 1995).

12. Frances Hesselbein, Marshall Goldsmith, and Richard Beckhard, *The Drucker Foundation: The Leaders of the Future: New Visions, Strategies, and Practices for the Next Era* (San Francisco: Jossey-Bass Publishers, 1996).

13. Karl Albrecht, *Social Intelligence: The New Science of Success Beyond IQ, Beyond EI, Applying Multiple Intelligence Theory to Human Interaction* (San Francisco: Jossey-Bass Publishers, 2006).

14. M. Y. Ganaie and Hafiz Mudasir, "A Study of Social Intelligence & Academic Achievement of College Students of District Srinagar, J&K, India," created November 3, 2015, accessed February 2, 2016, www.jofamericanscience.org/journals/am-sci/am110315/004_2810 7am110315_23_27.pdf.

15. Nicholas Humphrey, "Social intelligence," accessed August 5, 2017, https://en.wikipedia.org/wiki/Social_intelligence.

16. David Livermore, *The Cultural Intelligence Difference: Master the One Skill You Can't Do Without in Today's Global Economy* (San Francisco: AMACOM, 2011).

17. Hesselbein et al., *The Drucker Foundation*, 78–79.

18. Winthrop D. Jordan and Leon F. Litwack, *The United States: Conquering a Continent* (Englewood Cliffs, NJ: Prentice-Hall, 1987).

19. Jean Lipman-Blumen, *The Connective Edge: Leading in an Interdependent World* (San Francisco: Jossey-Bass Publishers, 1996).

20. Ibid.

21. Wendy Wang, Kim Parker, and Paul Taylor, "Breadwinner Moms," Pew Research Center, created May 29, 2013, accessed March 4, 2015, http://www.pewsocialtrends.org/2013/05/29/breadwinner-moms/.

22. Andrew Soergel, "US Job Market: Good, but Not Great," US News & World Report, created December 14, 2015, accessed November 11, 2016, www.usnews.com/news/articles/2015-12-14/us-job-market-good-but-not-great.

23. National Center for Education Statistics, "Digest of Education Statistics," accessed April 3, 2017, https://nces.ed.gov/prorgams/digest/d13/dt13_318.10.asp.

24. United States Census Bureau, "Current Population Survey: 2013 Detailed Tables," created May 1, 2016, accessed January 5, 2017, https://www.census.gov/data/tables/2013/demo/foreign-born/cps-2013.html.

25. Mark DeWolf, "12 Stats About Working Women," US Department of Labor Blog, created March 1, 2017, accessed May 12, 2017, https://blog.dol.gov/2017/03/01/12-stats-about-working-women.

26. Steve Odland, "A New Year's Resolution for the Boardroom," created December 22, 2015, accessed June 6, 2016, http://www.cnbc.com/2015/12/22/getting-more-women-on-boards-commentary.html.

27. Camille L. Ryan and Kurt Bauman, "Educational Attainment in the United States: 2015 Population Characteristics," created March 3, 2016, accessed February 5, 2017, https://www.census.gov/content/dam/Census/library/publications/2016/demo/p20-578.pdf.

28. Worldometers, "Countries in the World by Population, 2017," accessed April 7, 2017, www.worldometers.info/world-population/population-by-country/.

29. Laurie Burkitt, "China's Working-Age Population Sees Biggest-Ever Decline," *The Wall Street Journal*, Created January 22, 2016, accessed November 11, 2016, www.blogs.wsj.com/chinarealtime/2016/01/22/chinas-working-age-population-sees-biggest-ever-decline/.

30. Mark Hugo Lopez, Jeffrey Passel, and Molly Rohal, "Modern Immigration Wave Brings 59 Million to US, Driving Population Growth and Change Through 2065," Pew Research Center, created September 28, 2015, accessed November 9, 2016, www.pewhispanic.org/files/2015/09/2015-09-28_modern-immigration-wave_REPORT.pdf.

31. Richard Fry, "Millennials Overtake Baby Boomers as America's Largest Generation," created April 25, 2016, accessed January 2, 2017, http://www.pewresearch.org/fact-ank/2016/04/25/millennials-overtake-baby-boomers/.

32. David Giber, Samuel M. Lam, Marshall Goldsmith, and Justin Bourke, *Linkage Inc's: Best Practices in Leadership Development Handbook, Case Studies Instruments Training* (San Francisco: Jossey-Bass Publishers, 2000).

33. Ibid.

Chapter Six: The Succession Development Planning Process

1. Mitra Toossi, "Labor Force Projections to 2024: The Labor Force Is Growing, but Slowly," Monthly Labor Review, US Bureau of Statistics, created December 2015, accessed July 1, 2017, www.bls.gov/opub/mir/2015/article/labor-force-projections-to-2024.htm.

2. Jac Fitz-enz, *The ROI of Human Capital: Measuring the Economic Value of Employee Performance* (New York: AMACOM, 2000).

3. United Nations Population Fund and International Organization for Migration, "International Migration and Development Recommendation of the International System Report," created 2013, accessed April 4, 2015, www.publications.iom.int/system/files/pdf/ceb_gmg_web.pdf.

4. Kandeh K. Yumkella and Jeremy Rifkin, "The Five Pillars of the Third Industrial Revolution," accessed January 3, 2017, http://www.thethirdindustrialrevolution.com.

5. Margaret Rouse, "TechTarget: IoT Agenda," last updated September 2015, accessed April 23, 2017, http://internetofthingsagenda.techtarget.com/definition/Internet-of-Things-IoT.

6. *Wikipedia*, s.v. "future-proofing," accessed April 23, 2015, en.wikipedia.org/wiki/Future_proof.

7. Karie Willyerd and Barbara Mistick, *Stretch: How to Future-Proof Yourself for Tomorrow's Workplace* (Hoboken, NJ: John Wiley & Sons, 2016).

8. Rosabeth Moss Kanter, *Men and Women of the Corporation* (New York: Basic-Books, 1977).

9. Carol S. Dweck, *Mindset: The New Psychology of Success* (New York: Ballantine Books, 2016).

10. Ibid.

11. Karen Huffman, *Psychology in Action* (Hoboken, NJ: John Wiley & Sons, Inc. 2007).

12. Bruce D. Schneider, *Energy Leadership: Transforming Your Workplace and Your Life from the Core* (Hoboken, NJ: John Wiley & Sons, 2008).

13. B. Kim. Barnes, *Exercising Influence: A Guide for Making Things Happen at Work, at Home, and in Your Community* (Hoboken, NJ: John Wiley & Sons, 2015).

14. Daniel G. Amen, *Unleash the Power of the Female Brain: Supercharging Yours for Better Health, Energy, Mood, Focus, and Sex* (New York: Harmony Books, 2013).

15. James S. Nairne, *Psychology the Adaptive Mind*, 3rd ed. (Belmont: Wadsworth Thomas Learning, 2003).

16. Susan Cain, *Quiet: The Power of Introverts in a World That Can't Stop Talking* (New York, Crown Publishing Group, 2013).

17. Wendy Watson, *Personality and Blood Type: A Guide to Love, Work, and Friendships* (Lakewood, CA: Avid Readers Publishing Group, 2013).

18. William A. Kahn, "Psychological Conditions of Personal Engagement and Disengagement of Work," *Academy of Management Journal*, created December 1990, accessed January 2, 2017, http://dx.doi.org/10.2307/256287.

19. CBS Small Business Pulse, "US Bureau of National Affairs," created September 21, 2015, accessed April 4, 2017, http://www.cbspulse.com/2015/09/21/6-hr-facts-never-forget/.

20. Harvard Business Review, "The Impact of Employee Engagement on Performance," created September 2013, accessed December 12, 2016,

https://hbr.org/resources/pdfs/comm/achievers/hbr_achievers_report_sep13.pdf.

21. Amy Adkins, "Employee Engagement in US Stagnant in 2015," created January 13, 2016, accessed December 12, 2016, www.gallup.com/poll/188144/employee-engagement-stagnant-2015.aspx.

22. Jenn Mann, "The SAS Story: Building and Sustaining a Unique Culture," *The Huffington Post*, created June 26, 2015, accessed November 11, 2016, www.huffingtonpost.com/sas/the-sas-story-building-and-sustaining-a-unique-culture_b_5700489.html.

23. Adkins, "Employee Engagement in US Stagnant in 2015."

24. Leigh Branham, *The 7 Hidden Reasons Employees Leave* (New York: American Management Association, 2005).

25. Tom Rath and Barry Conchie, *Strengths-Based Leadership, Great Leaders, Teams and Why People Follow* (New York: Gallup Press, 2008).

26. Jeffrey Gitomer, *Little Black Book of Connections, 6.5 Assets for Networking Your Way to RICH Relationships* (Austin, TX: Bard Press, 2006).

27. Brian E. Becker, Mark A. Huselid, and Dave Ulrich, *The HR Scorecard: Linking People, Strategy, and Performance* (Boston: Harvard Business School Press, 2001).

28. Marlene A. Lee and Mark Mather, "US Labor Force Trends," *Population Bulletin* 63, no. 2 (2008), created June 2008, accessed January 3, 2017, www.prb.org/pdf08/63.2uslabor.pdf.

29. Robert M. Fulmer and Jay A. Conger, *Growing Your Company's Leaders: How Great Organizations Use Succession Management to Sustain Competitive Advantage* (New York: American Management Association, 2004).

30. Robert M. Fulmer and Marshall Goldsmith, *The Leadership Investment: How the World's Best Organizations Gain Strategic Advantage through Leadership Development* (New York: American Management Association, 2001).

31. Lynn Slavenski and Marilyn Buckner, *Career Development Programs in the Workplace* (Columbus: The Center on Education Research and Improvement, US Department of Education, 1988).

32. Peter M. Senge, *The Fifth Discipline: The Art and Practice of the Learning Organization* (New York: Doubleday, 2006).

33. William J. Rothwell, *Effective Succession Planning: Ensuring Leadership Continuity and Building Talent from Within*, 2nd ed. (New York: American Management Association, 2001).

34. Walter R. Mahler and Stephen J. Drotter, *The Succession Planning Handbook for the Chief Executive* (Midland Park, NJ: Mahler Publishing, 1986).

Chapter Seven: Workforce Competency Gap Analysis Case Study

1. Matt Thompson, "How Much Does It Cost to Hire a New Employee?," Dun & Bradstreet, created February 14, 2012, accessed May 12, 2016, https://www.dandb.com/smallbusiness/how-much-does-it-cost-to-hire-a-new-employee/.

2. Department of Commerce, "International Students Contributed Nearly $31 Billion to the US Economy in the 2014 and 2015 School Years," created November 16, 2015, accessed February 3, 2016, http://www.iie.org/Who-We-Are/News-and-events/Press-Center/Press-Release/2015/2015-11-16-Open-Doors-Data.

3. John Siegmund and Barb Rawdon, Department of Commerce International Trade Administration. "2016 Top Markets Report: Education," created May 2016, accessed December 12, 2016, www.trade.gov/topmarkets/pdf/Education_Top_Markets_eport.pdf.

4. Harvard University Competency Dictionary, accessed March 4, 2017, www.campusservices.harvard.edu/systm/files/documents/1865/harvard_competency_dictionary_complete.pdf.

5. Human Resource Systems Group, "Understanding General Competency and Technical Competencies," created November 2015, accessed May 1, 2017, http://www.hrsg.ca/understanding-general-and-technical-competencies/201511/.

6. Susan Ward, "Core Competency in Business: Small Businesses Can Have Core Competency Too," The Balance, accessed September 20, 2016, January 5, 2017, www.thebalance.com/core-competency-in-business-2948314.

7. *Business Dictionary*, s.v. "technical competence," accessed January 22, 2017. www.businessdictionary.com/definition/technical-competence.html.

8. Gary Hamel and Bill Breen, *The Future of Management* (Boston: Harvard Business School Publishing, 2007).

9. Society For Human Resource Management, "Leadership Competencies," created March 1, 2008, accessed March 5, 2016, www.shrm. org/ResourceAndTools/hr-topics/behavioral-competencies/leadership-and-navigation/Pages/leadershipcompetencies.aspx.

10. Greg Sekowski, "What Is Competency Modeling?," Human Resource Strategic Partners, Inc., accessed March 2, 2017, www.hrspartners. com/PDFfiles/HRSP_Competency_Modeling.pdf.

11. Dave Evans, "The Internet of Things: How the Next Evolution of the Internet Is Changing Everything," created April 2011, accessed July 10, 2017, www.cisco.com/c/dam/en_us/about/ac79/docs/inno/IoT_IBSG_0411FINAL.pdf.

12. Timothy Lagan, Margaret Barton, and Anne Holloway-Lundy, "Workforce and Succession Planning for Mission Critical Occupations," Office of Personnel Management, accessed December 12, 2016, annex.ipacweb.org/library/conf/07/lagan.pdf.

INDEX

ABOUT THE AUTHOR

A leading expert in the field of succession development planning, Douglas E. Fenner, EdD, is the founder and president of the Fenner Consulting Group. A professional executive and corporate coach, he pioneered the Department of the Navy's first succession-planning study.

Dr. Fenner's academic credentials include a bachelor's degree in electrical engineering, a master's in computer resources and information management, and a doctorate in leadership and educational sciences. He is a thirty-three year retired federal civil servant, and is a veteran of the US Navy.

In addition to being a certified professional executive coach with the International Coaching Federation, Dr. Fenner holds multiple certifications related to corporate succession development, leadership development, and emotional intelligence.

A member of the National Defense Industrial Association and Armed Forces Communications Electronics Association, Dr. Fenner also belongs to the National Society of Black Engineers. In his personal time, he coaches youth league sports and enjoys reading, running, swimming and cycling.

www.ingramcontent.com/pod-product-compliance
Lightning Source LLC
Chambersburg PA
CBHW061151220326
41599CB00025B/4437